Theory and Practice of Online Therapy

GW00671540

This innovative new resource outlines the process of conducting individual, family and group therapy online with the use of video conferencing tools, and explores the unique concerns associated with this increasingly popular and convenient approach to treatment.

Offering mental health practitioners a definitive presentation on how to use online tools to facilitate psychological intervention, the book will also enable readers to learn about the processes of virtual individual, couple, family and group therapy, specific concerns related to online group dynamics, as well as the responsibilities of the therapist and group leader in online sessions.

This is the perfect companion for counselors of all backgrounds and disciplines who are interested in offering or improving their approach to virtual services.

Haim Weinberg, PhD, is a clinical psychologist, group analyst and certified group psychotherapist. He is the past president of the Israeli Association of Group Psychotherapy and of the Northern California Group Psychotherapy Society. He taught at the Wright Institute in Berkeley, CA, and the Alliant International University.

Arnon Rolnick, PhD, is a licensed clinical psychologist with special interest in the usage of technology in psychotherapy. He is a certified supervisor in CBT and biofeedback and has written numerous articles on these subjects. Arnon is the head of a clinic in Tel Aviv, Israel, which integrates various psychotherapeutic approaches.

Theory and Practice of Online Therapy

Internet-delivered Interventions for Individuals, Groups, Families, and Organizations

Edited by Haim Weinberg and Arnon Rolnick

Routledge
Taylor & Francis Group

NEW YORK AND LONDON

First published 2020
by Routledge
52 Vanderbilt Avenue, New York, NY 10017

and by Routledge
2 Park Square, Milton Park, Abingdon, Oxon, OX14 4RN

Routledge is an imprint of the Taylor & Francis Group, an informa business

© 2020 Taylor & Francis

The right of Haim Weinberg and Arnon Rolnick to be identified as the authors of the editorial material, and of the authors for their individual chapters, has been asserted in accordance with sections 77 and 78 of the Copyright, Designs and Patents Act 1988.

Library of Congress Cataloging-in-Publication Data
A catalog record for this title has been requested

ISBN: 978-1-138-68184-2 (hbk)
ISBN: 978-1-138-68186-6 (pbk)
ISBN: 978-1-315-54553-0 (ebk)

Typeset in Bembo
by Integra Software Services Pvt. Ltd.

Contents

Contributors

Gily Agar is an Israeli clinical psychologist, founder of an online video-therapy service for Israelis abroad, and teaches therapists and other health-care providers how to create close and engaging relationships in video.

Lou Agosta, PhD, is an empathy consultant and psychotherapist in private practice, delivering empathy lessons (psychotherapy interventions) as a professor of medical education at Ross Medical University at Saint Anthony Hospital, Chicago, IL. He is the author of three peer-reviewed academic books on empathy, including *A Rumor of Empathy*.

Lew Aron is an internationally recognized lecturer on psychoanalysis who has made significant contributions to relational psychoanalysis. Unfortu-nately, he died in 2019 before the publication of this book.

Galit Atlas is a psychoanalyst known for her rethinking of the place of sexuality and desire in contemporary theory and practice.

Donna J. Dennis, PhD, is a leadership development professional, specia-lizing in solutions for leaders working in virtual and remote teams. She has conducted research on working virtually for the Gestalt International Study Center.

Nuala Dent is a systems psychodynamic researcher and practitioner with an interest in understanding group dynamics at the intersection of face-to-face and online ways of working.

Ryan M. Earl, Ph.D, is a Clinical Lecturer, Department of Psychology, at Northwestern University.

Bonnie Goldstein, LCSW, Ed.M., PhD, is founder and director of the Lifespan Psychological Center in Los Angeles, specializing in individual and group therapy for children, adolescents and families. She teaches at USC's School of Social Work and is on the faculty at the Sensorimotor Psychotherapy Institute, where she teaches internationally and has co-developed their child, adolescent and family treatment training program.

Shoshana Hellman finished her doctorate at Columbia University, Teachers College, NYC, in counseling psychology. She currently works in private practice both in Israel and the USA with individuals, couples and families, and is a licensed couple and family therapist – the only certified Gottman couple therapist and consultant in Israel. She worked as a senior supervisor for the Ministry of Education, psychological services in Israel for over 20 years and was a faculty member at the University of Wisconsin in Madison. She has several publications in the area of supervision and professional development of counsellors.

Katherine M. Hertlein, PhD, is a Professor in the Couple and Family Therapy Program at the University of Nevada, Las Vegas.

Ivan Jensen, MD, has worked with, taught and researched leadership and organizational development for more than 30 years, with a special interest in complex and virtual organizations. He is a founding partner of GestaltPartner in Sweden where he teaches, as well as provides consulting to organizations.

Ichak Adizes is an international consultant. He is the developer of the theory and protocols of the organizational therapy that bears his name.

Heather Katafiasz, PhD, is an Assistant Professor at the University of Akron. Her professional interests include expanding the systemic understanding of Intimate Partner Violence and its intersection with substance use.

Rakefet Keret-Karavani has been practicing organizational consultancy since 1994, focusing on leadership development. Her doctorate dissertation researched leadership in virtual organizations, as manifested in videoconference meetings.

Molyn Leszcz is president-elect of the American Group Psychotherapy Association. With Irv Yalom he wrote the 5th edition of Yalom's book *The Theory and Practice of Group Psychotherapy*.

Danielle Magaldi, PhD, is an Associate Professor at the City University of New York. Her research focuses on two areas: the effects of technology on human relationships and spirituality in psychotherapy. She maintains a private practice treating adults and children.

Pat Ogden, PhD, founder of the Sensorimotor Psychotherapy Institute, is a clinician, consultant, international lecturer and trainer, and groundbreaking author in the field of somatic psychology.

Rikki Patton, PhD, is an Associate Professor at the University of Akron. Her professional interests include improving treatment for marginalized populations with a focus on addiction work.

Michael Pennington, M.A.Ed., is a doctoral student in the Marriage and Family Counseling/Therapy program at the University of Akron. His professional interests include technology use in therapy, therapist self-care and cybersupervision.

Arnon Rolnick is a licensed Clinical Psychologist with special interest in the usage of technology in psychotherapy. He is a certified supervisor in CBT and biofeedback and has written numerous articles on these subjects. Arnon is the head of a clinic in Tel-Aviv which integrates various psychotherapeutic approaches.

Leora Trub is an associate professor of psychology in the school/clinical-child PsyD program at Pace University where she trains doctoral candidates in clinical work and runs the Digital Media and Psychology lab, which explores the intersection of technology and human connection. She is also a practicing psychologist based in New York City, working with adolescents, adults and couples.

Raúl Vaimberg Grillo is a Psychiatrist, Doctor of Psychology and Psychotherapist. He is the Director of the 'Postgraduate Course in Group Psychotherapy and Psychodrama' at the University of Barcelona.

Lara Vaimberg Lombardo has a Master's Degree in General Health Psychology, a Postgraduate degree in Group Psychotherapy and Psychodrama (University of Barcelona), and has participated in research projects on childhood, therapeutic groups and Autism Spectrum Disorders.

Haim Weinberg is a licensed psychologist, group analyst and Certified Group Psychotherapist in private practice in Sacramento, California. He co-edits a series of books about the social unconscious, wrote a book on Internet groups, and co-authored a book on Fairy Tales and the social unconscious.

Acknowledgments

As the editors of this book, we are pleased to acknowledge the help and contribution of our two co-editors who took a major part in editing two sections of our book: Shoshana Hellman who co-edited the Family and Couple section, and Rakefet Keret-Karavani who co-edited the Organizational Consultancy section. We are grateful for their work and patience with our many requests for revisions.

We are very grateful to our families and friends for tolerating our continuous preoccupation. Without their support and patience, we would have never been able to finish this project.

Last, but not least, we are grateful to our online patients who taught us so much about how to do online treatment properly.

Haim and Arnon

Introduction

Haim Weinberg and Arnon Rolnick

Ocean separates lands, not souls.

(Munia Khan, a Poet)

It is almost outdated to write that we are in a dizzying process of changes in a rapidly changing world.

Nobel prize winner Daniel Kahneman (2017) believes that the world of medicine, consultation and organizational behavior is going to change significantly due to technology in general and artificial intelligence in particular.

We, as clinical psychologists and psychotherapists, look at the changes that are taking place with a curious eye, examining cautiously but also with enthusiasm how these changes affect our lives. This book is edited and written from the same observing position, enthusiastic on the one hand and critical on the other.

One of the unique features of this book is that it is not only about one-on-one interaction and individual psychotherapy, but also on multi-participant interaction. Quite a bit has been written about remote treatment at the level of one-on-one (Scharff, 2018), and later in the book you will find reference to the knowledge accumulated in various articles and books. Human interaction and psychotherapy often exist in more than one-on-one format. Couples and family therapy is one example that we have chosen to expand on. Another unique challenge of this book is to discuss the possibility of remote group work. Group therapy is clearly less expensive and also effective, however, group therapists know the technical and practical difficulty of bringing a group of people together in one place at a time. We therefore found it very important to discuss the possibility of group therapy from a distance.

One of the sections in this book is certainly innovative and perhaps not classical to be included in conjunction with psychological treatments: this is the section of organizational consulting from a distance. The reasons for introducing this part are twofold. First, we have to acknowledge that the prevalence of group work in organizations is much greater than group therapy in clinical practice, and even more so, in organizations there is a tendency to neglect the importance of the interpersonal aspects of team work in general and from a distance in particular. Not neglecting the interpersonal dimension in organizational online work is one of the tasks of this book.

We want to emphasize that in this book we mostly focus on online videoconference therapy. Although there are some chapters that discuss text-based therapy, our main interest is in the more advanced technologies that make the sessions "closer to reality". Phone sessions, for example, has been practiced for several decades. However, their use was very limited, and they were always perceived as adjunct to the in-person therapy. This is not the case in videoconferencing, that threatens to replace the traditional face-to-face (f2f) meetings.

Theoretical and Practical Questions

In this book we aimed to encompass both the theoretical and practical aspects of online therapy and consultation. Some of the existing books and articles, focus only on one of these aspects (e.g. Essig & Russell, 2017 on theory, while Derrig-Palumbo & Zeine, 2005 on practice). We think that practical considerations stem from theoretical understanding and the specific school of thought. For example, in f2f group therapy, the question whether the group leader should always sit in the same chair depends on the theoretical orientation: In a psychodynamic one, a stable setting is very important, and the group therapist should stay in the same chair to allow for projections, while in humanistic approach, modeling and flexibility is more important, hence changing seats is recommended. What seems to be a simple practical question is influenced, in fact, by theoretical considerations. This same question, considered online, might affect the technology chosen for group work. Most of the programs nowadays do not enable the group therapist or consultant to choose the "seat" of the leader and participants on the screen.

The position of the editors and authors throughout the pages of the book is an observing position. We try not to fall into the following dichotomy: Is remote therapy good or bad? Are these treatments similar or different from conventional psychotherapy? Moreover, as researchers, we are interested not only in the question of whether tele-therapy is effective, but also the question: what can we learn about the mechanisms that work in treatment in the light of the existence of "non-body" treatment or treatment that is in different locations? The transition to remote treatment allows for dismantling the various therapeutic factors. The fact that disembodied therapy is possible, questions traditional assumptions of necessary conditions for therapy. Holding, for example (Winnicott, 1971), a major term in psychodynamic psychotherapy, is based on the actual maternal hands, hugging and encompassing the baby. In remote therapy not only "real" hugs are impossible, sometimes it seems that the therapist is a handless mother.

If we look at the changes that have taken place in the field of psychotherapeutic theories in the latest decades, Bowlby's theory of attachment stands out, as almost every psychotherapeutic approach nowadays uses some of his conceptual approach. Sroufe et al. (2005) claims that "Attachment can be considered 'perhaps the most important developmental construct ever investigated'." Proximity is the keyword in Bowlby's theory. Children seek closeness with a parent who can protect and take care of them. From here derives the assumption that the therapist should also be close in order to help the client repair the attachment ruptures. The question is whether being close means only physically. When Bowlby talked about proximity, did he mean "in the same location"? While interpretation-based theories did not place much emphasis on the element of physical closeness, in some of the attachment-based approaches this element cannot be ignored, thus questioning the validity of remote treatment. To sharpen this question, can we think of caring for small children without physical proximity? While we do believe that remote therapy is possible and effective, we hardly believe that it is suitable for very young children.

The question of physical presence is even more relevant in the frame of reference of interpersonal neurobiology modern theories. These theories, by Alan Schore (2003), Daniel Siegel (1999), Louis Cozolino (2013) and others, emphasize the importance of mutual regulation based on physical presence. For example, these theorists claim that what works in therapy are not just the words but the mutual regulation of brain to brain, body to body. Sometimes these theories focus on right brain to right brain communication and sometimes on the peripheral nervous system. Stephen Porges (2011) for example, argues that therapy is based on the experience of safety that a therapist provides to the patient. In Porges' opinion, two people in physical proximity immediately activate a mechanism that checks whether it is safe to be close with the other person. A major part of his Polyvagal theory is identifying the nervous system mechanisms that focuses on the other person's voice and face for that purpose. Ostensibly, these theories will question the adequacy of remote therapy as there is no body present to regulate the body of the other, so mutual regulation is impossible. A closer look shows that one of the important variables for Porges is the face (especially its upper part). However, facial expression becomes clearer and in higher resolution online – perhaps even more than in treatment in the same room. On the other hand, in remote treatment, usually only the face is seen while important information about posture, sitting, breathing, and various motor movements disappears. Smell and pheromones are also important and are missing online.

Some of these theoretical issues have clear practical implications. Several writers suggest solutions for creating a bonding experience in online family, group and organizational settings. For example, some recommend sitting more distant from the screen. To this end, we have attached a few pages to each section dealing with some possible best practice solutions for remote work, again from an observing and insightful position, discussing the advantages and disadvantages of any proposed solution.

We tried to summarize the main theoretical and practical issues that online therapists should deal with. Here is our list of topics to take into consideration:

1. *Presence.* All the authors writing about online therapy (e.g. Lemma, 2017; Russell, 2015; Weinberg, 2014) focus on the question of presence, wondering whether it is possible to create it in cyberspace and how much presence necessitates a body. Presence is actually essential for positive outcomes of psychotherapy. Nevertheless, it is quite an elusive term. In their book about therapeutic presence, Geller and Greenberg (2012) argue that it is the fundamental underlying quality of the therapeutic relationship and, hence, effective therapy. They describe therapeutic presence as the state of having one's whole self in the encounter with a client or a group by being completely in the moment on a multiplicity of levels – physically, emotionally, cognitively, and spiritually. Therapeutic presence is defined as bringing one's whole self to the engagement with the client and being fully in the moment with and for the client, with little self-centered purpose or goal in mind (Craig, 1986).

   The term 'face-to-face' means 'to be in each other's sight or presence'. Traditionally we mean the physical presence, since the participants in the communication are in the same physical space. However, when we move to cyberspace, and especially when we use video conferencing, presence acquires a different meaning. What is this online presence that is so crucial to therapeutic relationship? The presence of the other is usually felt through hearing the other's voice and seeing the other's face and body. Although traditionally, presence involves the body, actually this physical presence only supports subjective presence.

   The presence of the therapist involves his/her immersion, passion, attention, emotional involvement, reverie, and a readiness to be drawn into enactments (Grossmark, 2007). This can still be done online. Lemma (2017) writes that presence is the perception of successfully transforming an intention into action, and actions are not restricted to ones that we discharge physically. This can clearly occur in Cyberspace as well, although it might need specific focusing on how to transform the intention into action taking into consideration the limitation of online communication.

2. *Terminology.* We wondered what the right term for online therapy should be, especially one that is using video. Is it e-therapy (not exactly, as it implies using email for therapy), or online therapy? Certainly not "virtual therapy", as it implies that this therapy is only virtual. And how do we term therapy where all the participants are

physically present in the same room? Calling the latest f2f ignores the fact that in video therapy we also see one another face-to-face (and sometime better, due to the fact that the face is shown in a close-up). We noticed that the chapters' writers for this book struggled with this question as well, and we decided not to force a unified term, but allow each writer to use their own term. Thus, Ivan Jensen and Donna Dennis (Chapter 20) called it collocated work. Katherine Hertlein and Ryan Earl (Chapter 10) used a general term for online therapy and called it "Internet-delivered service". Leora Trub and Danielle Magaldi (Chapter 11) related to it as "in-person treatment". Nuala Dent (Chapter 21) chose 'face-to-face' to denote a group meeting in the same physical place and 'online' to denote a group meeting via technology specifically. She wrote:

> I search for words to distinguish these different face-to-face meetings. I could identify them as "physical" and "virtual" but this implies one is real and the other not-real. To describe a video conference meeting as "online" suggests that a meeting where all members are in the same room is "offline".

3. *Is it the same therapy or a different one?* A continuous debate in the literature about online therapy focuses on the question whether it is the same therapy as we do in-person or a different one. Sherry Turkle in an interview with Essig and Russell (2017) says: "Technology creates a new state of the self …. Online intimacies are real but operate with new dynamics" (242). Todd Essig (personal communication, 2017) agrees that online therapy is working but claims that it involves processes that are different from in-person therapy. Specific processes fundamental across psychodynamic therapies, such as analytic listening and attention to implicit processes, are inevitably changed and modified when subject to technological mediation. He is worried that we are lowering standards so that what takes place on screen qualifies as working. He and Russel suggest that the alluring convenience of remote treatment should not cause clinicians to either lose sight of or undervalue that which is unique to what we call "local therapy."

   We think that the split between "is it the same" or "is it different" is unproductive, and we prefer to look at both similarities and differences. For example, Weinberg (2014) argued that online relationship involves a different kind of intimacy and termed it *E-ntimacy*. It is not the kind of into-me-you-see that is praised in Hollywood movies and is based on self-disclosure and on privacy. As privacy cannot be guaranteed in Cyberspace, we should rethink of intimacy in new ways: "*Intimacy without privacy reinvents what intimacy means*" (Turkle, 2011: 171). Online E-ntimacy is more similar to the kind of intimacy that develops in Large Groups (see Chapter 15) and is based on an atmosphere of cohesion, "we-ness", and belonging.

Another example to different processes in online therapy is its meaning to ending and termination of therapy and relationship. We can continue therapy in circumstances that were unavailable in the past (such as moving to another country). Thus, online therapy and online connection perpetuates the fantasy that we can overcome human limitations of time and space, as we can continue our relationship whenever we want and wherever we are.

4. *Making it more "real"?* Related to the previous question of how similar or different online therapy is from in-person treatment, is the question how much we want to make it as closer as possible to the "real" experience. An approach wanting to replicate the circumstances in our clinic would insist that in online psychoanalysis the patient still lie on the couch even when the analyst is behind the screen. In our opinion this is a too rigid and even ridiculous. This question affects the decision whether to sit close to the screen, so that only our face is shown, or maintaining some distance from the computer, thus seeing our bodies as we are used to in our offices (we will address the distance from the screen in the practical guidelines). We believe that on the one hand we should try and replicate the basic conditions that exist when we see a patient in-person, but always taking into consideration the fact that it is a different media that dictates some different circumstances.

5. *The need to focus.* We agree that "an online environment may require a greater investment of time and energy to create and maintain a psychic space that supports learning through experience" (Nuala Dent, Chapter 21). In order to maintain presence, to stay focused and not be distracted by other stimuli (whether on the screen or in the therapist's environment), the therapist should be keenly aware and make a special effort.

6. *The disembodied self.* Many authors pointed out to the disembodied interaction online. This is only partly true, as each participant still have a body, and can sense it while sitting in front of the computer, which is not different than while sitting in our office with a patient (who is sitting or lying on the couch) in the same room. Lemma (2017) refers to therapy mediated by Skype as *embodied presence* because "in cyber-space we are still embodied. What changes is our experience of our own and the other person's embodiment" (92). All the members in online communication can feel their emotions, pain, body ailments and bodily needs while they communicate. What *is* missing is the body-to-body communication. It is missing because of two reasons: 1. Only part of the body (usually the head and shoulders) is seen, and most of the body is hidden. 2. The screen creates a barrier, so that we cannot smell or be sensitive to bodily cues that we are aware of (consciously or unconsciously) when we are in the same physical space. It reduces the communication from a full body, three dimensions, to a flat, two-dimension communication. So, indeed, something

is reduced in our ability to sense the other person's body. However, with some practice and becoming more focused, we can still catch hints of the physical sensations of the patient, or simply ask them how they feel in their body. Pat Ogden and Bonnie Goldstein (Chapter 4) give wonderful examples of how to use the body online, and Lewis Aron and Galit Atals (Chapter 5) in their interview bring interesting anecdotes about the existence of the body.

7. *Setting.* Normally, the therapist provides the setting, including the room, its furniture, a waiting room, tissues, or water. As Russell (2015) points out, in online therapy the setting can no longer be controlled by the therapist. This means that we therapists lost the ability to guarantee a safe environment and that "the lion's share of maintaining secure boundaries and providing his/her own environmental needs" (17) is upon the patient's shoulders. This change from the traditional situation in which patients come to our office and we can protect the space boundaries and provide their environmental needs, is not a small shift, and unfortunately, many therapists who work online ignore it. The psychotherapy setting is a combination of concrete and subjective elements in the psychotherapy framework that are set up to provide continuity, consistency and containment. A stable and safe environment helps patients feel free to explore and express their mind. Beside the consulting room, other elements of the psychotherapy setting include the session time and duration, the frequency, fees, absences and cancellations, breaks, communications, confidentiality and numerous others.

The setting is a crucial topic in psychodynamic treatment and many articles were written about its importance. Freud, in his technical writing, details the rules governing the analytic setting: they include temporal aspects (like time, length and frequency of meetings), space aspects (place and conditions in the room), financial aspects, and the analyst's position (abstinence, neutrality and anonymity). We can conclude that according to Freud, the setting is a group of constant variables that allow the psychoanalytic process to occur. Langs (1998) wrote an entire book about the setting and frame of the analytic situation. Bleger (1967) adds that the analytic situation is defined as a process, but as any process it needs a stable variable, which is the setting. He adds that we notice the setting only when it is disrupted. Modell writes:

> The psychoanalytic setting is [a] non-specific ... [frame] ... that recreates a dependency in which commonly shared developmental conflicts are experienced. These conflicts include dependency versus the fear of loss of autonomy; and the wish to merge versus the fear of being "swallowed up." These conflicts occur within the context of the need to reserve the safety and integrity of the self.
>
> (Modell, 1988: 587–588)

Modell (1989) sees the therapeutic setting as creating a warm, womb-like, safe and containing space, protecting the patient from the difficult reality outside the room. The function of the setting has been written about extensively and it is considered the essential background that provides containment and allows transference and unconscious processes to emerge.

Winnicott (1971) saw the secure setting as creating a space in which the patient can 'use' the analyst. He stated that the room is an extension of the patient's body and thus the therapist should accommodate this environment to the needs of the patient. Clearly, this cannot be achieved in online setting. In mediated therapy we cannot adjust the environment to the patient's needs, cannot guarantee a safe environment with no intrusion, and do not have the primary responsibility over the setting. The first thing is to recognize this fact, which, unfortunately, is ignored by many who do online therapy. Recognizing it requires some changes in the standard agreement, in order to guarantee that the patient will take care of the environment on his/her end (see the practical advice part in this book). Next, we should ask ourselves whether therapy still works even though the setting is different, and whether it is the same therapy. This is where writers on online therapy differ. Colleen Russell (2015) clearly states that "A safe holding environment cannot be established in the traditional way in the screen-to-screen relationship" (74), and later, while co-editing the special issue of *Psychoanalytic Perspectives* with Todd Essig (2017) about online therapy, they criticize psychotherapy going online and claim that "those routinely treating at a distance via screen relations are unwittingly serving the needs of technology entrepreneurs who want to replace therapists with apps and programs" (135). However, Gily Agar in this book (Chapter 5) argues that the fact that patients online are responsible to taking care of their needs encourages more self-reliance and conveys the message of trusting the patients' inner resources.

8. *Ignoring background information.* Most therapists ignore not only the fact that they do not control the setting and cannot create the conditions of the safe environment, but many other subtle events and incidents occurring online that they would never ignore when it is in-presence therapy. A cat that is walking on the table in front of the computer and its tail appears from time to time on the screen is a good example. If a patient brought a cat to our therapeutic session in our office, we would never ignore it, and probably try to explore the meaning of this appearance. Strange enough, most of us ignore this appearance online and take it for granted as part of the new environment.

In the epilogue of this book we gather the knowledge accumulated in all the sections and wonder how therapeutic and organizational interactions will evolve in the coming future. Some of the discussion points out to the growing centrality of existing technologies and wonders whether we can return to the "old" interactions we have been accustomed to over the past several centuries. We are very much aware that this book might seem obsolete soon after its publication, taking into account the accelerated rate of change we are facing. For example, evolving technology will probably allow, at some point in the future, a three-dimensional encounter, perhaps even a tactile one. Artificial intelligence techniques can identify emotions and might improve or harm human encounter.

References

Bleger, J. (1967). Psycho-analysis of the psycho-analytic setting. In J. Churcher and L. Bleger (Eds), *Symbiosis and Ambiguity: A Psychodynamic Study*. London: Routledge, 2012.

Cozolino, L.J. (2013). *The Social Neuroscience of Education: Optimizing Attachment & Learning in the Classroom*. New York: W.W. Norton & Company.

Craig, P.E. (1986). Sanctuary and presence: An existential view of the therapist's contribution. *The Humanistic Psychologist, 14*, 22–28.

De Las Cuevas, C., Arredondo, M., Cabrera, M., Sulzenbacher, H., & Meise, U. (2006). Randomized clinical trial of telepsychiatry through videoconference versus face-to-face conventional psychiatric treatment. *Telemedicine and e-Health, 12*, 341–350.

Derrig-Palumbo, K., & Zeine, F. (2005). *Online Therapy: A Therapist's Guide to Expanding Your Practice*. New York: Norton.

Dunstan, D.A., & Tooth, S.M. (2012). Treatment via videoconferencing: A pilot study of delivery by clinical psychology trainees. *The Australian Journal of Rural Health, 20*, 88–94.

Essig, T., & Russell, G.I. (2017). A note from the guest editors. *Psychoanalytic Perspectives, 14*(2), 131–137.

Frueh, B.C., Monnier, J., Yim, E., Grubaugh, A.L., Hamner, M.B., & Knapp, R.G. (2007). A randomized trial of telepsychiatry for post-traumatic stress disorder. *Journal of Telemedicine and Telecare, 13*, 142–147.

Geller, S.M., & Greenberg, L.S. (2012). *Therapeutic Presence: A Mindful Approach to Effective Therapy*. APA publications.

Grossmark, R. (2007). The edge of chaos: Enactment, disruption, and emergence in group psychotherapy. *Psychoanalytic Dialogues, 17*(4), 479–499.

Grubaugh, A., Cain, G.D., Elhai, J.D., Patrick, S.L., & Frueh, B.C. (2008). Attitudes toward medical and mental health care delivered via telehealth applications among rural and urban primary care patients. *Journal of Nervous and Mental Disease, 196*, 166–170.

Kahneman, D. (2017). A keynote lecture for Israeli Psychological association meeting, Tel Aviv, Israel.

Langs, R. (1998). *Ground Rules in Psychotherapy and Counseling*. London: Karnac.

Lemma, A. (2017). *The Digital Age on the Couch*. New York: Routledge.

Modell, A.H. (1988). The centrality of the psychoanalytic setting and the changing aims of treatment. *The Psychoanalytic Quarterly, 57*(4), 577–596.

Modell, A.H. (1989). The psychoanalytic setting as a container of multiple levels of reality: A perspective on the theory of psychoanalytic treatment. *Psychoanalytic Inquiry, 9*, 67–87.

Porges, S.W. (2011). *The Polyvagal Theory: Neurophysiological Foundations of Emotions, Attachment, Communication, and Self-regulation.* New York: W.W. Norton.

Russell, G.I. (2015). *Screen Relations.* London: Karnac.

Scharff, J.S. (2018). *Psychoanalysis Online 4: Teleanalytic Practice Teaching and Clinical Research.* New York: Routledge.

Schore, A.N. (2003). *Affect Dysregulation and Disorders of the Self.* New York: WW Norton & Company.

Siegel, D. (1999). *The Developing Mind.* New Yok: Guilford Press.

Sroufe, A., Egeland, B., Carlson, E., & Collins, A. (2005). Placing early experiences in developmental context. In K. Grossman, K. Grossman, E. Waters (eds) *Attachment from Infancy to Adulthood.* New York: Guilford Press, pp. 48–70.

Turkle, S. (2011). *Alone Together: Why We Expect More from Technology and Less From Each Other.* New York: Basic Books.

Turkle, S. (2015). *Reclaiming Conversation: The Power of Talk in a Digital Age.* New York: Penguin Press.

Turkle, S., Essig, T., & Russell, G.I. (2017). Afterword: Reclaiming psychoanalysis: Sherry Turkle in conversation with the editors. *Psychoanalytic Perspectives, 14*(2), 237–248.

Weinberg, H. (2014). *The Paradox of Internet Groups: Alone in the Presence of Virtual Others.* London: Karnac.

Winnicott, D.W. (1971). *Playing and Reality.* London: Karnac.

Section 1

General Considerations for Online Therapy

Edited by Haim Weinberg and Arnon Rolnick

1 Introduction to the General Consideration Section

Principles of Internet-based Treatment

Arnon Rolnick

Online Therapy
By Roni Frischoff

*With a heavy heart I sit in front of the computer, waiting for her to connect
    through Skype.*
Seven hours and an entire ocean separate us.
*I accepted her plea to continue distance therapy, accompanying her first weeks of
    moving to a faraway country.*
*I always felt her as distant, unavailable, detached. I expect the technology to
    alienate us further.*
I wish I had disagreed.
Leaning forward to see her better I click the connecting icon
Her face suddenly spread in front of me
Her big, glittering eyes, I can almost sense her breath.
A thin screen separates us
Just a kiss away

We begin this introduction by presenting two scripts from famous science-fiction art pieces: one from the novel *The Naked Sun* by Isaac Asimov, and the other from the movie *Her*.

In *The Naked Sun*, Asimov describes two possible forms of human interaction: Seeing, which means meeting face-to-face, and Viewing, which means encounters via technological devices.

A woman from another planet appears naked on the screen of an earthman who happens to be a policeman. The woman tells the policeman, Baley, that she would never do something like that in-person. Baley asks what the difference is between in-person and on-screen, saying to the woman that he can see her now, to which the woman responds:

> "No, you don't see me. You see my image. You're viewing me."
> "And that makes a difference?"
> "All the difference there is."

★★★★

In the movie *Her* the producer pursued a different futuristic concept of interaction that does not involve two humans, but rather a human-being and a computer. In an early conversation the human, Theodore, is told by the computer, Samantha, that she is made up of millions of personalities of the programmers who wrote her, but that she was also made to grow through experiences, just like a human. Later in the film, Theodore describes his relationship with Samantha in real, human terms, saying that at night when 'they're' in bed, he feels 'cuddled'.

We chose these two futuristic pieces to trigger a discussion on how forms of interaction may be changing, and how the psychotherapy world is dealing with these changes.

This introductory chapter discusses how psychotherapy interacts with new technological developments. While it is true that the short history of this profession is replete with debates over what exactly constitutes psychotherapy – modern technology and the Internet have certainly jarred the psychotherapy world like never before.

The possibility of using the Internet for psychotherapy confronts the therapeutic world with a fundamental dilemma. On one hand, it makes treatment accessible to populations that did not have access to psychological interventions beforehand and to individuals with problems that prevented them seeking such interventions. On the other hand, it threatens the conviction that genuine human contact is imperative for successful psychotherapy.

The review below demonstrates how theory and research in this field developed in very different directions, due to conflicting therapeutic approaches that often contradict one another.

We will attempt to show that the world of therapy has two significant aspects – one that emphasizes the therapeutic relationship as the primary component in achieving change, and another that presents the therapeutic techniques as the central element.

As this book is intended for a relatively wide range of professionals including psychotherapists, group facilitators, and organizational consultants, we will begin with a brief overview of the world of psychotherapy.

Two Approaches to Psychotherapy

For many years, the world of psychotherapy has been divided into two different camps. The main difference between the two camps was their view of the curative factor in psychotherapy that might produce the desired change (cf. Omer and London, 1988).

We will refer to one group as the Techniques Camp, and to the other as the Relationship Camp. Each of these camps view different components as central towards bringing about changes, and therefore their attitudes toward remote treatment will differ from one another, as explained in the introduction.

The Techniques Camp

The techniques camp emphasizes the importance of the treatment method and defines treatment protocols in which certain interventions are emphasized as the generators of change. This is easy to demonstrate in cognitive behavioral therapy (CBT), in which there is a clear and well-defined series of interventions that define the principles of the method.

There are different examples of such interventions that demonstrate the extent to which the transition to telemedicine affects the methods used by the techniques camp. For example, a cognitive therapist is expected to identify automated thoughts, and to use them to identify key beliefs or organizing schemes that manage the patient. In order to identify these thoughts and beliefs, the therapist will apply techniques such as the "ABC" model (A = Activating Event; B = Belief/thought; C = emotional and behavioral Consequence).

As its name suggests, this method also employs a series of behavioral interventions that are designed to improve the patient's condition. Methods of soothing the body through muscle relaxation have been fundamental techniques in CBT for many years. Although today there is a tendency to undervalue the importance of these components, they are still basic tools that therapists use. Upon entering the third generation of CBT, less of an effort was made to use these techniques. However, the acceptance approach and mindfulness ultimately emphasize both breathing and body scan.

In any case, this quick overview of CBT emphasizes the essence of the techniques camp. This leads us to the question of whether it is possible to translate these techniques for remote therapy and if so, how.

It is important to keep in mind that the techniques camp encompasses many other approaches beyond classic CBT. It includes approaches such as Acceptance and Commitment Therapy (ACT), as well as behavioral approaches such as DBT.

The Relationship Camp

Advocates of the relationship approach regard the therapeutic relationship as the curative factor that is the central facilitator of change. This camp maintains a series of assumptions about the origin and development of mental problems, which focuses particularly on the importance of the initial characters in the patient's life as designers of their worldview. It is assumed that an individual's central experiences as a child are those that shape his adult life. This approach is often considered to be inspired by Freudian thinking and his hypotheses about the necessary processes that the newborn undergoes while developing a relationship with parental figures. Over the years, this camp has evolved and now places great emphasis on the attachment processes, i.e. the extent to which the child experiences a pattern of secure attachment to the parental figure.

Thus, the relationship camp assumes that past relationships are the source of psychological problems in the present. Therefore, reconstructing those relationships and remedying them through a relationship with the therapist is the central component of therapy. Therapeutic approaches that explore the characteristics of the relationship between the patient and therapist were developed based on this assumption. This helps explain the development of concepts such as transference, i.e. how a patient relates to his therapist based on experiences with significant figures from the patient's past.

Dynamic therapists once placed a great deal of emphasis on interpreting relationships as "discovering the source of the patient's problem," however in recent years there has been an increasing tendency to perceive the patient's relationship with the therapist as therapeutic by itself.

Some of the central concepts that are often utilized by the relationship camp are "holding" and "containing". Though these terms have different meanings, both imply the importance of the supportive and accepting relationship. The relationship camp will then question whether holding and containing can be conveyed through Internet communication and impersonal screens.

How the Two Camps Use the Internet

The different approaches to Internet-based treatment that have been adopted by the two camps should not come as a surprise, as each camp has approached these developments in very different ways. In fact, there are significant publications about the use of Internet in psychotherapy, but each camp has developed its own approach to issues related to telemedicine that do not necessarily coincide with that of the other camp.

The techniques camp might have been expected to be the first to implement and document its application of remote interventions, as this camp is more likely to use technology than the relationship camp that sometimes attempts to detach the therapeutic process from the world of computers and telecommunication. Surprisingly though, the relationship camp was the first to begin writing about tele-therapy. As an anecdote, we might consider the fact that Freud would sometimes correspond with his patients though letters, which can be seen as the beginning of remote therapy.

The dynamic world has always been concerned with setting. Hundreds of articles have been written about the question of whether lying on the couch can be considered the same type of treatment as facing the therapist (cf. Grotstein, 1995). In other words, the question of the importance of face-to-face interaction has been pondered for many years.

Perhaps the first time that this camp dealt directly with remote therapy was when the telephone was introduced into the world of therapy.

Therapists began to address the question of how to continue treatment when the patient traveled on business trips and was unable to visit the therapist's office (see Saul, 1951). This was a crucial issue, as therapists at that time believed that therapy sessions should take place four to five times per week. Psychoanalysis by phone, without seeing the patient, would most likely have been acceptable as it does not significantly differ from laying on the couch without eye contact between the patient and therapist.

However, there was significant opposition to the idea of using the phone for psychoanalysis. For example, Argentieri and Mehler (2003) represented the conservative-traditional stance that this could not be considered psychoanalysis but rather "only a supportive treatment". Anyway, the need to teach psychoanalytic approaches and to train therapists in remote countries such as China caused some members of this camp to "break the rules" and to dare to provide remote supervision and later even remote psychoanalysis for therapy students. Other developments were the introduction of Skype software which significantly improved the visual image, and the increasing speed of the Internet which enabled higher video density and thus better-quality communication. It is clear that the transition to remote treatment challenges certain fundamental dogmas and principles that characterize for the relationship camp, which explains the availability of vast literature and discussions on this option, and on the legitimacy of remote care via the Internet. Quite a few books have already been written on this subject. *Distance Psychoanalysis* (Carlino, 2011), *Screen Relations* (Russell, 2015), *The Digital Age on the Couch* (Lemma, 2017) and the special issue of Psychoanalytic Perspectives (2017). The most impressive enterprise on this subject is undoubtedly a series of four books published between 2013 and 2018, entitled Psychotherapy Online (Scharff, 2013, 2015, 2016, 2018). Each volume offers a fascinating discussion on the significance of remote treatment and how it affects the therapeutic relationship.

Despite the abundance of books and articles, very little quantitative research on this subject has been conducted so far in this camp. Qualitative analyses and even research on the attitudes of psychoanalysts about remote therapy are still lacking.

The techniques camp did not ignore the possibilities offered by the Internet but focused mainly on the possibility of adapting techniques that were developed for face-to-face therapy for online therapy, without addressing the question of how this may interfere with the development of the therapist-patient relationship. In Albert Ellis' introduction to Debrig-Palumbo and Zeine's book (2005) on online therapy, for example, he writes that "a big myth in psychotherapy is that, in order to relate well to your clients, you have to show them fine empathy, support, and acceptance, and you have to see them face to face – Nonsense!" (xi).

Therefore, it is not surprising to see that much of what has been done in the field has not focused on face-to-face video meetings but rather on transferring CBT techniques over the Internet. In fact, it might be possible to say that the main focus of the techniques camp is to find ways to make their proven methods more widespread by using the Internet.

Barak, Klein and Proudfoot (2009) identified the main areas of online psychological therapy. Videoconference is only one example, and perhaps a less common one of Barak's list. In any case, it is very important to see that thanks to the techniques camp, hundreds of studies emerged within several years on the various aspects of Internet-based treatment. Gerhard Andersson, editor of the "Internet Interventions", a leading journal in this field, writes that in just a few years there have been over 200 randomized control studies in this field (Andersson, 2018).

The Approach Taken by this Book

The editors of this book believe that many roads lead to Rome, and that many psychotherapeutic methods can contribute to an individual's well-being. Yet we do believe that providing therapy for another human being is completely different than using a computer-based self-help program. However, our approach is to seek interesting ways to integrate the principles of the techniques camp with those of the relationship camp.

Over recent years, more complex models of what is called "blended interventions" have emerged. These are treatments that incorporate both face-to-face interaction and computer-based self-help programs (Fitzpatrick et al., 2018). Sometimes the face-to-face meetings are held while both the patient and the therapist are in the same room, but in principle a patient can see a therapist face-to-face online. The therapist can refer the patient to a site where he or she can practice behavioral cognitive methods, and once the patient has practiced them s/he will be able to return to the video conference with the therapist.

Both authors were raised on analytic approaches, but each sought unique ways to expand psychotherapy to make it more effective. Haim Weinberg, for example, has first studied many group interventions over the Internet that did not incorporate video or audio conferencing. Arnon Rolnick developed programs that allow the patient to practice self-help techniques that are based either on CBT or on biofeedback. Therefore, we have first explored options other than videoconferencing. It is important for us to emphasize that despite evidence that interventions without interpersonal encounters may be as effective as face-to-face interventions (Andersson, 2018), we believe that these are different types of interventions that offer a completely different human experience. Although we emphasize quite strongly that technology appears to be taking over a large portion of this discipline, we are convinced that a face-to-face encounter in one room or via video has important qualities that differ from computer-based exercises. On the other hand, we argue that there is no need to separate technique from relationship. We believe that effective treatment is sometimes obtained by structured interventions that have proven to be effective, and at other times, by developing the relationship between the therapist and the patient as a central component of treatment.

In sum, although many studies indicate that software that does not involve human intervention is effective and even creates a therapeutic alliance, we believe that this is another possible form of intervention. However, in cases of interventions involving more than one person (i.e. marital or family therapy, group therapy, or organizational intervention), it is difficult to imagine effective computer therapy without any personal encounter.

Do Not Throw the Baby Out With the Bathwater: Reclaiming (Video-based) Conversation

Sherry Turkle, one of the first to study online interactions in the early 1980s, was at first extremely enthusiastic about the role that computers play in our lives. She saw the online world as a place where people could express aspects of themselves that they typically repressed in their daily encounters (see *Life on the Screen*, 1995). However, as technology has developed, Turkle discovered the dangers that online interaction might present to human communication and became less enthusiastic (see *Alone Together*, 2012).

Recall the science fiction scenes presented at the beginning of the introduction. The possibility that humans will no longer meet other people in-person (like in *The Naked Sun*), or that they will seek loving relationships with a robot or operating system as in the movie *Her*, can be alarming for any psychotherapist or consultant.

In her book *Reclaiming Conversation* (2015), Turkle talks about how people prefer to send text messages than to talk or meet. We agree with this observation and her recommendation to reclaim conversation. We also agree with the message that she directs mostly to the techniques camp, that people and machines are not interchangeable. Turkle has conducted vast studies on human interaction with robots and alerts us to the possibility that a robot could replace emotional interaction with another human being.

As we noted above, we tend to agree with Turkle that the techniques camp might lead us to a situation like the one portrayed in the movie *Her*, in which computers or robots provide "psychotherapy". But unlike Turkle, we suggest not to throw the baby out with the bathwater. We believe that hybrid or blended interventions that involve both human-to-human interaction and self-help individual exercises using applications could be an integrative and powerful means of reducing human misery.

Turkle, however, takes the more extreme position of opposing all forms of online, video-based psychotherapy. She argues that therapists have a crucial role in defending the value of physical presence in today's digital culture. In an interview for *Psychoanalytic Perspectives* (2017), a psychotherapy journal, she said that "when analysts consider what screen relations will do to their enterprise, I don't think they take seriously enough that it will change its very nature" (239).

One cannot avoid comparing Turkle's view with Jean-Jacques Rousseau's notions of returning to nature. Rousseau believed that the more humanity deviates from its natural state, the worse off it would be. Rousseau taught that men are naturally free, wise, and good, and that instinct and emotion, when not distorted by the unnatural limitations of civilization, are nature's voices and instructions for living a good life.

This book takes a different view. As Lou Agosta writes, "the Genie – online communications – is out of the bottle, and turning back the clock is not an option. The future belongs to those who are able to interpret and manage the transference off-line – and online" (Chapter 3 in this volume) Agosta, who has already written a few books about empathy (cf. Agosta, 2010, 2018), deals with the question of whether empathy can be transferred over the Internet. He analyzes what constitutes empathy and suggests that video conferences can facilitate an emphatic process.

So, this cluster explores Turkle's position. We adopt Porges' (2011) focus on the important role of the face in human communication. Using his polyvagal theory, he points out that humans regulate each other based on facial expressions and tone of voice. One of the unique features of online therapy is that the faces that the patient and the therapist see are in fact clearer and bigger on screen than in a regular face-to-face session. Our experience using Skype for more than 15 years has shown that we see facial emotional responses much more clearly during video conferences than what we used to see in our clinics.

Ogden and Goldstein, whose psychotherapy is very much body-oriented, have contributed a chapter to this cluster (Chapter 4), in which they widen the scope to include issues related to the patient's movements, gestures and posture.

> The efficacy of the therapeutic journey between therapist and client can be heightened by thoughtful attention not only to the verbal narrative, but also to the somatic narrative – the story told by posture, movement and expression. With creative adaptations explored in this chapter, videoconferencing can be effectively used to tap the wisdom of the body, offering clients a valuable avenue to heal the wounds of the past and develop new competencies.
>
> (Chapter 4 in this volume)

Their chapter also offers an excellent example of how the relationship camp can be integrated with the techniques camp. While sensory-motor psychotherapy is very much associated with the relationship camp, their practical suggestions are a good example of using diverse techniques in psychotherapy.

The interview with Galit Atlas and the late Lewis Aron (Chapter 2 in this volume) shows the ability to present long-standing analytical thinking that takes a free, contemporary view in which psychoanalysts discuss distance therapy without any apologetics. Aron is considered a leading advocate of the relational movement in psychotherapy and writes quite a bit about the history of psychoanalysis, but clearly supports online psychotherapy. Atlas, who writes quite a lot on sexuality in therapy (2017), is not "alarmed" by the apparent absence of the body in remote therapy. Aron also discloses that today, much of his teaching and supervision work is done remotely.

Both the relationship camp and the techniques camp are dealing with online supervision. In this cluster (Chapter 6), Pennington, Patton, and Katafiasz write about Cybersupervision in Psychotherapy. They encourage the reader to consider how they may approach the concept of cybersupervision within the context of professional guidelines, research, and theory.

Another chapter by Gily Agar (Chapter 5) offers a refreshing perspective on the advantages of online therapy. According to Agar, there are also quite a few benefits of online therapy. Her title, "The Clinic Offers No Advantage over the Screen", describes several important aspects of transference that are more likely to exist in remote therapy.

Returning to Isaac Asimov who predicted that video conference technology would make us less human and less intimate, the objective of this book in general and this cluster in particular, is to find ways to prevent technology from hinder our humanity. To paraphrase Sherry Turkle, we seek ways for video interaction to reclaim conversation and allow the spread of psychotherapy. The practical considerations described at the end of this cluster are aimed at ensuring that video interaction maintains the humanistic elements we expect from psychotherapy.

References

Agosta, L. (2010). *Empathy in the Context of Philosophy*. London: Palgrave Macmillan.

Agosta, L. (2018). *Empathy Lessons*. Chicago: Two Pears Press.

Andersson (2018). Internet interventions: Past, present and future. *Internet Interventions 12*: 181–188.

Argentieri, S., & Mehler, J.A. (2003). Telephone 'analysis': 'Hello, who's speaking?' *Insight 12*: 17–19.

Asimov, I. (1991). *The Naked Sun*. New York, Toronto, London, Sydney, Auckland: Bantam Books.

Atlas, G. (2017). *The Enigma of Desire: Sex, Longing, and Belonging in Psychoanalysis*. New York: Routledge.

Barak, A., Klein, B., & Proudfoot, J.G. (2009). Defining internet-supported therapeutic interventions. *Annals of Behavioral Medicine 38*: 4–17.

Carlino, R. (2011). *Distance Psychoanalysis*. Karnac Books. London.

Debrig-Palumbo, K., & Zeine, F. (2005). *Online Therapy: A Therapeutic Guide to Expanding Your Practice*. New York: Norton.

Grotstein, J.D. (1995). A reassessment of the couch in psychoanalysis. *Psychoanalytic Inquiry: A Topical Journal for Mental Health Professionals, 15*(3): 396–405.

Her (2013). Jonze, S., director [Film].

Fitzpatrick, M., Nedeljkovic, M., Abbott, J.-A., Kyrios, M., & Moulding, R. (2018) "Blended" therapy: The development and pilot evaluation of an internet facilitated cognitive behavioral intervention to supplement face-to-face therapy for hoarding disorder. *Internet Interventions 12*: 16–25.

Lemma, A. (2017). *The Digital Age on the Couch*. New York: Routledge.

Omer, H. and London, P. (1988). Metamorphosis in psychotherapy: End of the systems era. *Psychotherapy: Theory, Research, Practice, Training 25*(2): 171–180.

Porges, S.W. (2011). *The Polyvagal Theory: Neurophysiological Foundations of Emotions, Attachment, Communication, and Self-regulation*. New York: W.W. Norton.

Russell, G.I. (2015). *Screen Relations*. London: Karnac.

Saul, L.J. (1951). A note on the telephone as a technical aid. *Psychoanalytic Quarterly*, 20: 287–290.

Scharff (2013). *Psychoanalysis Online*. London: Karnac.

Scharff (2015). *Psychoanalysis Online 2*. London: Karnac.

Scharff (2017). *Psychoanalysis Online 3*. London: Karnac.

Scharff (2018). *Psychoanalysis Online 4*. London: Routledge.

Turkle, S. (1995). *Life on the Screen: Identity in the Age of the Internet*. New York: Simon & Schuster.

Turkle, S. (2012). *Alone Together: Why We Expect More from Technology and Less From Each Other*. New York: Basic Books.

Turkle, S. (2016). *Reclaiming Conversation: The Power of Talk in a Digital Age*. New York: Penguin Books.

2 Interview with Lewis Aron and Galit Atlas

G = Galit Atlas; L = Lew Aron; H = Haim Weinberg; A = Arnon Rolnick

H: Let me start with the first question, if we agree that online therapy works, and it seems that it shows similar results, how can we explain it? The body is so important. How do we explain that it works without the body?

G: I want to say that for me there is a body in an online therapy. It's a different kind of body and it's a different format of a body but I have to tell you, one story that comes to my mind as you say that, is that I was on a Skype session with a patient. She is in Uruguay and I'm in New York and at some point, her dog barks, and she walks away and I see her vagina. She's completely naked underneath … so to say that the body doesn't exist is not correct [laughing].

L: I have very little experience with online therapy or analysis. I do a lot of study groups and about a third of my study groups are online. And I love it online. I work on Zoom all the time. And my experience with my study groups is that I feel absolutely as intimate and as connected to the students on Zoom as I do when they're in person. Sometimes, I have to say, even more. Because I feel I have everybody's face right in front of me.

A: And how about supervision?

L: I don't do a lot of supervision, but in general If you're used to seeing patients who are on the couch, and you can barely see their faces at all and you see their body from only a very limited angle, shifting to working with someone on Skype or Zoom, you're seeing more of their body that you've ever seen when they're in the room. And even if they were face-to-face … like now when we're looking at each other, I can see both of your faces with such clarity. And if you were in my office with all the distractions … here I have only your face and the top of your body, blown up. As a matter of fact, sometimes when I'm doing it with treatment, I will sit back further away from the computer, because I don't want to be so in their face. The whole idea, that you're not getting the body, doesn't hold true. And I had a story just like Galit. I had this one guy who was a finance guy and he was traveling around a lot. And he tended … also he would call me to keep his hour, he would call me sometimes it would be one in the morning, or 3 or 4 in the morning for him. He would wake up to have a session. And he would call me from his bed. And he's wearing his pajamas or his t-shirt and he's sitting in his bed and he just woke up for the session. I'm seeing more of his body that I want to see.

G: Sometimes it feels too close and there is a worry that … some therapists are afraid that the patient sees too much of them, not only that we see our patients from too close … how much I can control it. There is also something about that fact that when you have analysis on line you can usually also see yourself.

A: Right. Do you want to say something about that, the fact that you can also see yourself?

G: I think it's really interesting. I never thought about it, you know. Sometimes I see patients look at themselves instead of at me. I'm aware that with some patients I look at myself more than with others. There is something there to analyze and understand.

L: Yes. Since you're talking about it I can't stop looking at myself.

G: I know. You fix your hair, right? There is much more … we were talking and there is much more awareness, right? On how we look.

H: True, very true.

G: And I don't want to leave out of the picture the fact that something is left out of the picture. I mean the fact that my patient could sit in front without her underwear, and I don't even know that, right? There is a question what's in the frame. I can sit with my phone right here and somebody can text me, and I could look at it, if I want, right? I think that's a big question, how to keep boundaries where the other person sees only part of the picture.

L: Just in relation to that, it makes me think of the use of the phone, because for years I would have sessions on the phone before the internet and all of that. And I find that my concentration, staying with the patient, not getting distracted by the phone is much better on Skype or on Zoom than it used to be on the phone. With the phone, it was only sounds, my mind would wander and I was much more tempted to do other things or get distracted. With Zoom I feel more tuned in.

G: Right

A: But the question, maybe sometimes you want your mind to wander, you know.

H: But I don't think that it's the same. Do you agree, Lew? It's not a kind of reverie, it's a distraction.

L: Yeah.

A: I think that we might consider recommending to sit a little bit farther away. Maybe you should see a part of my body. Galit I can only see you from your chest and I want to see what is below. You see? How would it feel if I were to sit further back? [Arnon moves away from the screen].

G: But it bothers me that you went back, you know? Because now I feel too far from you. I want to ask you to come back. I feel like I can see more of your body, but I can see less of your face.

H: Galit pointed out something. The big question is whether you want to replicate exactly the conditions in the office, or not. So what would you say about lying on the couch and having the camera on the back of your head.

L: It's a different medium and you can't transfer it from one to the other. The idea that you look at the back of their heads just makes it absurd. It's very different than when they're in the room with you and they're on the couch and you have an overall understanding and view and context for what's happening. I think this is a really different medium and I do think it's going to take time and experimentation to think of all of the possibilities. Jonathan Slavin, whom you may know, does a lot of internet work. And he actually taught me, because he had much more experience than I did, this idea that when I'm working with patients, to sit a little bit further back and he uses headphones and the mic so that he doesn't have to speak into the mic on the computer, so he could be further away. And he said – and I think he's right – that it gets you away from only a headshot, you know, where it's nothing but the head. And people can feel like it's just head to head, too intrusive. I don't think there's a right answer about which is better. I think these all become options, and just like the patient in the room may choose to sit in one chair or another or the couch or get up and switch. Similarly, with Zoom or with the new technology, some people may feel comfortable being a little back further and that becomes one more thing to study and investigate, and understand what it means for them.

H: And to discuss, maybe.

L: Yeah.

H: Because many of the differences we simply ignore. And I think that we should not ignore them but discuss them like what you did, Galit, with Arnon. If you were a therapist or a patient, maybe we should discuss it: how close do you want me? Is it ok that I'll sit back?

G: I always try to discuss it, you know? Because the frame is different, right? I always ask the patient where are you exactly, do you want to show me around, or not? Because sometimes I'm in their bedroom. Sometimes I'm in their hotel. Sometimes other people walk into the room.

H: This is something we need to talk about, because the meaning of people walking into the room is that – and this is one of the biggest differences – that we do not control the setting.

G: Right.

H: And I wonder whether you want to relate to that, because the setting in psychoanalysis is so crucial, and suddenly we cannot create the setting that we want, because other people are walking in. what do you say about that?

L: In the times that I worked with patients this has been an issue ... we've had talks about it. For example, if somebody's traveling to a business conference and still they'll take an hour out to have a session. Where are they going to find private space? Can they get a room that they're sure is going to be private ... and their concern about who else might be able to hear them. If it's that they can go back to their hotel room and know it's private, that's a different situation. I think this is particularly complicated with college students. Many college students are speaking to a therapist back in their home-town, right? They started therapy before college or during high school or in the summer. Then they go off to college and they want to have a connection with the therapist. But now they're at their dormitory, and they have a roommate. How are they going to make sure they're going to call at a time when the roommate isn't coming in. and then the roommate becomes a part of their therapy, because the roommate has to be consulted about when you're going to be on Zoom. And so these are the kind of things that I think come up practically all the time.

G: We cannot go back to older ways. There is no going back, especially for the young generation, I'm talking about people in their 20s and 30s – that are doing Skype or Zoom everywhere. They do their meetings, their business meetings, online. They date online. They have sex online. Everything they do online. And that includes looking at yourself. It's part of the frame.... You know, it becomes almost something that you don't think about.

H: I think that it's back to the question how much do we want to copy exactly the conditions of the office or understand that it's a new media and we need to accept it differently and not relate to it as if it's the same.

G: Yes

L: You know ... talk again about going back, a lot of what we did was a historical accident. You know, neurologists in Freud's day had a certain kind of office. They made their living in a certain kind of economic model. Freud said himself that the reason he set up the office the way he did, the way he charged the way he did, and the policies, he said that's what tutors used to do, what music teachers used to do, when he was practicing in Vienna. He was doing what were the norms in Vienna in his day. And we keep doing it as if it's a holy ritual. So things shift. I'm very much in favor of not solving these problems with rules. And even in terms of figuring out what the policies are going to be, my feeling is that it's premature. We haven't had enough experience with yet, and I think, as an educator, we want people to experiment, and instead of this being something that's off to the side and they can't talk about it during their training because it doesn't count as kosher for the trainers, then they don't talk about it in the training seminars and don't talk about it with their supervisors because it's considered something not exactly right. I would much rather encourage that while the student is in their analytic training, that they bring this material in, and the student have a chance – with the supervisor, or with their class – to compare, what does it feel like when the patient I'm working with is online, what does it feel with the patient that comes to my office. What does it feel with the patient I'm taking a walk with. And bring it into the training. Don't keep it on the outside. If you keep it on the outside, and it's "against the rules", then we never really have a chance to work with it and learn from it and explore for ourselves "what does it feel like for me?". It may turn out for some of us, that it's not a good way to work. And for others of us it may be a very excellent way to work.

H: I have a couple of questions if I may, as a kind of devil's advocate. So, for example, you know that in online therapy the patient cannot really destroy the analyst. What do you say about that, if we think about Winniccotian ideas?

G: Why do you think they can't destroy the analyst? They can press a button and destroy...

H: You think it's the same? Like wanting to catch your throat and strangle you?

G: There are ways, I absolutely think it's the same. Not in the same form, but I think that of course they can destroy the analyst. It looks different maybe, but it's the same. The affect is the same, the impact is the same. It's just a different format.

H: Ok, good.

L: Even practically, they could do things to you that they couldn't do in the office. Online, they could be googling and searching, prying for information, getting into your personal life. There are all kinds of things they be doing that can be destructive.

H: Ok, ok. So we don't actually need the physical contact in order to feel that we are full of destructive drives. Ok. what about the opposite?

L: We're also presenting – and I understand you're doing it to play devil's advocate - but we're also discussing it now as if it's an all-or-nothing thing where you're only seeing the person online rather than some kind of combination, where you're seeing the person in-person part of the time and online ... you know and certainly I think it's worth if you're seeing somebody online having a certain amount of contact in-person as well, so … I don't think we have to be thinking of these in absolute alternative terms.

H: Ok, thank you. Good answer. Now I'll continue to be devil's advocate. A patient wants a hug from me, and online it's impossible … does it take away something that the patient cannot get what he wants, a real hug right now?

G: Yeah … you know, yes, but they might mean something else. I mean, it depends, right? If the hug is about a boundary … I have a patient that says before he leaves the room "consider this a hug". Which I really like. Again, it depends: is it a way to break a boundary, to get a hug? Is it a way of … fantasy of comforting the patient? Then, what are the other ways that we could find to replace this hug online. In some ways I feel that exactly like in analysis, if somebody has a need, it'll find its way. We will see it. if not through the hug, then through something else. It'll just have a different face.

L: I don't think that anybody … anyone would argue that it's exactly the same. There are going to be differences and they might be advantages or disadvantages at any given time. So I don't think that it's an argument that it's an exact equivalent. The issue is can you get to the things that you need to get to more or less so it's an effective vehicle, and some of the things may actually look pretty different and come about differently.

H: Yeah, well, I have the same conclusion. I want to go further. What about erotic transference?

G: Honestly, I cannot conclude that that's true for everyone, every-where. My personal experience is that erotic transference can actually become more intense, online.

H: That's interesting.

G: Yeah … even about porn, if you think about it, right? Or about any kind of sexual exchange that is not personal, it can be objectified a little bit. And there is something I think that in-person, some people might become inhibited, sometimes. I'm thinking about it especially from comparing patients that I see both in-person and online, that I feel that there is much more erotic transference when we're online, than when you're face-to-face. There is something actually about what you're saying about the absence of the body that allows that and the distance. And the fact that we cannot touch each other. Right?

H: And the fantasy works more, maybe.

G: Yeah. And I think it's more safe, right? I mean maybe that's even the basic thing. That it's a little bit more safe to have erotic material come up. And nothing can happen.

H: Ok, good. Arnon, do you want to ask …

A: Yes, if we think about interpersonal neurobiology people. They emphasize that everything is going via the body and, you know, right hemisphere to right hemisphere … if we try to include this into our discussion what would we make out of it?

L: I like keeping up with what is going on – particularly, I have to say, I like reading Mark Solms. I think that a lot of the neuro psycho-analysis is used very simplistically. And there's been a wholesale acceptance that right brain to right brain communication means that people need to be face-to-face and you need to have eye contact direct back… again, it's unwarranted, I think, and premature. And too big a generalization. It may be that some patients need that and this may help explain why it would be useful with some patients. I don't think that it's a general thing, that it's true for everyone. And I think that we have to be very careful about reaching conclusions about what's good and what works in a general way. People talk about "the therapeutic action" of psychoanalysis, as if there's one way of thinking about how people get better. And I always feel like there are many, many, many different therapeutic actions of psychoanalysis and it's not that they all work for everybody. They work differently for different people. Some people get better one way and other people get better another way. And we need experimentation and diversity and multiplicity. So I'm not persuaded that the right brain … it's not that it doesn't have a basis, it's being used in a very simplistic way. Peoples right brains tend to be connected to their left brains.

H: So here's another question that is a kind of devil's advocate. Some people think that the intimacy that is created online is not the same. And actually we cannot create the same intimacy. I know Lew that you said you feel differently. But I want to ask it as a clear question.

G: I can create intimacy anywhere.

H: Galit, I agree.

G: But I want to add something more. I'm a different person, slightly … my self-state, I would say, is different as a writer, or as a mother or as a therapist, probably online slightly. But I believe it depends on how much you are used to a format. I do a lot online, so looking at you online is not anxiety-provoking for me, it's not unusual to me. I assume that if it was my first time online I would be more anxious. What is it that we are used to or not used to, what creates more anxiety, less anxiety – for us, as analysts.

H: This is a very good answer, because it brings a frame of reference of the relational approaches, using the idea of self-states, we have an online self-state. So do you think of other relational ideas or concepts that might help us understand or be used about online therapy? Like enactment, or co-construction, whatever?

L: I mean, just off the top of my head, I think all those concepts would apply in the same way online. People are going to enact, whether they are enacting online, they're going to dramatize things, play things out, play out scenarios, take on characters, take on object relation scenarios, they're going to do that online and they're going to do that in-person. It seems to me, the idea of the medium brings up the whole idea of the analytic setting and the analytic stage, the potential space or transitional space, thinking about the nature of the medium extends what we usually think of as the frame, or the setting. It makes the frame and the setting a more dynamic one. One that is more everchanging depending on how the person is using it – how both people are using it. It seems to me there might be a potential, real advantage, in terms of training and education, if the patient were willing to have this used for educational purposes. In the same way that people use tape recordings. But, of course, this is more exposing. In the family therapy world, this has become a norm. So, it's about the culture. And it's about the way it's presented to patients. I do a lot of teaching of Harold Searle's work and he was a very strong advocate of doing live interviews and filming them. What he said was that it's a crazy way to teach a profession, to teach a skill, that nobody ever sees anybody do, other than their own analyst. This may have potential for training that we haven't even begun to explore.

A: The fact that recording is so simple here, you don't have to put a camera, you just …

L: In your experience now, because it's my experience, that the medium, the Zoom, has disappeared. I feel like we're in a room together talking. I don't think our conversation would've been any more intimate or intense or clear if we were sitting in a room together here, than it is now.

H: So very quickly the medium disappears. We feel as if we're not mediated, until there is a technological failure.

G: But you can also say this about in-person, right? I had a renovation next door to my office, they were drilling the whole time. In my mind, in my experience, there are less and less technological failures and there are many failures in the room. I had a leak in my office a month ago, in the middle of a session. Like water came….. In the middle of the room. There's no technological failure that can look like that. You know?

A: I think Lew is in the best position to speak about changes in psycho-analysis, the whole question of being orthodox versus moving and playing with it.

L: Orthodox versus Reconstructionist.

A: Exactly, so I wonder if you could say something about this. How internet therapy is just another step in the change psychoanalysis is experiencing.

L: You know, Freud didn't like talking on the phone. Even to friends and family. He would prefer to write a letter. So from the very beginning of psychoanalysis, the medium mattered. For Freud, the letter had an intimacy and directness and also a chance to revise and think about what you're writing, that the phone didn't have. He didn't like the technology and that's even before his surgery. It's not because he couldn't speak. He didn't like the phone.

I think that one of the biggest issues that we have to think about: how much is psychoanalysis part of the culture, is embedded in the culture, has to fit into the culture in order to work in the culture, and how much psychoanalysis has to be removed, apart from the culture. If we completely adopt the culture, then we don't have a place to be critical of it. On the other hand, if we're so far removed, then we're not relevant to the people in the culture. And it seems to me that … you know I talk about it in terms of optimal marginality. That we need to be marginal, but not so marginal that we're irrelevant. And I think that to refuse these things, to say "oh, it's not the same, it's whoring down psychoanalysis, it's not kosher", that so removes us from where the culture is, that we're no longer relevant. But on the other hand, to completely adopt it, uncritically, without reservation, makes us so much a part of the culture that we may lose the critical edge. So to me, the evolution of psychoanalysis is always in relation, dialectically, to being a part of the culture and yet apart from it.

H: You can replace the word "culture" with "online therapy" and it would be a wonderful bottom line I think, for our interview. Yeah, I think you phrase it wonderfully.

I thought of asking the last provocative question. It's clear from what you say, and from what we talked about, that we need to adjust something, mostly practical things. I want to bring a radical idea. That we need to develop a new theory about online therapies, beyond the practical issue. There must be some new idea that is not exactly the same as face-to-face. What do you think about this idea? A new theory that will be more relevant and more suitable to online psychoanalysis.

L: A new theory…. I have to ask you what you mean: a new theory of what? A theory of therapeutic action? A theory of technique? A theory of mind? A theory of development? A theory of pathology?

H: More a theory of technique actually. Taking into consideration every-thing we talked about but somehow not just detailing "you need to do this, you need to do that" but more understanding it broader terms. For instance, intimacy. I think you are right, Galit, that you create the intimacy, and it doesn't matter when or where. However, I do think that there might be something different about the kind of intimacy that you can create online and we need to talk about it in theory as well.

G: I absolutely agree with that. We don't have enough data. Everything I tell you is from my personal experience. Even when I talk about intimacy I talk about my experience. I didn't even ask my patients about their experience of intimacy. So, everything we talk about is very limited in some ways because what we need is more data, more research, more theory, more everything. And, therefore, I absolutely agree with you. We don't know enough about it. We have to research it. We have to really understand what it means.

L: It reminds me of one story. When I started as director of NYU Postdoc a little more than 20 years ago, I introduced that we'll have a listserv. And it was the first time that the program had a listserv. Twenty years ago those were just developing anew. And the analytical institutes tend to be a group of older people. So, among many of the more senior people there was a lot of resistance to the idea that we were going to start using email and listservs and we decided not to have a print newsletter. We used to mail out a newsletter where everybody got it in the mail, hardcopy. We shifted doing it through a listserv. And at first people were very, very anxious. Many of the older people didn't want to give their emails and sign up for it, and the rationale was that it was going to make the community less personal, less intimate, it was everything was going to be done technologically. We wouldn't see each other anymore. The fact is that that listserv became the heartbeat of the community. That is the thing that now links the whole community together. Even when something deeply personal, we have a loss, someone dies, and we immediately can reach the whole community and everyone knows, everybody can send condolences and a memorial. The internet did not have the effect of making the community less personal, it in fact had the result of making it a much more coherent community. And that was unpredictable. And I think that's the important thing. When we're talking about these new technologies.... Steve Mitchell used to say that the biggest secret of doing therapy is how much of it is trial and error. And I think that's relevant here. We need trial and error. That's the way we're going to learn.

G: I want to add one last thing to that. It's obvious to me that there is a lot of anxiety about online therapy. And that's the main thing we're dealing with. And I'm interested to hear, because you guys have much more experience than us thinking about it, I believe, that maybe the anxiety is also about losing. I was interviewed for the *New York Times* about two years ago about apps. Therapy apps. I think it was an Israeli company that developed a therapy app. And the whole anxiety I believe is really about the fact that technology can replace us. Not only in therapy – in everything. Today I was at a parent–teacher conference and a teacher says: soon you won't need teachers; everything is going to be online. If there is some anxiety that not only is this a tool, but it becomes something that replaces us. And the whole idea about therapy apps, instead of therapists, you have an app that does it.

L: It's annihilation anxiety.

G: Yeah, annihilation anxiety.

H: Yeah, I think both of you touched on important issues. I agree with you very much, Lew, that listserv can be an amazing supportive and community reach-out device, tool. I don't know whether you know but I direct, or manage, or conduct a listserv about group psychotherapy for 22 years and it became such an amazing connecting device. The other thing that I want to say, regarding what you mentioned about the anxiety, that when the telephone was invented the newspaper wrote "that's a disaster. People will stop meeting one another and only talk with each other on the phone. We'll lose the connection". It's exactly the same anxiety.

      Ok, I want to thank you very much. I really enjoyed talking to you.

A: I enjoyed it too. and I felt your presence so close to us on the screen. I think that the content is great. I think we could really use it in our book. Thank you very much.

3   Empathy in Cyberspace
The Genie Is Out of the Bottle

Lou Agosta

Empathy as the Foundation of Authentic Human Relations

The short definition of empathy is that empathy is a method of data gathering about the experience of another person's experience, which is further processed in understanding the other person and responding in such way that the other person is able to assess whether he or she has been understood.

The longer definition of empathy is that the "experience of another person's experience" in the person doing the empathizing is a vicarious experience. Key term: vicarious. A vicarious experience is a form of empathic receptivity: openness to the experience of the other person. It is not a merger with the other person's experience; but rather a representation of the other's experience such as one might have in going to a movie or the theatre, reading a novel or narrative, or listening to person talk about his or her life. This vicarious experience is further processed empathically in understanding, interpretation, and responsiveness.

Empathic understanding is an essential part of empathy. Empathic understanding requires cognition and thinking, but is not mere thinking. The understanding is existential in that it requires comprehending who is the other person as a possibility. The person shows up for therapy as anxious, depressed, or upset; but even within the presentation of the upset, the possibility exists of a break through to shifting out of upset and into human flourishing. Empathic understanding works to grasp and process the possibility of such a shift into well-being.

Empathic interpretation is the folk understanding of empathy: take a walk in the other person's shoes and take the perspective of the other person – "as if" in the other's place – with the other person's character and inclinations in so far as one can grasp them imperfectly in the moment. Empathic interpretation works to make explicit and articulate the other "as if" one had his perspective. Empathic interpretation is not separate from understanding, but a derivative form of understanding that the listener makes explicit. This making explicit is especially important if one finds oneself unable to relate due to differences of character or context.

Empathic responsiveness is an important part of empathy as a complete process. At some point, the would-be empathizer must try to communicate to the other person what the listener has grasped in his experience. This empathic responsiveness may be a concise expression such as an acknowledgement of the other's courage or persistence or humanity (and so on) in experiencing what the other has experienced. This gives the other person an opportunity to validate (or invalidate) the proposed empathic response by providing additional relevant material. So, the process of empathic receptivity, empathic understanding, empathic interpretation, and empathic responsiveness forms a circle. If the proposed empathic response is off the mark or incomplete, then go back to the top and iterate. This definition of empathy is summarized in Figure 3.1. (For further details on applying this definition of empathy see Agosta, 2010, 2013, 2014, 2015, 2018.)

The remainder of this chapter takes this definition of empathy and explores the transformations and obstacles that arise in applying empathy in the four possible combinations (or modalities) in (1) one-on-one psychotherapy sessions in-person, (2) psychotherapy groups in-person, (3) one-on-one psychotherapy sessions online, (4) psychotherapy groups online. Note that here "online" is defined and exemplified as using an Internet-based media of communication such as Skype or Google Groups with a visual image of the other person available on the screen.

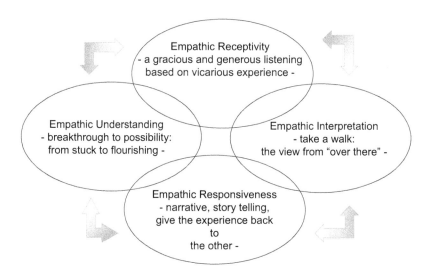

Figure 3.1 How empathy works: four phases of empathy

For educational purposes, the following is a useful sequence in present-ing empathy: empathy individually, empathy in group, empathy individu-ally online, empathy in group online. Thus, at first glance, one may get the impression that the persons are totally available in-person in immediate bodily presence to one another in the traditional one-on-one talk therapy session, but become progressively less available as additional persons are added to form a "group," dividing the therapist's resources and attention; and, even further, availability is further watered down and attenuated by going online and diluting presence by adding additional people in a group. The progression seems to be from authenticity in relating personally to an expanding inauthenticity as one goes online and become personally remote. However, nothing could be further from the truth. The operative terms here is "seems," and this is something of a "straw man."

The average everyday way of thinking about empathy – especially in psychotherapy communities – reduces empathy to a psychological mechanism that is more-or-less effective as the one individual is listening to the other. Nothing is wrong with such an approach, but it is incomplete. If one shifts from thinking of a psychological mechanism to thinking of empathy phenomenolo-gically as a way of being, then empathy expands to encompass the entire context of relatedness. Empathy forms the foundation of intersubjectivity, the founda-tion of community, and is the form of authentic human relatedness regardless of milieu. The result? Each of these milieus – individual and group, offline and online – has its own distinctive way in which empathy shows up and succeeds or fails. It is not as if going online suddenly renders human relations inauthentic, though going online may indeed present new challenges to authenticity. Relating online is a relatively new possibility for human relatedness. Humans may be expected to use and misuse online milieus to succeed or distort or resist possibilities for survival and flourishing in diverse human ways.

Advantages and disadvantages – trade-offs – definitely exist between individual and group, off-line and online, therapy. We now explore the trade-offs in each modality.

The first point is to underline that human beings are empathic in every situation that humans find themselves in. No exceptions. Human beings are even empathic in situations in which they decide (and try) to "turn off" their empathy (for example, they are in a battle with bullets and bombs and want to survive (and decide that turning off empathy will help them to survive)). The second point is that not only does empathy emerge (as we shall see) in the "virtual" group online in cyberspace, but this "virtuality" *already* is present and lives in individual and group psychother-apy in-person. It is sometimes called "transference." Any therapy oriented towards being in the "here and now" activates patterns of feeling and behavior relating to parents and past experiences that "live on" in ways that constrain the client's possibilities. That is why the person came to therapy! The final point is that empathy succeeds or fails in diverse ways in all cases: individually, in groups, off-line and online.

The Individual is Part of the Group, the Group is a Part of the Individual

Empathy is notoriously difficult to conceptualize at the group level. I do not believe or endorse in a group spirit as a practical or workable alternative. However, every individual has within her- or himself the distinction "other person". This is rather like George Herbert Mead's "generalized other" (Mead, 1934). In particular, while the individual participates in the group, the group also participates in the individual. The group lives in the individual as a function of coordinating the responses of multiple members of the group, who, in turn, are trusted or feared, welcomed or shunned. The individual is part of the group; and the group, part of the individual.

Now consider this conversation in the direction of in-person group interactions, for example, in the group psychotherapy practice developed and described in detail by Irvin Yalom (2005). A spontaneous, unstructured, and freely interacting group (Yalom, 2005: 137) aims at a many-to-many interaction in which the participants relate directly to one another, not only to the therapist. In a group setting empathic receptivity, empathic understanding, empathic interpretation, and empathic responsiveness go from one-on-one to many-to-many. However, at least initially, one-on-one empathy is enacted – and succeeds or fails – in a public, community context.

For practical purposes here, we shall not try to solve the problem of a "group spirit" or some entity separate from the individuals in the group coordinating their efforts (or not). The recommendation is rather to work in terms of a service level agreement – group norms. The rules of the group – the rules of engagement, for example: ask for time from the group to discuss a problem or issue; be honest and authentic in expressing one's feelings in the moment; take turns instead of everyone trying to talk at once; or when people speak simultaneously, stop and negotiate, one person speaks at a time; do not tell another person how the other person feels, rather tell the other person how one feels; speak in the first person "I feel ...," "I think ...," "I believe ...," "I disagree ..." and so on. (This list is not complete.)

The participants in a psychotherapy group are peers. They bring with the issues and limitations that caused them to seek treatments for the emotional constraints and self-defeating behaviors that are stopping them from advancing towards their life goals. In no way are participants in the group trained therapists; and their interventions may or may not have the empathic responsiveness that we expect from a professional. However, since space is limited in this format, we go straight to the payoff for group psychotherapy (regardless of milieu). If the therapist tells the client Ben, "Your meaning making machine is working overtime, Ben, and you are making it up that Ruth is angry at you," Ben may or may not "get it." But if one of Ben's peers, Joseph, in the group tells him the same thing, then the statement has an impact that demands a level of in-depth consideration not given to the "authority figure" of the therapist. In addition, one may turn to the group and say: "What do you think? How do you feel?" One may even turn to Ruth and ask her: "Were you angry or was it indigestion?" Naturally, none of the responses is the truth with a capital "T," but, if the group is a relatively coherent and authentic one, then Ben may experience possibilities that he had not previously appreciated. The treatment advances for all, especially Ben.

Furthermore, the accuracy of the particular content of the intervention rapidly becomes less irrelevant than it at first seemed. If attributing anger to Ruth is a way for Ben to avoid acknowledging that he is uncomfortable because he finds Ruth attractive in a romantic way, then we arrive at what makes groups powerful: the process orientation. Go up a level and look at how the interaction repeats patterns in the moment that also occur in one's life outside the group. To be sure, such dynamics occur in individual therapy, too, but they must be brought in from one's experience in life outside the room, slowing the development and conversation. As Irv Yalom points out, process is the power source – and power cell – of the group (Yalom, 2005: 150). It is the value-added contribution of the group approach. Now shift that process online.

The Genie is Out of the Bottle

The day that the first therapist invited his one-on-one client (who had an urgent need for a conversation but an inability to get to the office) to put down the phone and dial into Skype, the genie escaped from the bottle. The reader will recall that in the *1001 Arabian Nights* the Genie was very powerful but a trickster and nearly impossible to control. Making wishes is tricky, and if one is not careful, the sausages end up stuck to one's nose and one must waste the last wish to get them off. In this case, the Genie is Internet technology such as Skype and Google Groups and the emerging conveniences, affordances, complexities, entanglements, and even resistances that it offers. In the *Arabian Nights*, the hero, Aladdin, had to trick the Genie to getting back in the bottle by appealing to his narcissism. "You are not all powerful," Aladdin said. "A large creature like you could not possibly fit in that small bottle!" The Genie's wounded narcissism caused him to prove that he can indeed fit back in the bottle. Aladdin puts the stopper back on – trapped! However, in the case of the Internet and online communication tools, do not look to be able to turn back the clock.

But there is good news. The human face is an emotional hot spot. It is rich in micro-expressions many of which are available and visible even though the "real estate" on the screen in less rich in detail than an in-person experience. Indeed, it is not even clear that the face as presented online is "less rich". It is the only thing being displayed, and the viewer is led to concentrate on it in detail. But here the trade-off of bodily presence versus the imaginary comes into the foreground.

The criticism fails that the online conversation between persons lacks the reality of the in-person encounter. But this criticism fails, in a surprising way. The criticism fails *not* because the online media is so real. Rather the criticism fails because the in-person psychotherapy encounter is shot through-and-through with the imaginary, with symbolism, the imaginary and irreality. The "irreal" includes the symbolic, the imagined, the fictional, the part of reality which is distinct from the real but includes the past and the future and the imaginary, which are not really present yet influence reality.

In psychotherapy, the in-person encounter is precisely about the symbolic and the imagined – the transference. The basic definition of "transference" is that the person relives emotionally the relationship to objects (persons) from the past, persons who are not physically present in the room (or in the virtual space online). What we are calling the "virtuality" of the technology media adds an additional dimension of irreality to the symbolic and imagined transference relationship. Yes, the media is the message (as Marshall McLuhan famously wrote), but with the arrival of online therapy the media is first and foremost the transference. The message now occurs with a strike-through, ~~message~~. The online technology itself becomes a source and target of transference.

The one thing that immediately occurred to us: Psychotherapy invokes a virtual reality all of its own – even without cyber space. This is especially the case with dynamic psychotherapy that activates forms of transference in which one relates to the therapist "as if" in conversation with a past or future person or reality, the latter not physical present. Indeed, with the exception of being careful not to step in front of a bus while crossing the street on the way to therapy, we are usually over-confident that we know the reality of how our relationships work or what people mean by their communications. This is less the case with certain forms of narrowly focused behavioral therapies, which are nevertheless still more ambiguous than is commonly recognized. Never was it truer that meaning – and emotions such as fear – are generated in the mind of the beholder.

While virtual reality (VR) goggles as such are not a part of any online therapy group process, VR goggles are currently being used in individual psychotherapy with clients who are dealing with phobias and related individual issues.[1] For example, it is much easier for someone with a fear of flying to put on a set of VR goggles in the therapist's office and take a virtual trip to the airport, board an airplane (in VR), and be taxing down the run away (in VR), than it is to do this in the real world. The next step in a group process is to create an avatar that resembles one's individual physical self, warts and all, and to join the other avatars in an online virtual reality group session. New possibilities are opened up by this form of therapy for dealing with all kinds of emotional and mental issues that are beyond the scope of this article.

Here the point is just to look at how virtual reality ("virtuality") already lives in the in-person psychotherapy session even as it might have been conducted in 1905. There is a strong sense in which the conversation between a client and a psychodynamic therapist already engages a virtual reality, even when the only "technology" being used is a conversation in English or other natural language. For example, when Sigmund Freud's celebrated client, Little Hans, developed a phobia of horses, Freud's interpretation to Hans' father was that this symbolized Hans' fear of the father's dangerous masculinity in the face of Hans' unacknowledged competitive hostility towards his much-loved father. The open expression of hostility was unacceptable for so many reasons – Hans was dependent on his father to take care of him; Hans loved his father (though he "hated" him, too, in a way as a competitive for his mother's affection); and Hans was afraid of being punished by his father for being naughty. So, Hans' hostility was displaced onto a symbolic object, the horse. Hans' symptoms (themselves a kind of indirect, "virtual reality" expression of suffering) actually gave Hans power, since the whole family was then literally running around trying to help him and consulting "The Professor" (Freud) about what was going on. In short, the virtual reality – now remove the quotes – made present in the case is that the horse is not only the horse but is a virtual stand-in for the father and aspects of the latter's powerful masculinity. So add one virtual reality of an imagined symbolic relatedness onto another virtual reality of a simulated virtual reality (VR) scenario, the latter contained in a headset and a smart phone. Long before VR technology, therapists of all kinds, including behaviorists, used VR by activating the client's imagination by asking him or her to imagine the getting on the feared airplane. One may try to escape virtual reality by not going online, but the virtuality follows as long as human beings continue to be symbolizing, imagining creatures.

The Media Is the ~~Message~~ Transference

Transference to the online technology becomes the obstacle and the enabler of the process of online therapy (both individual and group). The technology itself becomes the two-ton elephant in the living room going unnoticed like most elephants. The strike through of the word ~~message~~ of Marshall McLuhan's slogan "The media is the message" is intentional. The "media equation" suggests that we relate to media as we relate to aspects of our humanity – with distance, involvement, and a certain respect (see Byron Reeves and Clifford Nass 1996/2002). The fantasy that, thanks to the technology, the therapist can read your mind is not as farfetched (or limited to the paranoid) as it might at first seem.

To err is human, to cause a complete breakdown requires the Internet! Technology is a great leveler. Anyone can experience an online technical outage at any time. A new level of vulnerability opens up thanks to the possibilities created by technology. I was talking with a potential new client online. I begin by explaining that in case of an interruption to the session, I will call her back. One of her issues was anger – anger at the world. For reasons we will never know, the online sessions freezes, goes into a suspended state, and hangs up. Attempts to reestablish contact do not succeed. In desperation – I am now getting anxious – I try to reboot my computer, taking up even more time. I try calling by a land line. She does not answer the telephone. It keeps going to voice mail. She is too angry? The cellular service is intermittent? (More technology!) The relationship never recovers. Empathy does not get a chance to be restored. The recommendation for additional therapy norms? Before beginning a series of online sessions, reboot the computer to clean up and considerate computer resources such as memory and connectivity. Have land line and cell phone numbers available, and an explicit agreement to try to restore communication if the service is interrupted. As if the therapist does not already have enough things to manage already! A new challenge emerges. In addition to managing schedule, fees, framework, client agreements, client crises, the therapist is now in charge of the Internet Help Desk. This has never before been a part of her or his job description.

The Fundamental Rule of Online Transference, Whether Individually or in Group?

What a person does off-line the person does online, too. While a generalization, the rule of thumb is that whatever a person does in her or his life off-line, the person does online, too. Whatever the person does in the non-electronic world of personal encounters, the person also does online. That is why online group therapy works in the first place and to the extent that it does work. Yet sometimes being online encourages uninhibited, self-expression. No one can hit me for being self-expressed or provocative. One can feel safe that way online. On other occasions, being online discourages self-expression. The sense of unreality that accompanies talking to postage stamp size representations of people on a screen discourages self-expression. However, in general, if a person is shy offline, the person will be shy online. If the person is mean or a bully offline, the person will bully online, too. However, there is one nuance. The online world may increase a person's sense of anonymity. This is reflected in the celebrated *New Yorker* magazine cartoon, which, admittedly, precedes, social networking: "On the Internet no one knows you are a dog." With the dog sitting at the computer terminal, typing. That is perhaps still true even of Facebook and social networking where fake identities are a new and disturbing trend. Less so in the case of being connected in the moment via a conversation in real time with one's moving, animate representation online. However, the anonymity and impersonality of the online milieu can reduce inhibitions in people who are looking to behave uninhibitedly. Online a person may be able to "let it all hang out" in words – whether authentically or not – because the behavioral consequences are remote.

There is no one else in the room. Once again, such lack of consequences was supposed to be an original feature of the safe in-person psychotherapy session where a person could imagine (for example) the consequences of anger as a part of working through the emotion without enacting the consequences. However, the point is that the online environment may amplify the dis-inhibition in certain individuals. It's *not* "just like" the in-person session. Yes, a person may feel safer in an online group since no one can harm her or him physically – but it may also make it easier for him to avoid the issue of safety and trust – in effect, fooling himself.

Thus, we ask: Is it easier to fool yourself online? Not easier, but different. Humans beings are really sneaky. They are good at "hiding out." If they have been abused or mistreated, they are deeply conflicted about it. They are both ashamed and want to hide from the upset and they want to be known and treated empathically as a survivor. People can "hide out" in a group in-person – but being online can provide new variations on "hiding out." Just as in-person one agrees to turn off or silence one's cell phone; so too online one has to put barking dogs and crying children outside the room. For example, a person is pouring one's heart out overcoming one's shame and inhibitions for a full two minutes – oops, the person was "on mute" and no one heard about it. How is this like the person's life? A voice crying in the wilderness? On a daily basis, this person feels his contribution is not recognized. This must be taken up a level and interpreted at a level of process that requires grasping transference to the technology.

The Zen master understands that the behavior of the computer system is "empty and meaningless." It is what we make it mean that counts. Here "it" lives as the impersonal, the implicit, the un-thought in the background, the meaning we as humans project onto the arbitrary behavior of the automated system in our attempts to reach out and establish an empathic relationship. "Empty and meaningless," yet one can predict with almost absolute certainty that the person who is the most helpless and dependent in his or her life in the real world of traffic jams, lost car keys, and smelly kitchen garbage, will relate to the technology in exactly the same way. This person will be helpless and dependent in relation to the technology of the online session. One will "accidently" hit the wrong button. One will be unable to find the controls required to make the headphones work and reduce the audio echo, enabling clear and clean communication. One will pour his heart out – on mute. One will be unable to get rid of the echo or persistent buzz coming from the unadjusted volume control – the echo of the past?

We get a whole new class of slips of symptomatic actions and slips of the tongues. You know how after one has a fight with one's spouse, he or she accidently drops the birthday gift vase or kitchen appliance and breaks it? It was not done intentionally, but it was done quasi-intentionally due to mixed feelings, ambivalence, and lurking emotional conflict. Online, the favorite "slip" is a "technical difficulty" – when something emotionally charged occur, there is "coincidentally" an interruption in the Internet service for the given individual. Once again, this is not intentional, yet it unwittingly wittingly occurs – the person hits the wrong button.

Technology Shifts the Possibilities of Empathic Relatedness Online

The "gold standard" remains being in the bodily presence of the other person. Human beings are embodied creatures. The philosopher Wittgenstein famously said that the human body is the best picture of the human soul. While some facial micro-expressions are available in the two-dimensional picture of the face, they are much reduced in size. Likewise, gestures such as holding one's palms open and outwards as one talks are correlated with empathy; but the visual information is greatly reduced online (see Chu et al., 2013). The overall disposition of the body is attenuated to the extent that it is nearly impossible to read the body language. Smell is also a powerful way in which the presence of another human being is decisively enacted in relating. It is simply gone in an online mode.

Encountering an individual who is 6.5 feet tall, weighing 250 pounds (195cm, 114kg) who is upset about something, is an emotionally challenging situation. The would-be empathizer has to manage both his sense of other person's upset as well as his own fear that the individual may escalate to violence. In that sense, the online environment can offer a measure of security since the individuals are in separate physical spaces. The possibility of violence no longer exists, and, in general, that is a good thing. On the other hand, without the implicit possibility of escalation being acted out, one does not have the opportunity to demonstrate mastery of it. Yes, I am big, but I can control myself and the therapist does not have to summon "back up" security.

In the online world one does not have a sense of the physical presence of the other person in the same way that one has when bodies occupy the same space. For example, if the therapist has a bias against people who are over-weight, then that is front and center when the over-weight individual is physically present. There is no way to disguise it. When one is connecting using teleconferencing, then that is irrelevant. A benefit? In general, removing prejudices from the space is a good thing and allows treatment to proceed with expanded empathy. On the other hand, being present with the bias would enable the therapist to master her or his own counter transference and expand the authenticity of the empathic encounter.

No matter how advanced the media, the embodied self of the human being in an in-person presence in an in-person psychotherapy session is a powerful actuator of empathic relatedness. Even if one is lying alone on the psychoanalyst's couch where the transference is stimulated by the imaginary quality of the analyst's voice (and not visual presence!) over one's shoulder, one can still hear human sounds of physical presence: the analyst breathing, the chair squeaking as the analyst moves subtly and adjusts position and weight, the nose sniffing, the stomach growling. What are these sounds? They are the sounds of the real presence of our shared humanity. We may debate whether they are directly therapeutic in themselves; but they are part of the structure and framework within which empathic relatedness occurs. The dis-embodied nature of the online environment – whether individual or group – is one of the chief disadvantages of the online approach.

If seven people are sitting in a circle in the same physical room, people do not have to click a button or raise their virtual hand to be taken off mute in order to speak. They look around and prepare their own spontaneous, unstructured, freely interacting irruption of speech. Online – and rather like old style radio – if you don't speak, you don't exist. The online therapist who is quiet may disappear, lose power. In contrast, imagine Irv Yalom sitting quietly in-person for the majority of the group session, stroking his beard, being a powerful presence in the space. When this is reduced to a postage-sized presence on the screen, the power of the presence is also reduced. One may say: "Well, what about getting a two-meter-wide screen?" A good idea! It might just work. However, such an investment significantly raises the bar financially and technically. It might be simpler just to leave extra time to fight your way through traffic blockages to get to the clinic.

In an online milieu, the bodily dimension is contracted and the virtuality is expanded. *The empathic receptivity is reduced and the empathic understanding and interpretation are expanded.* The net result (no pun intended) is that empathy continues to be on the critical path of success but different dimensions of empathy are highlighted. Are online group norms different than those that occur when people are sitting around a circle in a group in the same physical space? My sense is that online seems to favor "taking turns" – as opposed to unstructured, spontaneous, freely interacting – since one literally cannot see the details of the facial expression in the online window in enough detail to read empathically that someone just has got to be self-expressed in the next moment or he will explode emotionally. Online it is easier to walk out – you just click "end" and pretend that the Internet connection failed. No easy answer here except that if someone really needs to walk out in the moment, then maybe they should do so. This is one example and raises the general question as to how group norms shift in the online mode.

The distinctive feature of online empathy is precisely an appreciation of how the technology shifts the possibilities of relatedness. In an online milieu, the bodily presence of empathic receptivity is "dialed" down; the need for empathic interpretation – imaging what is going on "over there" with the other – becomes more critical path. The point is that all aspects of empathy are present but the constraints of the technology – the empathic possibilities – may highlight empathic interpretation rather than empathic receptivity due to these constraints. Technology provides both client and therapist with new ways to express ambivalence, mixed feelings, psychic and emotional conflict. Note that such online "Freudian" slips of behavior, of the tongue, and (now) of technology cannot simply be dismissed. The individuals in the group speak and express themselves; and as they do so the unconscious also takes an opportunity to express itself. In plain English, people have blind spots and as they interact, they do so out of those blind spots, many of which are powerfully present and evidence to everyone in the group. Everyone except the person who is speaking. And that is the power of a peer pointing out to the speaker: "Hey, it is no accident that your technology failed at that confronting moment just now. Would you be willing to take look at that?" It may be necessary for the therapist to undertake some basic training in the use of the technology (both as student and instructor!) in order to be able to call out and interpret such symptomatic acts and behavior. These are ways of advancing the treatment by inquiring into and investigating the process as an online process – and are consistent with online therapy, individually and in group. The Genie – online communication – is out of the bottle, and turning back the clock is not an option. The future belongs to those who are able to interpret and manage the transference off-line – and online.

Note

1 See www.psious.com – an engaging start-up which is promoting the VR goggles for psychotherapists. The author (Lou Agosta) reports: I have no financial relationship with this company, and I wrote a blog post in 2016: "A Rumor of Empathy at Psious": https://tinyurl.com/jyuxedq.

References

Agosta, L. (2010). *Empathy in the Context of Philosophy*. London: Palgrave Macmillan.

Agosta, L. (2014). *A Rumor of Empathy: Rewriting Empathy in the Context of Philosophy*. New York: Palgrave Pivot.

Agosta, L. (2013). "A Rumor of Empathy: Reconstructing Heidegger's Contribution to Empathy and Empathic Clinical Practice," *Medicine, Health Care and Philosophy: A European Journal*, doi:10.1007/s11019-13-9506-0

Agosta, L. (2015), *A Rumor of Empathy: Resistance, Narrative, Recovery*. London: Routledge.

Agosta, L. (2018). *Empathy Lessons*. Chicago: Two Pears Press.

Chu, M., Meyer, A., Foulkes, L. and Kita, S. (2013). "Individual Differences in Frequency and Saliency of Speech-Accompanying Gestures: The Role of Cognitive Abilities and Empathy," *Journal of Experimental Psychology: General*, Advance online publication. August 5, doi:10.1037/a0033861

Mead, G.H. (1934). *Mind, Self and Society from the Standpoint of a Social Behaviorist*, C. W. Morris, ed. Chicago: University of Chicago Press, 1962.

Reeves, B. and Nass, C. (1996). *The Media Equation: How People Treat Computers, Television, and the New Media Like Real People and Places.* Palo Alto, CA: CSLI (Stanford) Publications, 2002.

Yalom, I.D. with Leszcz, M. (2005). *The Theory and Practice of Group Psychotherapy*, 5th edition. New York: Perseus (Basic) Books.

4 Sensorimotor Psychotherapy from a Distance

Engaging the Body, Creating Presence, and Building Relationship in Videoconferencing

Pat Ogden and Bonnie Goldstein

Sensorimotor Psychotherapy values body-related communications and the "somatic narrative": the story told by posture, gesture, facial expressions, movement and eye gaze. In this approach, attention is given to how the body itself holds the legacy of trauma and attachment inadequacies, and to how this legacy can be changed through awareness of the body and its movement patterns. Because physical habits reflect and sustain implicit processes, some of which are shaped in the brain and body before the acquisition of language, the somatic narrative can reveal patterns that are not told with words. In Sensorimotor Psychotherapy, the correlations between the body, beliefs, and emotions are paramount. For example, a limiting belief such as, "I don't have any support," or an emotion such as disappointment, will correspond to patterns of physical sensation, posture, gesture, breath, gait, autonomic arousal, and movement. Clients become aware of these procedural habits, and eventually acquire skills to change the ones that reflect and sustain outdated working models that interfere with satisfaction and richness in current life.

To help clients discover and change the non-conscious habits that diminish well-being, Sensorimotor Psychotherapy prioritizes mindful awareness of the moment-by-moment *experience* of physical, emotional and cognitive patterns over engaging in conversation, or "talking about" (Kurtz, 1990; Ogden & Minton, 2000; Ogden, Minton & Pain, 2006; Ogden, 2015). Mindfulness is often characterized as a non-verbal, internal endeavor, taught as a as a solitary, silent activity, even when practiced in group settings. In contrast, Sensorimotor Psychotherapy's "Embedded Relational Mindfulness":

> is integrated with and embedded within what transpires moment-to-moment between the therapist and client through the co-created relationship. Therapists encourage clients to observe internal experience in the present-moment, and verbally share what they observe as their experience is occurring.
>
> (Ogden & Goldstein, 2017: 68)

Embedded relational mindfulness encompasses several critical elements: the therapist observes visible elements of clients' here and now experience, directs them to become aware of this experience (*Let's stay with that hollow feeling in your chest and the sadness that goes with it*) and asks mindfulness questions (*What do you notice in your body right now? Is that hollow feeling staying the same or changing?*). Through these interventions, clients become mindful of their internal organization of experience in the moment, and verbally report what they notice to the therapist.

Although this approach is traditionally an in-person treatment, it lends itself well to a videoconferencing format, where the client receives psychotherapy services at a different site from the therapist's location but where parties can see and hear one another in real time. Hilty, Ferrer, Parish, Johnson, Callahan and Yellowlees (2013) concluded "Videoconferencing appears to be as effective as in-person care for most parameters, such as feasibility, outcomes, age, and satisfaction with a single assessment and consultation or follow up use" (15). However, since working with the client's movement, gesture, posture as well as the body-to-body conversation between therapist and client are essential elements of the approach, Sensorimotor Psychotherapy via videoconferencing presents specific challenges. To elucidate these challenges and their possible solutions, we present a composite case study of a client – "Lea" – who suffers from a history of trauma (molestation by a friend of the family), attachment disturbances (divorce and abandonment), and the diagnosis of obsessive compulsive disorder (OCD).

Introduction to Lea

Lea, a 21-year-old college student, experienced uncontrollable worries and doubts that had become obsessions. When these emerged, she performed repetitive habits that decreased the anxiety caused by her obsessions. She complained that these time-consuming rituals caused her additional distress and interfered with her studies and relationships. Lea's symptoms included many of those typical of OCD: repeated hand washing, fear of touching "germy" objects, repeated checking (e.g. to see if doors are locked), needing things to be in a certain order, needing to do things "just right."

Lea's symptoms began prior to her parents' divorce when Lea was eight years old, leaving Lea, an only child, in the full-time care of her father. Her mother went on to remarry, move out of the country, and start a new family. Those who struggle with OCD are particularly sensitive to stress, and tend to focus on negative thoughts, and Lea was no exception. She talked about the "rejection" and "abandonment" she felt, and wondered aloud what was wrong with her. Her feelings of inadequacy led to difficulty forming close bonds with others, and Lea tended to isolate herself from her peers. The rituals she compulsively performed exacerbated the self-criticism she felt about her OCD, creating a vicious cycle of behavior from which she could not easily escape, characteristic of those with an OCD diagnosis. Lea's feelings of abandonment, isolation, and low self-esteem were complicated by sexual harassment and molestation by a friend of her father's over a period of two years when in her early teens, a trauma that Lea did not reveal to anyone until she entered therapy.

Beginning Videoconferencing: The Physical Setting and Preparation

In videoconferencing, the therapeutic alliance can become unfocused and weakened, especially when casual formats, such as FaceTime, are used. Creating a physical setting for videoconferencing that mirrors in-person therapy and using that setting consistently, can strengthen the therapeutic container. The work environment should be quiet and support a focused intention. At their first meeting, Lea and her therapist each designated a room for their videoconferencing sessions, which helped to establish a sense of continuity and predictability. They also discussed disabling their phones and any distractions on the computer, such as the feed of email, text messages or alerts, to reduce the tendency to multitask or become sidetracked by these temptations.

Since Sensorimotor Psychotherapy depends upon mindfulness, allowing the time to shift gears and quiet the mind prior to the session is helpful. If the therapist arrives at a videoconferencing session in a speedy "action" or "to-do mode," the client might respond in kind. Mindfulness is facilitated when the client can also quiet the mind and be aware of internal experience rather than "do." Quieting the mind was challenging for Lea, and she and her therapist decided to start each videoconferencing session with a few moments of a quiet body scan to help shift gears to a more mindful "being" mode.

Lea's therapist initial goal was to build rapport with Lea in order to form a strong, collaborative therapeutic alliance with her. Sensorimotor Psychotherapy is an attachment-focused approach that emphasizes the role of the therapeutic relationship to foster safety and heal the aftermath of adverse experience. In contrast, although remote Cognitive Behavioral Therapy (CBT) has been found to be an effective modality for OCD (Aly, 2017), CBT relies on self-help protocols, with minimal client-therapist interactions (Rees, Anderson, Kane & Finlay-Jones, 2017). Of note is that the therapeutic alliance is established not only with words, but through implicit body-to-body affective communication. As Bowlby asserted decades ago,

With attachment theory in mind, a therapist will convey, *largely by non-verbal means*, his respect and sympathy for his patient's desires for love and care from her relatives, her anxiety, anger and perhaps despair at her wishes having been frustrated and/or denigrated.

(1980: 180, emphasis added)

Similarly, Schore (2009) writes:

At the most fundamental level, the work of psychotherapy is not defined by what the therapist explicitly, objectively does for the patient, or says to the patient. Rather the key mechanism is how to implicitly and subjectively be with the patient.

(41)

Essential to the therapeutic relationship is state-sharing, a reciprocal embodied consciousness conveyed and experienced through body-to-body affective communication. Clearly, this presents challenges in online videoconferencing.

State sharing in videoconferencing requires that the therapist be able to meet the client in resonant emotional territory in the absence of physical proximity. Because it is non-verbal and implicit, state sharing may be more difficult to attain during videoconferencing, especially when using a small screen. Lea and her therapist decided to use their large screen computers, rather than laptop or cell phone to allow for non-verbal details such as body posture and facial expression to be more easily noticed and felt by each party.

State sharing also requires that therapists are aware of how they use their voices to connect with clients. In the therapeutic relationship, "right-brain to right-brain prosodic communications ... act as an essential vehicle of implicit communications....The right hemisphere is important in the processing of the 'music' behind our words" (Schore & Schore, 2008: 14.) Vital to establishing the relational safety and state sharing in videoconferencing is the therapist's ability to match client's prosody – timbre, volume, pace of their words – as well as their eye contact, facial expression and physical movements (leaning towards, taking a deep breath, tilting the head and so forth) to appropriately to join with the client. Thus, therapists need to be in touch with themselves, their bodies, and their own state, including countertransference, defenses, enactments, and so on.

In Sensorimotor Psychotherapy, tracking the body's posture, expression and movement is essential. During the first session, Lea and her therapist talked about the importance of addressing the body and the challenges this presents in videoconferencing as compared to in-person therapy. For example, tracking the body is limited when only the client's face, rather than the whole body is visible on the screen.

Moving chairs further from the camera allows more of the body to become visible, however doing so renders it difficult to track the subtleties of facial expression. Together Lea and her therapist established some guidelines to work with these challenges.

They chose rooms that were large enough to move their chairs closer and more distant from their computers, and they each utilized rolling chairs. They explored each moving closer to the camera and further away, checking Lea's reaction to each position. With her therapist's prompting, Lea decided that the "default" view that was most comfortable for her was to be able to see the therapist's head and shoulders. This became the therapist's normal position in videoconferencing with Lea, but was adjusted according to their guidelines throughout each session. They also agreed to move their chairs further from the camera when exploring posture and movement to make the body more visible, and move closer to the camera at other times, especially when Lea felt emotionally vulnerable and needed to clearly sense her therapist's resonant empathy that shows most in facial expression and eye contact.

The therapist also asked Lea to pay special attention to her body, and be sure to report any physical changes she experienced, since these might not be visible to the therapist. Providing a menu of what might be important – such as "tell me when someplace in your body becomes tight, or you feel a tingling sensation, or a little movement, like a lifting of your fingers or a pressing down with your feet" helped Lea understand what her therapist was asking of her.

Lea's therapist also requested permission to frequently ask Lea questions about her body to compensate for the limitations in tracking the body in videoconferencing, and also asked Lea to tell her if any of these questions felt uncomfortable. For instance, questions such "When you bring up the molestation, what do you notice in your body? Can you sense any movement, maybe in your legs or somewhere else?" are asked when Sensorimotor Psychotherapy is conducted in-person, but become even more frequent and critical during via videoconferencing to continually call upon the body's movement, posture and sensation to address the client's concerns.

Additionally, they discussed that the therapist would also pay attention to her own body and share her somatic response to something Lea might say, for example, "I feel like my stomach is tightening and I'm pulling back as you mention your aloneness – I wonder if that corresponds to what you're feeling in your body?" The therapist may also contact what transpires between therapist and client, emotionally and physically such as by saying, "There's a real shift in the emotion between us," or "It seems like you move back in your chair as I lean forward."

Once these initial guidelines were established, Lea and her therapist were prepared to commence Sensorimotor Psychotherapy via video conferencing. Lea's primary initial goal was to modulate anxiety and hyperarousal and reduce the OCD behaviors she found so challenging, so therapy began with developing somatic resources – physical actions that would ease Lea's anxiety "just a little." The goal was not to eliminate her anxiety altogether, but rather discover a variety of gestures or movements that would help her quiet it slightly.

Somatic Resource: Hand on Heart

Lea had a great fear of illness from the germs she might contact, a fear she admitted was irrational. Her stated goal was to refrain from washing her hands after contact with objects, particularly when she was in public. However, when she tried to refrain, her anxiety escalated causing her heart rate to increase. The somatic resource Lea discovered was to place her hand on her heart, which helped her to soothe the anxiety and gain a sense of self-regulation. Lea and her therapist both moved their chairs so that each of their torsos, rather than just the face, was visible. Slowly, and mindfully, the therapist suggested that they bring their hands gently to their hearts, and to notice the effect. The therapist and Lea's executing this somatic resource together strengthened their attunement and allowed the therapist to model a gentle, nourishing self-touch action. As she repeated this somatic resource over and over, she began to recognize that nothing bad happened when she refrained from washing. With this new awareness, Lea built her confidence in drawing upon her own body to manage her anxiety.

In Sensorimotor Psychotherapy clients and therapists collaborate to discover somatic resources. This is especially important for those with OCD because reassurance seeking (i.e., from parents, teachers, and therapists) is a predominant response when anxiety or obsessive thoughts are experienced as unmanageable. However, looking for reassurance from a therapist or caretaker can foster an endless cycle, with clients fearing they will not be able to tolerate the uncertainties that arise if they do not get the reassurance they seek. Lea's discovery of a somatic resource was a tangible tool that she could use independently rather than seek reassurance from others, which she found empowering.

Somatic Resource: Posture

Lea's anxiety about eating at restaurants began after her parents divorced, and became so profound that she obsessed about avoiding any food she considered "unhealthy." She became unable or unwilling to go to a restaurant without prior reassurance that the venue would accommodate her ever-growing concerns. During videoconferencing, Lea was in the throes of anxiety as she spoke of this issue. Her therapist noticed that Lea's whole body tightened and her posture became both tense and droopy. This tight, slumped posture further diminished her sense of confidence and control, leading her even more anxious.

Lea and her therapist collaborated to find ways to relax the tension and shift her posture. They both moved their chairs back from their computers far enough so that they could see each other's posture. This presented an opportunity for the therapist to model different postures— both a slumped and an upright, aligned posture – and describe the difference she experienced with each of these two stances, sparking Lea to experiment as well. Lea compared each posture and her therapist asked her to notice the different emotions, thoughts, and degrees of self-esteem. Lea had recently seen the Broadway production of *The Lion King* and was reminded of when the young Simba gained confidence. She described that his whole body shifted as he held his head high and his posture became tall and powerful. Lea's therapist observed and named similar shifts in Lea's body as she spoke, encouraging her to exaggerate this posture to attain a taller, more powerful stance.

Since both Lea's and her therapist's rooms were large, they could easily move far enough away from the camera to allow a view of their full bodies when standing. Doing so, they explored contrasting Simba's aligned stance with a collapsed one, and Lea immediately noticed that she felt more fearful, anxious and less willing to notice her surroundings when her posture was collapsed. She recognized that an upright posture decreased her fear. Her therapist suggested that they practice this upright posture while walking. They each took a few minutes to walk around their rooms, noticing how it felt to walk with a tall, upright posture. When they came back face-to-face in front of the computer, Lea reported that she felt more engaged with her environment in an upright posture, and imagined walking into a restaurant in this posture, which then became her homework. Lea found that she felt stronger, more powerful, and more confident and could explore eating in a restaurant when she maintained an aligned, tall posture.

Somatic Resource: Boundaries

Lea had difficulty setting boundaries with others who came "too close" to her personal space, or asked her to do something she did not want to do. Drawing upon a Sensorimotor Psychotherapy boundary exercise, traditionally used to establish a felt sense of physical safety, Lea's therapist suggested they explore saying "no" with their bodies, rather than with words. Pushing their chairs away from the camera for more visibility, they tried out different ways of physically saying "no": tensing their bodies, using facial expressions, narrowing their eyes and putting their hands up with palms facing outward. It should be noted that such a pushing action by the therapist can appear distorted if the outward facing palms fill up the screen of the client. The therapist must be aware of how their actions come across on the client's screen. Lea's therapist kept one eye on the window that reflected her own body to assure that her demonstration of actions the pushing motion appeared as intended to Lea, and did not appear warped.

Lea liked the boundary exercises. She said she felt a strong "no" inside and she would like to stomp her feet. Her therapist suggested, "Perhaps you would like to stand and stomp your feet to say 'No'." Lea hesitated, saying she would be embarrassed for anyone to see her stomping. Her therapist suggested she might mute the sound on her computer and try the stomping out of view of the camera. With the ability to control her environment and exclude the therapist, Lea felt safer and more comfortable. After she tried the exercise, came back to the camera, and turned on the sound, her face glowed and she reported a felt sense of freedom. Giggling, she said she stomped on the floor so fiercely that she worried her roommate, who came running from the other room.

This foundational boundary work was then applied to real-life situations when Lea's anxiety and her OCD symptoms encroached on her well-being. For example, she said "no" when her concerns about germs arose. She envisioned Simba and his powerful stance, and laughed as she described Simba trying to find his roar; when he tried, only the tiniest of roars was vocalized at first, yet he persisted. Lea imagined herself roaring "no" in a restaurant, and even laughed aloud as she described all the diners roaring back in her imagined scenario. Her therapist suggested that maybe they could both roar "no", in a message of solidarity with Lea in her newfound assertion and joy. Face-to-face at their computer screens, the therapist counted to three, and then both roared, much to Lea's delight.

This joyful collaborative experience was enhanced by the video-conferencing format, as Lea could control the volume on her computer, move out of view of the therapist, and silence her therapist or herself when she felt the need by putting her sound on mute. In this way, she could assert her sense of control over her environment and give herself safety as she tried new actions. This mitigated the sense of awkwardness or even shame that might inhibit exploring new actions. In this respect, videoconferencing offers more options than does in-person work.

Somatic Resource: Breath

Lea compulsively used social media, which had turned into an overarching obsession. Only a generation ago, social exchanges were limited to family members and select friends, and people carefully selected who was privy to their personal thoughts and actions. Now, however, young and old alike post on Facebook, Instagram, and Snapchat; write personal blogs; and send tweets, often fueling an escalating need to let others know of one's actions and thoughts at any given moment throughout the day. This culture in which it is so easy to document our lives can foster addictive behavior, although clear diagnostic criteria remain to be defined (van Rooij, Ferguson, Van de Mheen, & Schoenmakers, 2017).

Several factors lay the groundwork for this phenomenon. Posts on social media often leave out the more challenging moments in life, including self-reflective posts that process one's hurts, frustrations, sadness, and anxieties. Instead, a deliberate attempt is made to portray a persona that conveys the message "all is great." This false self, in turn, generates a sense of longing, envy, feelings of being left out in others, and unrealistic expectations about how their lives should be.

Lea aspired to be an "influencer" on social media by generating followers and obtaining sponsors to pay her for product placement. Lea experienced an addictive, obsessive, never-ending pressure to post, tweet, and so forth, similar to phenomenon that occurs in the addictive cycle of any substance (Borba, 2016; Pantic, 2014). Concomitantly, she experienced anxiety about the negative feedback she received online and lived in constant fear of online haters. She also felt painfully excluded whenever she discovered she had not been invited to an event or party others she knew were attending. She acknowledged that she tended to withdraw, avoid, and shut down when feeling wounded. She described an entire summer during which she saw no one in-person, and remained solitary in her room, connecting solely through social media. As her social withdrawal escalated, she became more isolated in all aspects of her life.

Feeling under pressure to create new and ever-more witty, beautiful, or dramatic online content, Lea found herself spiraling downward. She described a rapid escalation of overwhelming feelings as she waited for acknowledgment and responses to her posts. Her self-destructive thoughts increased, her already low self-esteem plummeted, and she became ensnared in depression. Her anxiety further escalated after a brief dating relationship when her former partner began posting photos to show that he had moved on. Lea felt humiliated, especially in contrast with others' supposedly perfect relationship status updates. Her addiction to social media grew unbearable, leaving her feeling abandoned, left out, with the sense that the world was going on without her, stimulating the attachment wound of losing her mother.

Videoconferencing offers a powerful forum to address anxieties and addictions related to social media. The therapeutic setup can be compared to one in which the therapist is trying to work with an alcoholic client while alcohol is present, tempting and preoccupying the client. The agreed upon guideline that Lea would refrain from using social media during sessions proved difficult for Lea to achieve. Posts showed up on her computer or phone during videoconferencing, and rather than disabling this feature, Lea tried to conceal her use of social media from her therapist. Eventually she confessed that she was "cheating" by checking her social media during sessions, and exclaimed, "Do they have a rehab for this?" Indeed, her therapist had noticed her hunched shoulders and anxious expression as Lea attempted to maintain dual attention—both on the session and on the feed from her social media. As they discussed this issue, Lea said she felt simultaneously empty and filled with anxiety (i.e., tremors or shaking).

Lea's therapist encouraged her to look at social media during the session, and pay attention to how she held her body, particularly her shoulders. Lea discovered that she hunched her shoulders, became very still and held her breath for extended moments when she gazed at social media. Her therapist suggested they explore shifting these physical reactions. She pushed her chair further away from the screen to model opening and relaxing her shoulders and gently expanding her chest by bending her elbows and moving her arms and shoulders backwards, suggesting that Lea also explore this movement and notice what changed, if anything, in her body. Lea reported that pushing her shoulders back allowed her spine to lengthen, and she could breathe more deeply, smoothly and easily. Homework between sessions included Lea watching how she held her body, and how that posture linked to her breath throughout her day-to-day use of social media. She realized that hunching her shoulders and holding her breath deepened her anxiety and panic and the contrast of doing the breath work exercise helped her recognize the adverse impact this holding of breath had on her whole body.

Encouraging Lea to journal her thoughts and feelings as they arose, and coupling this with newfound awareness of her breath and body lay the foundation for even deeper work as videoconferencing sessions continued, and exercises and handouts from *Sensorimotor Psychotherapy, Interventions for Trauma and Attachment* (Ogden & Fisher, 2015: 389, 697–719) were integrated into the session and practiced as homework. Her obsession lessened as she continued to integrate the breath work exercise when she engaged social media.

Somatic Resources: Reaching Out

Proximity seeking actions, like reaching out, secure the nearness of attachment figures (Bowlby, 1969) and are "based on that person's forecasts of how accessible and responsive his attachment figures are likely to be should he turn to them for support" (Bowlby, 1973: 203). Thus, proximity seeking actions are adjusted depending on the response of attachment figures. Ogden (2015) states that reaching out with the arm(s) "can be executed in a variety of styles that reflect and sustain unsymbolized meaning: palm up, palm down, full arm extension or with bent elbow held close to the body, relaxed or rigid musculature, shoulders curved in or pulled back". Lea was fearful of social interactions and tended to isolate herself rather than pursue relationships. She was reluctant to reach out to others, stating that "no one would be there."

Lea's therapist implemented creative ways of mirroring one another as they playfully explored proximity seeking, such as moving closer to the computer camera and then apart, leaning towards the screen, and reaching towards one another with their eyes and eventually with arms, with Lea reporting the changes she noticed with each. Sensorimotor Psychotherapy capitalizes on mirror neurons by therapists' modeling certain actions to primes the client to execute the same. As Lea observed her therapist demonstrating the movement of reaching out, motor neurons in her brain fired as if she were executing the same action, essentially 'rehearsing' the action herself (Rizzolatti & Craighero, 2004; Rizzolatti, Fadiga, Gallese & Fogassi, 1996). Lea was then more willing to then explore reaching out with her hands toward the screen, mirroring her therapist's gesture. The therapist made sure so have her chair far enough back from the camera that the reaching action was not distorted on Lea's computer screen. In this supportive, playful manner, Lea could try out new proximity seeking actions by mimicking her therapist's modeling of them and together they explored the meaning of Lea's actions. For example, as Lea reached out as if to touch her therapist's hand through the computer screen, the words that accompanied the reaching were: "I have help and I'm going to get through this," referring to her struggles with OCD. Lea began to consider that she was not alone, that she did have help, and that maybe she could reach out to others.

In addition, the therapist suggested that they each select a small object that represented support. Lea had a collection of crystals on her desk and she selected a large polished amethyst. Her therapist had a basket of polished stones in her office, and selected one of them. Together, they practiced reaching out at the same time to grasp the object that symbolized support. As they explored the meaning therein, Lea said she felt supported by the amethyst because of its dense weight, smooth texture, and familiarity. Keeping the amethyst with her in her purse or pocket represented deserving support and taking a bit of nourishment. This exercise too helped her combat feelings of isolation, and allowed her to begin to let others in from a position of more internal strength.

Traumatic Memory: Restoring Empowering Action

All the somatic resources described above helped Lea develop self-regulatory capacities, paving the way for more complex processing of painful memories. As she practiced these resources in her daily life, her confidence in herself increased, and eventually she felt ready to directly address the molestation by her father's friend, someone she had trusted, when she was a young teen. She expressed shame and self-critical thoughts like, "Why did I let that happen? I didn't even try to stop him," not realizing that during the actual event she instinctively froze and became unable to take action to defend herself.

Sensorimotor Psychotherapy work with traumatic memory addresses the instinctual protective physical defenses that emerge automatically during threat. These defenses fall into two general types: *mobilizing* defenses, such as calling for help, fighting, and fleeing, and *immobilizing* defenses such as freezing and feigning death or shutdown (Ogden, Minton & Pain, 2006). Discovering and physically executing instinctive mobilizing actions when immobilizing ones have become default defenses helps diminish feelings of being out of control or helpless, replacing them with the experience of empowerment and control.

As Lea talked about the molestation, she reported that her body felt "shut down," and "mostly numb," indicative of immobilizing defenses. Her therapist asked her if there was any part of her body that was less numb, a question intended to prompt an impulse to take defensive action. Lea reported slight tension in her arms and hands. Since tension is often a precursor to action, the therapist directed Lea's mindful attention to the tension and asked what her body "wanted" to do. Lea said she felt an impulse to push. In the prior section on boundary work, the boundary actions were practiced devoid of memory content, whereas in this case, these actions emerged from her awareness of her body during traumatic memory processing. The defensive impulse to push away that could not be executed at the time of the molestation appeared spontaneously as Lea directed mindful attention toward the tension in her hands as she remembered the incident.

In person-to-person therapy, this pushing action could be executed against a pillow held by the therapist, which would allow a client to sense the physical capacity to defend in the here and now. Since this is not possible in videoconferencing, Lea's therapist suggested that she might push using the large exercise ball that Lea had in her room to push against the wall instead. She instructed Lea to place this ball against the wall, which provided some give-and-take as Lea pushed against it, simulating the effect of pushing against a pillow held by the therapist. Lea felt a surge of energy as she pushed hard against the ball. She reported that the movement felt "really, really good" and that she felt angry that the molestation had happened to her. Anger serves to support instinctually driven defenses (Frijda, 1986; Hobson, 1994; Rivers, 1920), and as Lea's anger energized the pushing action, she experienced a physical sense of empowerment and strength. Lea had felt disempowered and helpless to defend herself until she was able to experience the gratification of physically executing a defensive action fully and with vigor. Afterwards, she reported a newfound confidence in interactions with others and less isolation. Her "freezing" in the face of presumed threat that she implicitly experienced when she was with others was replaced with a bodily sense of confidence in their ability to protect and defend herself.

Attachment-Related Memory and Strong Emotion

Bowlby (1980) states that "many of the most intense emotions arise during the formation, the maintenance, the disruption, and the renewal of attachment relationships" (p. 40).

> Lea had always done her best to minimize the intensely painful emotions related to her mother's leaving. Until she had developed the resources to regulate her anxiety and arousal, her window of tolerance (a term coined by Dan Siegel, 1999) was not wide enough to tolerate emotional intensity. Lea and her therapist felt that her tolerance for emotions had increased sufficiently so that she was now prepared to address the powerful emotions pertaining to the abandonment she had experienced as a child.

Addressing strong emotions presents challenges in videoconferencing because clients need a compassionate other – the therapist – to attune to, accept, and "hold" the vulnerability of emotions, as well as help regulate their intensity if needed. It is imperative that clients can sense and receive empathic support from the therapist, which was typically absent during the original event(s). A crucial element is the therapist's own tolerance for emotions, which will determine the kinds, strength, and variety of emotions that are expressed or denied by the client (Schore, 2003). In videoconferencing, therapists need to assess their own affect tolerance and pay attention to their own verbal and non-verbal communications to assure that their ability to welcome emotions can be clearly seen and felt by the client.

> Lea's therapist noticed that when she spoke of her mother, her spine slumped slightly. Whereas previously Lea had developed an aligned posture as a resource for her anxiety, at this point in therapy, the therapist asked Lea to exaggerate the slumped posture instead. Studies show that when subjects embody a certain posture, they are likely to recall memories and emotions in which that posture had been operational (Dykstra, Kaschak & Zwann, 2006). Indeed, as Lea allowed her posture to slump a little more, she said she felt terrible about herself, and a vivid memory from her past came to her mind; an image of watching her mother walk away from their home, get into the car and drive away. Realizing the importance of experiencing and expressing the pain of this memory in her presence, Lea's therapist encouraged her to focus on the image as she allowed her spine to slump, which escalated Lea's emotions of sadness and grief.
>
> Making sure to convey her emotional resonance over the distance, the therapist made comforting, encouraging, nonverbal sounds as Lea cried. She wanted to communicate without words that she was present with Lea in this heart-wrenching moment even at thousands of miles away, so that Lea could sense that someone who was able to share the intensity of her feelings accompanied her as she revisited this old wound. Such non-verbal sounds, uttered in a manner so that the client knows that the therapist "gets it," can convey a degree of empathy that often eludes words.
>
> Emotions are reflected prominently in facial expression, which are registered implicitly by others, who "make inferences about intention, personality, and social relationship" (Ekman, 2004: 412). Lea's therapist made sure to lean toward the camera, so that her facial expressions of empathy and compassion and the softness of her eyes were clearly visible to Lea. Leaning towards also communicates a desire for proximity, which is usually needed by clients when they are in pain. The non-verbal sounds, facial expression, eye-gaze, and seeking proximity all convey to Lea that her therapist resonates with her internal emotional state, and fosters her ability to feel and express deep emotions in a safe attuned relationship.
>
> As Lea's sobs subsided, the therapist used short, simple sentences of empathy, understanding, and encouragement, which prompted Lea to continue to experience her emotions. These statements, said tenderly

with resonant prosody, included, "Oh, there's so much pain … how hurtful for such a little girl … this image has haunted you all your life … you never really got over it, huh" and so forth. Statements like, "the pain makes you just want to curl up, huh" also include the body, and upon hearing this, Lea curled up more, which in turn deepened her emotions further. It was important for the therapist to track Lea's reaction to each statement, most of which resonated but some of which did not. One statement that Lea did not resonate with was, "You must have wished she wouldn't leave." The therapist noticed the knitting of Lea's brow, knew her statement did not resonate, and immediately recovered, saying, "That's not quite it, is it – maybe it would have been worse if she stayed." Lea nodded as her tears spilled over, saying, "All they ever did was fight!" The therapist's ability to track and recover from a statement that did not resonate helped Lea feel understood and again deepened her emotions.

The embodied presence and state sharing that Lea's therapist demonstrated during videoconferencing created the safety for Lea to fully feel and express the emotional pain of her past. After her sobs quieted, Lea could more easily recognize the inaccuracy of the meaning she had made from her mother's abandonment. The limiting beliefs of being unworthy and underserving of love were exchanged for the realization that the abandonment had nothing to do with her worthiness, and that she, like all of us, did deserve love. Lea's habitual collapsed posture, which had reflected her feeling unworthy, did not support this new realization. After this session, Lea and her therapist together embodied an aligned posture and full breath that expanded Lea's chest and uplifted her chin, all of which reflected and helped to sustain Lea's new belief, "I do deserve love."

Conclusion

At first glance, Sensorimotor Psychotherapy as a body-oriented therapy may not seem to lend itself well to videoconferencing, because working with movement, posture, and gesture is essential to this method. However, with the following adjustments, Sensorimotor Psychotherapy via videoconferencing can be an effective way to serve clients.

- Designate a physical workspace that mimics a therapy room and limits interference during sessions.

- Use a large enough room so that you can stand, and move away from the computer without adjusting the screen to make the entire body visible to track and model posture, stance, walking, and so forth.
- Use a large screen computer rather than a laptop or phone to broaden the visual field.
- Use a rolling chair to easily adjust distance and proximity to the computer screen to more easily demonstrate posture, gesture, and other movements.
- Discuss the challenges of a body-oriented approach with clients and ask them to stay aware of their movement, posture, and body sensation and report to you what they notice, especially the movements that are not visible on the screen.
- Collaborate with clients to establish a visual picture that will be your norm (face only, full body, or torso), noting also that Sensorimotor Psychotherapy's work with the body requires adjustments – moving back at times to see full body, closer for facial expression, etc.
- Encourage having props (e.g., therapy balls, pillows, and ropes for boundary work) available to both you and your client.
- Realize that arm gestures, such as reaching out or pushing away, can be distorted in videoconferencing, and make sure the distance from the computer allows for a normal-looking gesture on your client's screen.
- Pay extra attention to facial expression, eye contact, and prosody, and make sure that these are fully visible to the client when needed, because these are primary means to communicate empathy.
- Request clients' permission to ask numerous questions about the body, because it is invariably more difficult to track the body during videoconferencing.
- Use menus related to the body (such as, "maybe you feel tight, or sense a movement in your body, or a sensation like tingling or buzzing, maybe your heart rate changes," and so forth) to prompt your clients' awareness of the body.
- Provide a menu that might indicate preparatory movements – such as "maybe someplace in your body becomes tight, or you feel a tingling sensation, or a little movement, like a lifting of your fingers or a pressing down with your feet."
- Appropriately share your own experience of your body to model comfort with body awareness and encourage clients to do the same.
- Stay mindful of the moment-to-moment body-to-body interchange,
- Use a slow pace to encourage mindful awareness, giving clients plenty of time to sense the body.
- Support emotional state-sharing through awareness of what is happening in your own body, along with curiosity about what is happening in the client's body.

Kocsis and Yellowlees (2017) conclude that online therapy offers novel ways to reach and form strong psychotherapeutic relationships with many different types of patients, and proposed that this may foster therapeutic intimacy in ways that in-person psychotherapy cannot. Sensorimotor Psychotherapy at a distance may be especially befitting for clients with high degrees of shame, body or social phobia, or awkwardness or self-consciousness related to their body, those with a need for greater control or those who might feel safer and more comfortable engaging in body-oriented therapy from the security of their own homes. The benefits of Sensorimotor Psychotherapy via videoconferencing also may enhance cost-effectiveness and continuity of care, by increasing accessibility and serving communities without access to local Sensorimotor Psychotherapy-trained therapists.

Implicit processes are not always accessible through words because they exist beneath cognitive awareness and verbal language. The efficacy of the therapeutic journey between therapist and client can be heightened by thoughtful attention not only to the verbal narrative, but also to the somatic narrative – the story told by posture, movement and expression. With creative adaptations explored in this chapter, videoconferencing can be effectively used to tap the wisdom of the body, offering clients a valuable avenue to heal the wounds of the past and develop new competencies.

References

Aly, R. (2017). Remote cognitive behavior therapy for obsessive-compulsive disorder in Egypt: A randomized trial. *European Psychiatry*, *41*. doi:10.1016/j. eurpsy.2017.01.1992

Bowlby, J. (1969). *Attachment and Loss. Vol. 1*. New York: Basic Books.

Bowlby, J. (1973). *Attachment and Loss. Vol. 2. Separation: Anxiety and Anger*. New York: Basic Books.

Bowlby, J. (1980). *Attachment and Loss. Vol. 3. Loss: Sadness and Depression*. New York: Basic Books.

Borba, M. (2016). *UnSelfie: Why Empathic Kids Succeed in Our All About Me World*. New York: Simon and Shuster.

Dijkstra, K., Kaschak, M.P., & Zwann, R.A. (2006). Body posture facilitates retrieval of autobiographical memories. *Cognition*, *102*(1): 139–149.

Edelman, G.M. (1999). *The Remembered Present: A Biological Theory of Consciousness*. New York: Basic Books.

Ekman, P. (2004). *Emotions Revealed: Recognizing Faces and Feelings to Improve Communication and Emotional Life*. New York: Henry Holt.

Frijda, N. (1986). *The Emotions*. Cambridge: Cambridge University Press.

Hilty, D.M., Ferrer, D.C. Parish, M.B., Johnson, B., Callahan, E.J., & Yellowlees, P.M. (2013). The effectiveness of telemental Health. *Telemedicine and e-Health*, *11*(4): 398–409, doi:10.1037/a0034963

Hobson, J. (1994). *The Chemistry of Conscious States*. New York: Back Bay Books.

Kocsis, B.J., & Yellowlees, P. (2017). Telepsychotherapy and the therapeutic relationship: Principles, advantages, and case examples. *Telemedicine and e-Health*, doi:10.1089/tmj.2017.0088

Kurtz, R. (1990). *Body-centered Psychotherapy: The Hakomi Method*. Mendocino, CA: LifeRhythm.

Ogden, P. (2015). 'I can see clearly now the rain has gone': The role of the body in forecasting the future. In J. Pertrucelli (Ed.), *Body-states: Interpersonal and relational perspectives on the treatment of eating disorders* (pp. 92–103). New York: Routledge.

Ogden, P., & Fisher, J. (2015). *Sensorimotor Psychotherapy: Interventions for Trauma and Attachment.* New York: W.W. Norton.

Ogden, P., & Goldstein, B. (2017). Embedded Relational Mindfulness (ERM)© in child and adolescent treatment: A sensorimotor psychotherapy perspective, in K.D. Buckwalter, and D. Reed. *Attachment Theory in Action*, Building *Connections between Children and Parents.* Blue Ridge Summit, PA, Rowman and Littlefield.

Ogden, P., & Minton, K. (2000). Sensorimotor psychotherapy: One method for processing traumatic memory. *Traumatology*, Vol VI, 3(3): 1–20.

Ogden, P., Minton, K., & Pain, C. (2006) *Trauma and the Body: A Sensorimotor Approach to Psychotherapy.* New York: W.W. Norton.

Pantic, I. (2014). Online social networking and mental health. *Cyberpsychology, Behavior, and Social Networking*, 17(10): 652–657.

Rees, C.S., Anderson, R.A., Kane, R.T., & Finlay-Jones, A.L. (2016). Online obsessive-compulsive disorder treatment: Preliminary results of the "OCD? Not Me!" self-guided Internet-based cognitive behavioral therapy program for young people. *Journal of Medical Internet Research*, 3(3), e29, doi:10.2196/mental.5363

Rivers, W. (1920). *Instinct and the Unconscious: A Contribution to a Biological Theory of the Psycho-neuroses.* Cambridge: Cambridge University Press.

Rizzolatti, G., & Craighero, L. (2004). The mirror-neuron system. *Annual Review of Neuroscience*, 27: 169–192.

Rizzolatti, G., Fadiga, L., Gallese, V., & Fogassi, L. (1996). Premotor cortex and the recognition of motor actions. *Cognitive Brain Research*, 3: 131–141.

Schore, A.N. (2003). *Affect Regulation and the Repair of the Self.* New York: W.W. Norton.

Schore, A.N. (2009). Right-brain affect regulation: An essential mechanism of development, trauma, dissociation, and psychotherapy. In D. Fosha, D. Siegel, & M. Solomon (Eds), *The Healing Power of Emotion: Affective Neuroscience, Development and Clinical Practice* (pp. 112–144). New York: W.W. Norton.

Schore, J.R., & Schore, A.N. (2008). Modern attachment theory: The central role of affect regulation in development and treatment. *Clinical Social Work*, 36: 9–20. Available online at http://link.springer.com/article/10.1007%2Fs10615-007-0111-7#page-1

Siegel, D. (1999). *The Developing Mind.* New York: Guilford Press.

van Rooij, A.J., Ferguson, C.J., van de Mheen, D., & Schoenmakers, T.M. (2017). Time to abandon Internet addiction? Predicting problematic internet, game, and social media use from psychosocial well-being and application use. *Clinical Neuropsychiatry*, 14(1): 113–121.

5 The Clinic Offers No Advantage over the Screen, for Relationship is Everything

Video Psychotherapy and its Dynamics

Gily Agar

Introduction

"How might anyone think that it was possible? This was a violation of the setting!"

That was the first reaction of analyst Anna Kudiyarova, who directs the Psychoanalytic Institute for Central Asia, when she first heard about psychoanalysis by video-calls (Kudiyarova, 2013) and her response is by no means exceptional. In this chapter, I wish to bridge the gap between angry, contemptuous responses from psychotherapists who hear about video psychotherapy (Kudiyarova, 2013; Aryan, 2013), usually without experiencing it, and the abundance of clinical and research testimonies, indicating that its results are just as good as those of face-to-face meetings (for example: Mizrahi, 2017; Wagner, Horn & Maercker, 2014). In the past eight years, in which I have practiced video psychotherapy and led a team of 20 video therapists, I have come to realize that due to its technical attributes, video psychotherapy encourages certain types of transference relations constituting a unique expedited space for change and growth, by direct contact with contents and core processes, which in the clinic take us longer. The ideas I explore in this chapter, are the outgrowth of my deep curiosity about those special clinical characteristics that are facilitated by using video as a medium by which the therapist and the patient meet.

Aspects of Video Therapy that Encourage Idealizing Transference, Twinship Transference and Merging Transference

Video psychotherapy and psychoanalysis are considered controversial (Mazri & Fiorentini, 2017). Interviews in the media on the subject, the refusal of certain therapists to use online treatment and a humoristic television series[1] that ridicules the matter, all make it clear to the public that not every therapist practices video therapy. The patients who contact us face the same criticism and are therefore aware that they are contacting a therapist who has made a choice that is perceived as novel and daring. In addition, a significant percentage of persons applying for remote therapy still do so due to geographic limitations or mobility restrictions and often, without the therapist's flexibility, the patient would not be able to get therapy. A concrete aspect of reaching out is therefore inherent to this situation. Those factors might form an idealizing transference (Kohut, 1971) towards the therapists even before the session begins, inasmuch as patients know that their therapist has made an unconventional and possibly brave professional choice to make the therapy accessible to them.

Not only the therapist, but the patient himself, has also made a choice that cannot be taken for granted, by choosing video therapy. This mutual knowledge of the similar choice type made by both parties may engender another element of transference and countertransference, with characteristics of resemblance and twinship (Kohut, 1984) before therapy even begins. Once therapy does begin, the therapist and patient become not only similar in their choice of video therapy, but also partners, who together take part in something innovative that in certain communities is still perceived as revolutionary or even subversive.

Technical issues might also affect the relationship from its outset. The programs used for video-calls today differ in their displays on the screen. The question whether each party sees only the other party or himself too on the screen, and at what size, is significant in the formation and representation of the therapeutic relationship. This joint visual presence may have valuable meanings. For example: a display in which the patient sees himself[2] as a smaller image may encourage certain patients to be preoccupied with "who is bigger", even unconsciously, or relive an emotional experience of diminution and difficulty in occupying space (Bachar, 2001). However, I hypothesize that the joint visual presence of the therapist and patient on the screen in most cases has the potential to form a feeling of "togetherness" and encourage transferences and fantasies of merging from an early stage in the therapeutic relationship (Kohut, 1984). In contemporary "selfie culture" whenever we share a screen, however momentarily, with another person, there is an emotional illusion that this will form a connection, a partnership, closeness and merging. That may account for people's intense affection for being photographed with celebrities and uploading their photographs to Facebook. A fascinating study in the field of cinema research has shown that home-made commemoration videos that families make for their loved ones have great emotional meaning owing to the family members seeing themselves, however briefly, in the same space with their loved ones, and their main experience as a result of this is an experience of momentary merging with a person whom they have lost (Melamed, 2013).

Aspects of Video Therapy That Transform the Therapist into a Tabula Rasa (Of Sorts)

There are many types of signals and pieces of environmental information that the patient perceives consciously and unconsciously and attributes to his therapist during the clinical session, which are neutralized or significantly reduced when the session is held by video. In a session held in the clinic, the patient walks into the therapist's world by arriving at the town, neighborhood and building housing the clinic, and the information that he or she picks up along the way, consciously or unconsciously, constitutes a transferential and contextual origin of the therapeutic session. My clinic, for example, is situated in the Israeli town Jaffa, which is a mixed city populated by Jews and Arabs, and my choice of location, reveals some of my social and political opinions. For many patients who come to my practice, the journey here engenders various feelings, from happiness about the opportunity to get to know this stylish area to anger over the need to encounter the Arab population.

In video therapy, in contrast, patients cannot study the neighborhood in which I have chosen to locate my clinic or the clinic's design. The therapist's dress style and build are also only partially perceivable to the patient by video-call. In addition, through this means, some of the therapist and patient's physical gestures are not fully communicated to the other side. By video, the patient cannot see whether the therapist is moving his legs in irritation or whether they are still, the therapist cannot see whether the patient is fidgeting with his fingers, placing them on his knees or pulling threads out of his armchair as though it were a transitional object. The intuitive discomfort at not having the possibility of perceiving the body language of the other party in full is compounded by new studies that show that our decoding of the other party's emotional state lies in his body language more than his facial expressions (Aviezer, Trope & Todorov, 2012).

What makes up for this information deficiency, which allows the therapeutic relationship by video to materialize nonetheless? These lacunas in the patient's knowledge about the therapist and his/her surroundings render the therapist, in the initial stages of therapy, into more of a tabula rasa than in the clinic. As a result, video therapy has greater potential for the onset of transference fantasies, particularly at the beginning of the therapy, and this approaches somewhat the classic idea of the therapist sitting so that the patient cannot see his facial expressions as a means of releasing free associations (Carlino, 2011).

But does this reduce the therapist to a mere object? Clinical experience shows that it does not. A possible explanation is that video therapy (unlike therapy by telephone or correspondence) involves significant patient exposure to the therapist's facial features and expressions. When using a video-call, people tend to sit close to the computer both in order to see and hear properly, and to feel as close as possible to the other person. As a result, facial details are enlarged, revealing more visual information of both parties. The familiarization with the therapist's body language however, is partial and gradual due to the mediation of the screen is less. As the therapy progresses and sharing experiences and mutual revelations accumulate, the patient learns the repertoire of his therapist's reactions, better identifies his expressions and affective state, and through this process his fantasies and projections make way for the encounter with reality. This transition represents a unique opportunity for the patient and therapist to advance from the object world to the subject world within the therapeutic relationship.

Aspects of "Environment Mother" and Childish Omnipotence in Video Therapy

Throughout the history of psychoanalysis and psychotherapy, the physical therapy room is perceived as a significant basis for a therapeutic setting and is experienced as a symbolic container for the patient's inner world (Lunn, 2002). In video therapy, this element is conspicuous in its absence, particularly for professionals who have been practicing for years in the clinic that they have designed, and of which they are accustomed to thinking as part of the therapeutic function. Patients who hear about video therapy after having had face-to-face therapy are also aversive in some cases to the idea of therapy without a clinic, and describe the extent to which they perceive the therapy room as a safe space. Surprisingly, similar reactions to video therapy may be heard from people who have never had therapy, but have formed an image of what therapy is, based on films and books, in which therapy session is represented visually and stereotypically as including a couch, armchair, subdued lighting and a tissue box.

In the absence of a common room, the therapeutic space that is available to the video therapy patient is the therapist's own internal setting, which is the zone in which reality is defined by symbolic, metaphoric or unconscious meanings (Parsons, 2007). This inner zone is an active container, which changes and forms throughout the therapeutic process (Quinodoz, 1992) and forms in a process of joint creation by the therapist and patient as a one-off therapeutic space that Lunn aptly referred to as the "potential room" (2002).

In the absence of a concrete meeting with the physical realness of the video-therapist, both the therapist's concrete and symbolic figures seem to converge with the therapeutic function. This corresponds with the emphasis Winnicott (1963) places on the mother functionality of the term "mother environment", a term that stresses that for the infant, the mother is not experienced as another individual but as a functional environment. Bollas (1979) continues to develop this idea, adding that the mother is not identified by the infant as an object, but as a process consisting of a collection of extrinsic and intrinsic gratifications, through which she is experienced as a "transformational process". The search for an object in adult life, according to Bollas, is the search for a signifier of this existential transformation process, a yearning to surrender to the metamorphosis that the other can engender in me. Video therapy has the potential to revive this transformation process, owing to the functional-environmental quality of the transference, which encourages contact with early object experiences.

Moreover, it seems that the video therapy situation allows the patient to connect in a certain sense with a quality of childish omnipotence too, and momentarily sustain the illusion of control and exclusivity over the potential room, and as part of it over the therapist as well (Winnicott, 1952). Whereas at the end of the session in the clinic, the patient sees his armchair empty or his waiting room vacant for other patients, in video therapy, the patient may retain the illusion that the therapist exists for him alone. Another aspect of the illusion of controlling the therapist is related to the relative vagueness concerning the therapist's figure on video directing the patient to phantasmatic primary mental activity of reliving the primary internal transition from good enough to ideal. In this state, there is greater freedom to experience the therapist as exact and feel possession of him as an ideal good object (Klein, 1952).

When face-to-face therapy takes place in the clinic, in addition to the potential room there is also the concrete physical therapist's room into which the patient steps at the beginning of the session and which he exits at its end. In this room, there is seldom any great flexibility for the patient's physical preferences (such as the room's lighting intensity) and the room itself, in terms of style, location and furniture chosen by the therapist, that remains without any visible change when the patient leaves the clinic. In some cases, this dimension of physical permanency of the room which we take for granted in the clinic, may have a re-traumatization effect on the injured self, that once again meets an inflexible, insufficiently adaptive environment. As an acquaintance of mine wrote on Facebook: "I came out crying from the session with the psychologist, and on the way out her dog pounced on me and gleefully licked me. It was the most inappropriate thing that could happen considering how I was feeling".

For the video patient in contrast, the potential room is the only shared room that exists, and is wholly furnished using abstract "furniture" that may be experienced by the patient as having been "created" solely for him at that point in time. This attributes to the container and setting of video therapy a quality of joint, more adaptive creation for the therapist and patient, which is formed from the one-off contact and dialog between them. At the end of video sessions, the potential room is "painted" with unique colors that have been produced during that specific session through a mutual process, reminiscent of the way a child therapy room looks at the end of a session.

But do the better match and the contact with childish omnipotence not leave the patient in video therapy in a passive position that encourages regression and dependency? Here too, clinical experience shows this not to be the case. The explanation is related, to having a greater part for the patient in matching the physical aspects of the "mother environment" to his needs in video therapy. Discomfort at the clinic related to aspects such as the physical distance between the therapist and patient, the armchairs, the room temperature or the volume of the therapist's voice – is not under the patient's control. In video therapy, contrastingly, the patient has essential influence and greater control over these physical and symbolic aspects of the "mother environment". The patient may get closer or move away from the screen at his convenience at any given time, increase or decrease the volume, control the room temperature according to his needs and thus be an active partner and have agency over the degree of suitability of the therapeutic space for himself. Since many patients lack the habit of identifying and fulfilling their needs, the video therapist can relate to these aspects and make sure that the patient is indeed in an environment that is comfortable for him during the session. The fact that the therapist draws attention to the patient's physical needs, puts an emphasis on their importance and may engender a change in the way in which the patient is in touch with them.

Ghent (1995) describes how in one of his sessions he put a warm blanket on his patient's lap, and in response, she tearfully said: "I didn't even know I was feeling cold". In video therapy, the therapist cannot tell that the patient's room is cold through his own physical experience, but he can sense it from the way in which the patient is dressed, from his body language and through active interest. Such a moment in which the patient notices through his therapist that he is cold, but he is the one who brings himself the blanket, illustrates how video therapy encourages the patient to be an active partner in adapting the "mother environment" to his needs while maturely using an object (Winnicott, 1969). It allows the patient to own his needs and answer them, supporting an agency experience. These processes may help the patient to gradually internalize this function.

People relate to technological devices (mobile phones, tablets, etc.) as an integral part of themselves and as an almost physical extension of their bodies and minds (Carlino, 2011). It contributes to experiencing the therapist on the same screen as an extension of the patient's body. It gives this screen image qualities of a transitional object, allowing the patient to carry on the representation of the therapist and the functions of the potential room even after the therapy conversation has ended, enhancing the internalization of the therapist and his/her function.

We can conclude that many characteristics of video therapy increase contact with primary processes, especially at an early stage of the therapeutic relationship, alongside elements that preserve a sense of agency and encourage the patient to provide his own answer to his needs.

Video Therapy Encouraging Relational Mutuality

Many of the transferential emphases mentioned above characterize "one person psychology" approaches. Idealizing transference and merging, projections and fantasies, and the rise of childish omnipotence, all triggered by a vague therapist figure, give the impression that video therapy erases the therapist's subjectivity and encourages treating him as an object (Winnicott, 1969). However, this is not the case. First, some of these characteristics, such as the relative vagueness of the therapist's figure, are salient at the beginning of the therapy, before any familiarity or relationship has formed. Throughout the process, as the relationship progresses, the patient has the opportunity to learn subjective aspects of the therapist. In this process, the therapist and patient have an opportunity to learn how fantasies and projections gradually encounter aspects of reality and how this change becomes organized in the patient's inner world.

All the factors mentioned above as encouraging transferences that are characteristic of "one-person psychology" are due to the technical aspects of video therapy. It must be remembered that all these factors are compounded by the therapist's unique personality, therapeutic approach and the way he approaches all these transferential issues. These, when interacting with what the patient introduces, will dictate the type of transference and countertransference that will eventually form during the process.

In addition, video therapy simultaneously encourages transferential aspects that are characteristic of "two-person psychology", due to the fact that technical cooperation between the therapist and patient is required. They are required to cooperate regarding audio synchronization in the conversation itself and around coping with inevitable technical challenges. Sentences like: "Can you hear me properly?", "Maybe we should check our Internet connections?", "Could you move the camera higher so that the light behind you doesn't dazzle me?" are common in video therapy, originating from the therapist and patient alike. Concerning these parts, the therapist and patient have an identical, symmetrical role. This inevitable partnership of structuring the video therapeutic space may be treated in two ways. In the basic sense, and in the terms of contemporary Freudian theorists (Kris, 1982 in Aron, 1996), the technical involvement of both parties underlines the classic idea of a "therapeutic alliance" and the therapy being "a project with a common goal", for whose results the patient also has a commitment to and is responsibility for.

I recall a patient of mine who said that she felt that the technical difficulties connected us together during the therapy, owing to the need to cope with them together. However, this ostensible technical mutuality may also be considered as symbolizing the relational conception of therapeutic mutuality, which expands towards the classic idea of an "alliance" or "cooperation". It is inevitable in a therapeutic process for the therapist and patient alike to be subjected to some extent to the influence of their own and each other's unconscious (Aron, 1996). Symbolically, both the therapist and patient have "unexpected line faults". The absence of a hierarchy between the therapist and patient is prominent here, and this underlines them being two human subjects who depend on each other for forming continuous communication. The encounter with the therapist's technical difficulties may introduce aspects of his humanity and vulnerability and therefore encourage relating to him as a subject, which affords, from an early stage in the relationship, a possible contact with the pleasure of a meeting and of cooperation between two subjects (Benjamin, 1995).

Moreover, many therapists are not very good at overcoming technical obstacles in real time. Thus, often it is the patient who is the one to suggest solutions to the therapist when a problem occurs. These situations constitute symbolic concretization of the mutual influence concept in relational theory, whereby the therapist also learns, is supported and develops through the patient in the therapeutic process (Aron, 1996; Mitchell, 2000). That same patient of mine who felt that technical difficulties brought us together, came from a technological background and gave me useful technical recommendations throughout the conversation. Her affection for those moments was related not only to the alliance that formed due to "coping with a common enemy" but also the deep validation that these moments gave her, sensing that she has an influence and being able to "save" and correct me and the therapeutic situation. During those moments, I was not the only one who possesses knowledge, influence and corrective ability, for she did too.

In conclusion, this duality gives the patient a basis to experience the therapist in projective tones and in transferences that are characteristic of "one-person psychology", while extending a basis to experience the therapist as a subject and form a mutual relationship in terms of "two–person psychology".

The following brief example exemplifies how this duality occurs.

In one of the video sessions in which I wore a new outfit that I was extremely fond of, the patient started the conversation by gladly saying: "I see you're in pajamas too!". The surprise on my face was instantly discernible. A moment later I realized that the top of this outfit, which I thought was very presentable, could look like a pajama without the context of the outfit itself. This is an excellent example of the way in which the concrete stimulus of my attire was sufficiently vague and partial to allow the patient to "create" me and experience me as an object, thus expressing some element of her need for twinship that we could later touch upon. At the same time, the patient could have learned about my subjectivity when she saw my surprised reaction and heard me telling her it was not a pajama but an outfit that I had thought was very smart. She could also experience mutuality and feel that she had influence over me when

I added that I could understand through her how not everyone would consider that outfit to be smart, which I would take into account in the future. I was both an object and subject in that situation, and both aspects had value in the therapeutic process.

Knowledge is Better Than Discovery, or: What Do You Need to Know Besides Turning on a Video Camera?

The aspects cited above illustrate the pivotal importance of the video therapist's familiarity with the characteristics of video therapy, and the therapist's ability to "translate" them correctly. This calibration is dramatic for the therapist's ability to maintain core therapeutic functions. Basic terms such as setting and therapeutic boundaries have to be translated into the new situation, in which there is no physical room and both parties are partners in forming the therapeutic space. In effect, most of the terms and dynamic tools that we tend to use for thinking in the clinic, assume a different appearance or manifestation in video therapy (Mazri & Fiorentini, 2017).

One example of a term that must be translated and uniquely calibrated into the situation of video therapy is Winnicott's "the capacity to be alone" (1958). At the concrete level, remote therapy occurs when the patient is eventually alone, at home or in his room. This therefore requires special attention for structuring a remote therapy situation of being alone in the presence of the other person, rather than of being alone against the other person.

Intuitively, it would seem that video provides a feeling of "being in the presence of another person" (Suler, 2000). Patients have a clear feeling that their video therapist sees them and the space they are in, and the patients themselves can see how their therapist sounds and looks, and which space the therapist is in, and most importantly: whether the therapist is oriented and attentive only to them. However, to develop the ability to be alone, according to Winnicott, a good enough mother figure must be internalized, allowing her infant to stay alone for long enough in her company. But not every mother-infant dyad yields a successful end of this process, and many patients come to us after an environmental failure that did not develop their ability to be alone (Mitchell & Black, 1995). When treating a person due to impairment in this axis, the therapist's ability to create a continuous, holding therapeutic environment is critical for the revival and correction of the damaged self-functions.

The issue of continuity is challenging in video therapy, due to factors over which the therapist has no control, such as Internet connection and equipment failure that might lead to a sudden hang up. During these times, the patient remains alone in the most concrete sense, possibly at the climax of a significant moment in his therapy. The therapist has the responsibility to consider such disconnections, and to establish in advance responses and alternative communication channels. He/she must also address it in a way that keeps the therapeutic goals in mind, using those interruptions as an opportunity to deepen the work.

Critics of video therapy consider these disconnections as a grave drawback, but events of such unintended nature are not confined to video therapy. I was treated by a psychoanalyst in a clinic. She used to escort me from the stairwell through the waiting room into the room, and when exiting the room, through the waiting room back to the stairwell. This accompaniment had various meanings for me. I remember the only occasion in which my therapist took a bathroom break in the middle of the session, leaving me alone in her "space" for the first time. Being left alone in the space for the first time I felt abandoned and alienated. This became worse as it went unmentioned afterward. In contrast, when I took video therapy as a patient, I never interpreted such disconnects as a difficulty or abandonment, particularly owing to the opportunity to discuss them afterward. Therefore, there is a need to prepare in advance alternative ways of communication for cases of disruptions and to comment on them afterward, enabling patients to express what it was like for them. Without doing so, therapy may result in reliving primary experiences of omission and inconsistency of maternal figure, and instead of helping the patient build up his ability to be alone, it might deepen its absence.

Another matter that is crucial for forming a correct therapeutic space in video therapy is the seemingly technical matter of positioning in front of the camera. It constitutes an essential basis for the success of the video therapy. Studies that examined the concept of presence in remote therapy have shown that it is dramatically influenced by the ability of both parties to be drawn into the illusion that the other is really sitting across them rather than on the screen (Lombard & Ditton, 1997 in Russell, 2015). This ability is strongly affected by the skill of the therapist in technically structuring the therapeutic situation and his positioning in front of the camera, particularly as we know that a lot of information on the emotional state of the other party may be found in his body language rather than his face (Aviezer, Trope & Todorov, 2012). Also of significance is the ability to establish eye contact by video, i.e., to give patients the impression that I am looking into their eyes, and to get the impression that they are looking into mine. It is difficult to imagine how a sense of attentive presence may form in a therapeutic conversation in which patients feel that the therapist's gaze is constantly diverted away from them.

Without contemplating all these and many other issues, it is very difficult to form a similar feeling to the one that forms when two people sit facing each other in the clinic. Regrettably, therapists who are not aware of this knowledge, make failed attempts at video therapy that leave both parties disappointed or with unjustifiably negative views on this medium. In my mind, these situations are a significant tier in understanding the gap between the advocates and critics of video therapy.

Summary

Video therapy, owing to its unique characteristics, introduces several types of transference and countertransference relations from an early stage of the therapeutic relationship. Interestingly, the elements that stimulate them are often elements related to the medium's technical limitations. Both the choice of video therapy by the therapist and patient, and their co-presence on screen, have meaning at the transferential and counter-transferential level, gaining a quality of partnership, twinship and merging. The video-call therapist becomes a vaguer figure than the therapist in the clinic, which makes him more of a tabula rasa in the first stages of therapy than in the case of therapy in a clinic, allowing for live contact with object relations and the inner world of fantasy.

The absence of the physical therapy room leads to blurring the boundary between the therapist as an object and the therapist as a therapeutic function. This converging of therapist's figure and function is reminiscent of Winnicott's "environment mother" idea (1963). Video therapy has qualities that encourage the patient to feel momentarily that he is "creating" the therapist, allowing childhood omnipotence fantasies to surface in therapy (Winnicott, 1952). The therapist appears in the patient's home space and on the computer screen in front of which the patient spends a significant portion of the day. The computer is experienced as an extension of the patient's body and self. All these factors expedite internalization of the therapeutic functions and create a symbolic continuity of therapeutic relationship between sessions.

Some of these transferential modalities stem from the technical characteristics of the medium and have a quality of "one-person psychology" as the object relations and fantasies of the patient are more projected than influenced by realistic stimuli. However, the video-therapeutic contact also has inherent aspects that characterize the "psychology of two people". These aspects bestow the therapeutic relationship elements of relational mutuality and let the patient richly encounter the therapist's subjectivity in a unique, live manner from an early stage of the relationship.

The transference that occurs in video therapy is therefore characterized by duality. On the one hand, projective and phantasmatic transference qualities of "one-person psychology" occur, and on the other hand, there are qualities of mutuality and a rich encounter with the therapist's subjectivity in "two-person psychology" terms. These two poles do not cancel each other out, but coexist, providing a unique dualism from an early stage of the relationship. One should remember however, that those transferential elements are just a starting point and will go through endless changes as the therapeutic relationship unfolds.

In conclusion I assert that the therapist's mastery of the unique aspects characterizing the video-mediated therapeutic relationship is of utmost importance for "translating" and calibrating the situation according to their therapeutic approach in a manner that will preserve the core therapeutic functions.

I shall end with a personal anecdote. About 80 years ago, in snowy Romania, a country doctor rushed by coach between the scattered homes of patients that needed his help. Sometimes he arrived too late. That man, my beloved grandfather, carried those people in his heart until his last day. If he had the opportunity to use telemedicine, he could have saved the lives of more of them.

I consider extending access to medical and mental treatment by video as a possibility of revolutionizing the field of health and psychotherapy. If this chapter gives even a single therapist the opportunity to rethink video therapy and consider it as a legitimate option, I have done my part in contributing to this awaited transformation.

Notes

1 *Web Therapy* – An American comedy series that was broadcast on Showtime between 2011 and 2015.
2 The use of male gender for the patient or therapist is for convenience reasons only.

Bibliography

Aron, L. (1996). *Relational perspectives book series, Vol. 4. A meeting of minds: Mutuality in psychoanalysis*. Hillsdale, NJ: Analytic Press, Inc.

Aryan, A. (2013). Setting and transference countertransference reconsidered on beginning teleanalysis. In J.S. Scharf (Ed.), *Psychoanalysis Online* (pp. 119–132). London: Karnac.

Aviezer, H., Trope, Y., & Todorov, A. (2012). Body cues, not facial expressions, discriminate between intense positive and negative emotions. *Science, 30*: 1225–1229.

Bachar, E. (2001). *The Fear of Occupying Space: The Self-Psychology and the Treatment of Anorexia and Bulimia*. Jerusalem: Magnes Press.

Benjamin, J. (1995). *Like Subjects, Love Objects: Essays on Recognition and Sexual Difference*. New Haven, CT: Yale University Press.

Bollas, C. (1979). The transformational object. *International Journal of Psycho-Analysis, 60*: 97–107.

Carlino, R. (2011). *Distance Psychoanalysis*. London: Karnac.

Ghent, E. (1995). Interaction in the psychoanalytic situation. *Psychoanalytic Dialogues, 5*(3): 479–491.

Klein, M. (1952). Envy and gratitude. In *The Writings of Melanie Klein*. London: Hogarth Press, (1975).

Kohut, H. (1971). *The Analysis of the Self: A Systematic Approach to the Psychoanalytic Treatment of Narcissistic Personality Disorders*. New York: International Universities Press.

Kohut, H. (1984). *How Does Analysis Cure?* Chicago: University of Chicago Press.

Kudiyarova, A. (2013). Psychoanalysis using Skype. In J.S. Scharf (Ed.), *Psychoanalysis Online* (pp. 183–193). London: Karnac.

Lunn, S. (2002). The psychoanalytic room. *Scandinavian Psychoanalytic Review, 25*: 135–142.

Lombard, M., & Ditton, T. (1997). At the heart of it all: The concept of presence. *Journal of Computer-Mediated Communication, 3*(2).

Mazri, A., & Fiorentini, G. (2017). Light and shadow in online analysis. In J. S. Scharf (Ed.), *Psychoanalysis Online 3* (pp. 65–83). London: Karnac.

Melamed, L. (2013). Close to home: Privatization and personalization of militarized death in Israeli home videos. *New Cinemas: Journal of Contemporary Film, 11*(2–3): 127–142.

Mitchell, S.A. (2000). *Relationality: From Attachment to Intersubjectivity*. New Jersey: The Analytic Press.

Mitchell, S.A., & Black, M.J. (1995). *Freud and Beyond: A History of Modern Psychoanalytic Thought*. New York: Basic Books.

Mizrahi, C. (2017). The analyst's closeness in long-distance psychoanalysis. In J. S. Scharf (Ed.), *Psychoanalysis Online 3* (pp. 65–83). London: Karnac.

Parsons, M. (2007). Raiding the inarticulate: The internal analytic setting and listening beyond countertransference. *The International Journal of Psychoanalysis, 88*: 1441–1456.

Quinodoz, D. (1992). The psychoanalytic setting as the instrument of the container function. *International Journal of Psycho-Analysis, 73*: 627–635.

Russell, G.I. (2015). *Screen Relations: The Limits of Computer-Mediated Psychoanalysis and Psychotherapy*. London: Karnac Books.

Suler, J.R. (2000). Psychotherapy in cyberspace: A 5-dimension model of online and computer-mediated psychotherapy. *CyberPsychology and Behavior, 3*: 151–160.

Wagner, B., Horn A., & Maercker A. (2014). Internet-based versus face-to-face cognitive-behavioral intervention for depression: A randomized controlled non-inferiority trial. *Journal of Affective Disorders, 152*: 113–121.

Winnicott, D.W. (1952). Psychosis and child care. In *Collected Papers* (pp. 219–228). New York: Basic Books, 1958.

Winnicott, D.W. (1963). *The Development of the Capacity for Concern. Bulletin of the Menninger Clinic, 27*: 167–176.

Winnicott, D.W. (1969). The use of an object and relating through identification. In *Playing and Reality* (pp. 86–94). California: Psychoanalytic Electronic Publishing.

6 Cybersupervision in Psychotherapy

Michael Pennington, Rikki Patton and Heather Katafiasz

The purpose of this chapter is to provide an overview of the current state of cybersupervision literature in psychotherapy, with an emphasis on systemic cybersupervision. It will 1) provide a historical context of cybersupervision, 2) review definitions and conceptualizations of cybersupervision, 3) discuss the logistics of initiating and maintaining the cybersupervision relationship, and 4) examine the various forms and platforms of cybersupervision. In addition, ethical and legal risks considerations associated with cybersupervision will be infused throughout the chapter. In doing so, this chapter can serve as a learning resource for therapists who plan to engage in cybersupervision.

History of Cybersupervision

The American Association for Marriage and Family Therapy (AAMFT) published its first cybersupervision documents in summer 2001, when the movement toward online therapy was in its infancy (Bacigalupe, 2010). In those documents, questions related to the potential ethical ramifications of cybersupervision and the potential usage of videoconferencing as a means of supervision were posed (Fialkov et al., 2001; Greenwalt, 2001). Neighboring mental health fields were also looking at the legal and ethical concerns related to providing supervision and therapy primarily through online mediums. Consequently, this led to exploring the how technologically provided therapy and supervision compared to traditional therapy and supervision, in terms of quantity and quality (Panos et al., 2002). These discussions were largely in response to the rapid advances in technology during that period, in addition to the legal implementation of the Health Insurance Portability and Accountability Act (Health Insurance Portability and Accountability Act of 1996, Pub. L. No. 104-191, 110 Stat.1936). Although some findings were mixed, research has largely identified that technology, such as email or texting, could enhance traditional supervision, and that cybersupervision could be used as an equivalent experience to traditional supervision (Chapman et al., 2011; Clingerman & Bernard, 2004; Nelson, Nichte & Henriksen, 2010; Stebnicki & Glover, 2001).

Though the implementation of HIPAA forced a dramatic shift in the ethical and legal understanding of cybersupervision across mental health professions, the use of technology in supervision was not new to the field of systemic supervision. Foundational family therapy training utilized live supervision as a main form of synchronous supervision, providing immediate feedback to therapists learning how to engage clients (Bernard & Goodyear, 2014). Live supervision was initially performed in the same room as the therapist and the client, and then later, behind a one-way mirror (Bernard & Goodyear, 2014; Jordan & Fisher, 2016). As technology advanced, live supervision transformed into "raw" supervision (Bernard & Goodyear, 2014; Boyle & McDowell-Burns, 2016), which continued to include, added the usage of video or audio recordings to traditional live supervision, so the sessions could be either watched in real time (synchronously) or recorded to be later reviewed during supervision (asynchronously). This form of live supervision allowed supervisors to digitally watch sessions in a separate room or a separate geographical location entirely. Additionally, enhanced video recording software now permits supervisors to watch multiple therapy sessions simultaneously (albeit only listening to one session at a time). Some supervisors choose to engage in delayed feedback, only providing feedback on a live session after the session has concluded; however, other supervisors provide immediate feedback by interrupting the session (Bernard & Goodyear, 2014; Boyle & McDowell-Burns, 2016). In the early years of family therapy training, live supervision could be disruptive, as the supervisor would interrupt the session by knocking on the door and forcing the therapist to "break"; however, with newer technologies, supervisors are able to interrupt sessions much more seamlessly using telephones, "bug-in-the-ear" (Bernard & Goodyear, 2014; Boyle & McDowell-Burns, 2016; Jordan & Fisher, 2016), and instant messaging/texting (Bernard & Goodyear, 2014).

Rousmaniere, Abbass, Frederickson, Henning, and Taubner (2014) emphasize the shift toward increased utilization of technology in supervision is occurring rapidly. As of 2013, supervisors have been providing training via videoconferencing in almost all therapeutic disciplines, including emotion-focused, cognitive-behavioral, dialectical-behavioral, acceptance and commitment, and eye-movement desensitization (Rousmaniere et al., 2014). Among training programs, most accrediting bodies have accredited clinical programs that utilize distance learning as a primary means of supervision (COAMFTE.org, n.d.; CACREP.org, n.d.). Further, the Commission on Accreditation (CoA) for the American Psychological Association (APA) specifies that up to 50% of the supervision occurring in psychology programs can be cybersupervision (CoA, 2010). Additionally, when training future supervisors, AAMFT specifies that supervision mentoring should include "live or recorded supervision sessions" (AAMFT, 2016: 9) and that supervision should include at least 20% raw data (AAMFT 2016).

In looking at current guidelines related to cybersupervision, we are left with three main principles: 1) we must follow applicable codes of ethics and laws/regulations, 2) we must be HIPAA compliant, and 3) the supervisor must be competent in this form of supervision (AAMFT, 2015; ACA, 2014; CoA, 2010). Further, regardless of the specific mental health profession, consensus agrees that the "burden for determining that technological delivery complies with applicable ethics and law is placed upon the" supervisor in cybersupervision (AAMFT, 2014: 9). While these main principles are straightforward, understanding the nuances of how to be ethically and legally compliant can be challenging as applicable laws vary from state to state and many states do not have specific legal guidelines regarding cyber-therapy or supervision (Pennington, Patton, Ray, & Katafiasz, 2017). Additionally, ethical codes vary in how much guidance is provided regarding ethical competence of cybersupervision depending on the professional organization (AAMFT, 2015; ACA, 2014; APA, 2017). The following sections of this chapter will provide more clarity about defining cybersupervision and discuss potential ethical considerations regarding cybersupervision, especially when considering different technological forms of cybersupervision. The following is meant to provide an overview and should the reader want a more in-depth discussion of cybersupervision, please refer to Rousmaniere and Renfro-Michel (2016).

Conceptualization of Cybersupervision

The CoA for the APA defines cybersupervision as, "clinical supervision of psychological services through a synchronous audio and video format where the supervisor is not in the same physical facility as the trainee" (CoA, C.28, 2010). Other professional associations further define cybersupervision as including, "asynchronous two-way electronic communication including but not limited to telephone, videoconferencing, email, text, instant messaging, and social media" (AMFTRB, 2016: 16). The addition of asynchronous elements denotes that any supervision that utilizes technology should be considered cybersupervision. However, based on a review of the literature, the key aspect to supervision that delineates cybersupervision from technologically enhanced supervision is the aspect of distance (Carlisle et al., 2017).

Specifically, the CoA for APA distinguishes cybersupervision from in-person supervision, which is defined as, "clinical supervision of psychological services where the supervisor is physically in the same room as the trainee" (CoA, C.28, 2010). When the supervisor and the supervisee are in geographically different locations and are unable to physically meet, the ensuing supervision is considered "distance" or cybersupervision. Additionally, the understanding with cybersupervision is that it will occur primarily utilizing technological means. Although traditional supervision was previously distinguished by its face-to-face component, with the advent and wide usage of videoconferencing software, face-to-face supervision is no longer limited by the physical proximity between the supervisor and supervisee (Carlisle et al., 2017).

The Cybersupervision Process

The advent of technology has afforded supervisors the ability to move beyond the physical boundaries that are inherent in physical supervision (i.e. geographic location) and into the online world. While there are similarities between traditional supervision processes and cybersupervision processes, there are considerable nuanced aspects within cybersupervision that require additional considerations. As such, supervisors need to consider the following topics: a) contracting for supervision and establishing the relationship; b) cybersupervision forms; c) technology platforms, d) maintaining the therapeutic relationship, and the overall benefits and challenges of using cybersupervision. As we examine the cybersupervision process, we must also account for ethical and legal considerations within cybersupervision. Based on a review of the extant literature in the Marriage and Family Therapy, Psychology, Counseling, and Social Work fields, we have identified the following four ethical and legal areas for consideration. These areas include: 1) understanding current professional guidelines for the use of technology in supervision, 2) following the ethical guidelines, 3) ensuring confidentiality and security, and 4) developing and maintaining the supervisory relationship. Understanding these major factors, and the related ethical and legal considerations, as they relate to cybersupervision can help the supervisor approach cybersupervision with a more informed lens.

Contracting for Supervision: Establishing the Relationship

As technology continues to grow and change, both supervisors and supervisees need to learn how to use these methods effectively, with the supervisor facilitating the process (Boyle & McDowell-Burns, 2016; Layne & Hohenshil, 2005; Rousmaniere et al., 2014; Vaccaro & Lambie, 2007; Watson, 2003). While supervisees should have a background in using the technology, it is the ethical obligation of supervisors to train supervisees in the use of the specific technology (i.e. videoconferencing software) used in their sessions (AAMFT, 2015). It is recommended that supervisors and supervisees should also engage in simulations or role-plays via the technology platforms planned for supervision. This ensures that the process will go smoothly, and that all participants 1) will be aware of their role, 2) will have time to become accustomed to the technology, and 3) be able to work out any issues that they may run into (Rousmaniere et al., 2014).

Once adequate cybersupervision competence is determined, and supervisees are adequately trained, supervisors can begin establishing the logistics of supervision. Procedurally, supervisors should sign into the videoconferencing software with both a username and password and then invite supervisees to do the same. For more information on the physical setup for videoconferencing in cybersupervision please refer to Rousmaniere et al. (2014).

Supervisors are asked to ensure that, when identifying a physical space, it is secure and HIPAA compliant so that discussions of confidential information about both supervisees and clients be protected. If we consider a case:

> Melinda is a 40-year-old Hispanic female and Steve is a 23-year-old African American male. Melinda has served as Steve's MFT supervisor for the past year. Melinda and Steve have conducted supervision both in-person and via a supported online platform (e.g. VSee), and both are comfortable and competent in the use of technology in supervision. When Melinda initiated supervision with Steve, and each time she and Steve engaged in cybersupervision, Melinda verified with Steve that his location was private, to ensure confidentiality would not be breached. Both Steve and Melinda typically engaged in supervision at their therapy offices, with the door closed and a white noise generator on; however, occasionally, they engaged in cybersupervision when one or both were at home

It is not uncommon for our families to interrupt our work if we are working from home, so it is imperative that protocols be set during supervision so that all participants are aware of how to respond in these instances. Regardless of the location (home or business), supervision should be conducted in a closed and private location where information cannot be seen/overheard by others (Glosoff et al., 2016). For this case, when either Steve or Melinda needed to engage in cybersupervision from home, they needed to establish a protocol to identify a private space to initiate the cybersupervision session, to wear headphones to prevent significant others from overhearing, and to pause the conversation if a significant other entered the room during cybersupervision.

For cybersupervision to succeed, communication between supervisors and supervisees must be concrete and based on trust. Prior research has reported that utilizing technology to conduct cyber-counseling can have a significant impact on the communication and social-emotional information conveyed between participants, with text being read as more emotionally charged than when presented through audio-visual mediums (Wilczenski & Coomey, 2006). These same processes could also occur in cybersupervision. Glosoff, Renfro-Michel, and Nagarajan (2016) highlight that an effective supervisory relationship entails a collaborative, trustworthy relationship, and that the inclusion of technology in the supervisory relationship may impact the development and maintenance of alliance and rapport in the supervisory relationship. Considering Melinda and Steve again:

> Melinda sends Steve the following text message: "I really need to have a conversation with you." In this example, Melinda intends to convey to Steve that she needs to speak with him because she unexpectedly needs to reschedule supervision. However, the content of this message could be interpreted in different ways, as the inflection is difficult to convey through text. Steve could very easily misconstrue this message as more emotionally charged than it was intended, such as there is an emergency or that he has done something wrong.

Glosoff, Renfro-Michel, and Nagarajan (2016) provide several strategies to consider when developing and maintaining a supervisory relationship, which include being knowledgeable of the requisite skills to provide effective supervision, having a firm understanding of the technology being used, and understanding how to integrate effective supervision skills with technology utilization. Further, Haberstroh and Duffey (2015) directly discuss suggestions for developing and maintaining a supervisory relationship when using cyber-supervision. Their suggestions include attending to and mirroring the supervisees writing style, engaging professionally within the space created for supervision, being competent in the use of technology, and intentionally attending to the supervisory relationship. Let's consider another example from Melinda and Steve:

> As part of their supervisory relationship, Melinda and Steve agreed on using asynchronous supervision, specifically email, in between in-person supervision on an as-needed basis. Steve sent the following email to Melinda on Monday:
>
> Dear Melinda,
> I have a supervision question that I would like to process before next meeting. I met with a family yesterday that triggered my self-of-the therapist issue we have been discussing. I wanted to discuss some strategies for bracketing my own reaction. Thank you for any tips.
> -Steve
>
> Melinda responded several days later, on Friday, with this email:

Hey Steve,
That really sucks! I hope you are ok now. ☺ Did you try the other strategies we have discussed before???
–Melinda

In this practical example, Melinda did not follow all the strategies outlined for maintaining a supervisory relationship. For instance, she did not respond in a timely manner, she did not mirror the supervisee's language, and she did not attend to the supervisee's requests. It is imperative that supervisors attend to the development and maintenance of the supervisory relationship by accounting for the multiple nuances involved in the way we communicate and support our supervisees. Multicultural considerations are another important factor related to maintaining a supervisory relationship. Multiple scholars have also identified how multicultural issues are infused in the supervisory relationship, and the importance of culturally competent supervision practice as a prerequisite to effective counseling and supervision (Baltrinic et al., 2016). Baltrinic, O'Hara, and Jencius (2016) identify several guidelines for maintaining cultural competence specifically in cybersupervision including a) modeling to your supervisees by sharing your own worldview; b) providing enough time and space in the supervisory relationship to develop an understanding of your supervisee's worldview; c) openly and consistently discuss culture during the supervisory communications; d) continue your own multicultural training; and e) continue your own cybersupervision training.

Cybersupervision Forms

In the last ten to 15 years, technology that had been widely used for supervision and has gone from being standalone hardware, into being infused with software. Devices are now engineered to be connected. This connection is constant, and always communicating through its ability to share data, update automatically, and potentially, socially available to a multitude of users. Many of these enhancements have made tasks such as putting together the logistical aspects of supervision easier (Nagel & Anthony, 2016; Rousmaniere, 2014), or allowing for a multitude of options for communication, including email, text messaging, instant messaging, video conferencing, etc., to be used in the cybersupervision process (Arnekrans et al., 2014; Negal & Anthony, 2016; Rousmaniere, 2014; Stokes, 2016). However, along with these advances, additional nuanced considerations must be made when choosing the form of supervision.

Synchronous vs. Asynchronous

The different forms of communication technology used in cybersupervision can be characterized in two ways; synchronous and asynchronous (Bender

& Dykeman, 2016; Vaccaro & Lambie, 2007). Synchronous communication is done in real-time; i.e. through instant messaging or text-based chat, audio chat, phone calls, video conferencing, etc. Asynchronous communication is done in delayed time, i.e., over email, discussion threads, electronic based mailing lists, etc. Both COAMFTE and AAMFT require that cybersupervision occur synchronously (e.g. in real-time) whereas the APA accreditation standards do not have specific standards regarding this aspect of cybersupervision (CoA, 2010; SoA, 2017.). However, the statements made are general ones and are up for interpretation. The literature makes note that from this point on, the cybersupervision process functions similarly to physical supervision (Carlisle et al., 2017). Knowing that there are still some areas that cannot be completely translated from physical to cybersupervision, the authors want to caution both supervisors and supervisees to make sure they have a clear and established protocol for cybersupervision in place. Of the forms of cybersupervision mentioned here, email and instant messaging (or other text-based chat), and videoconferencing appear to be the most popular ways of conducting cybersupervision and they will be discussed in detail (Chapman et al., 2011; Rousmaniere, 2014; Stokes, 2016).

Email

Email-based communication has been used as a main form of supervision, as well as in combination with other synchronous and asynchronous forms. Email can be useful due to its ability to keep information constantly circulating between supervisor and supervisee. It also can act as a built-in filing cabinet, as the records may be kept in a specific inbox or smart folder, and can be readily accessible at any time. Research has shown that supervisees who used email in their group supervision meetings felt more supported by supervisors, and reported that the communication between the supervisor and supervisee was less tense due to the increased level of access afforded (Chapman et al., 2011). Supervisees also reported feeling more comfort disclosing their feelings in meetings, and an increased want to have thoughts clarified by all participants (Chapman et al., 2011). Email also allows for both supervisor and supervisee(s) to respond to each other in a timely manner, especially during critical issues when feedback is needed from multiple sources. There is also the added ability for all participants, whether in individual or group supervision, to have equal participation in case discussions, therefore enhancing conceptualization (Chapman et al., 2011; Stebnicki & Glover, 2001).

Clingerman and Bernard (2004) note that constantly using email can be useful, but how useful is uncertain. This could be because it is time-delayed; potentially resulting in problems with trying to engage in meaningful discussions due to language barriers associated with written text. Confidentially is another issue. Completely protecting email messages is not feasible due to the possibility of messages being seen by others, especially if the computer or device being used is a public one. To help avoid this, email limits should be outlined when training of both supervisors and supervisees, as well as having all parties, including clients, sign an informed consent to safely store emails. Messages should also be sent over a secure network and should be encrypted (Mallen et al., 2005; Vaccaro & Lambie, 2007; Watson, 2003).

Chat or Instant Messaging

Chat-based communication is considered synchronous and refers to any type of text-based messaging or texting that occurs between devices over a cellular network from one person to another. Instant messages are text commutation that is delivered through a system or software application used for sending and receiving messages electronically, i.e. an Apple iMessage. Chat communication may also refer to "chat room" communication in which multiple users who are connected to the same platform or chat channel can communicate to each other all at once (Arnekrans et al., 2014).

This form of cybersupervision can be a real benefit in both work and group cybersupervision settings. In group supervision, the supervisor utilizing a chat/text messaging platform such as iMessage, Android messenger, or WeChat could invite supervisees to engage in a group chat through a specific channel in which all members could participate in real time. This could also be accomplished within group messaging if multiple supervisees utilize different platforms (i.e. iMessage with an iPhone or Android messenger with a Pixel; Nagal & Anthony, 2016).

Utilizing chat and instant messaging technology in supervision also create challenges with confidentiality. Encryption is key, and today it is relatively easy to do with chat, as most chat platforms have built in encryption tools. Research has also shown that using this in a group or agency setting for in supervision has been seen as a way for supervisees to help foster a sense of community and feeling supported by others (Anthony & Goss, 2009; Nagel & Anthony, 2016; Vaccaro & Lambie, 2007).

Videoconferencing

Videoconferencing is the most widely used new technology for cybersupervision practices. Videoconferencing was originally conceptualized to be used as a cybersupervision tool for trainees and professionals practicing in distant or rural areas. However, due to the ease of access, it is currently being used to provide supervision as well as training in almost all major therapeutic settings, including students, trainees, and professionals out practicing in the field (Rousmaniere et al., 2014). Its use has allowed clinicians to receive training from experts at multiple sites, which could even span great distances from each other. Supervisors can also work from a central location when supervisees are spread across many sites (Caldwell, 2016). Recent software enhancements allow videoconferencing from multiple locations simultaneously. Videotaped sessions can also be utilized within video conferencing applications so that supervisors can review sessions while conducting live supervision (Abbass et al., 2011). This can be helpful in group supervision, as supervisors can communicate and process with multiple supervisees while watching recorded sessions.

Research has noted that due to the newness of videoconferencing technology as a form of cybersupervision, the trend seems to be looking at whether or not it is comparable to traditional supervision (Rousmaniere, 2014; Rousmaniere et al., 2014). The limited research conducted thus far has demonstrated that it is effective for individual and group supervision, as well as teaching (Jencius & Sager, 2001; Rees et al., 2009; Rousmaniere et al., 2014). According to Rousmaniere et al. (2014) supervisees reported feelings of safety in the relative distance from their supervisor afforded through videoconferencing, which was found to increase their level of self-disclosure and reduce disinhibition.

There has been research regarding using videoconferencing as an effective formal supervision for both cross-cultural and international supervision (Panos et al., 2002). However, there is the risk that cultural miscommunication could potentially be increased due to the physical distance between a supervisee and supervisor (Powell & Migdole, 2012; Rousmaniere et al., 2014). Let's consider another case example:

> While miscommunication has not been a challenge for Melinda and Steve, Melinda engages in cybersupervision with another supervisee, Saeko, whose native language is Japanese, but who also is fluent in English. Melinda and Saeko engage in supervision in English, which at times creates communication challenges. Melinda must be even more conscious, both in her written communication as well as verbal communication, about the message she is conveying, to ensure clear and direct communication with Saeko.

Other concerns include the possibility of the modality not being as effective as traditional supervision (Sholomskas et al., 2005). The inability for either the supervisors or supervisees to understand nonverbal cues through electronic communication could also be present, as well as the possibility that anxiety could become increased among supervisees (Rousmaniere et al., 2014; Sørlie et al., 1999).

There is a concern, both ethically and legally, regarding whether or not the participants understand the laws and rules of their own state regarding cybersupervision through videoconferencing. This uncertainty creates a possible ethical gray area for supervisors and supervisees and all parties should examine and become familiar with their local laws and regulatory boards and consult with them when they have questions (Abbass et al., 2011; Rousmaniere, 2014; Rousmaniere et al., 2014).

Videoconferencing also suffers from reliability issues, just as other technologies. There are times it may not work, therefore supervisors must have a backup or workaround prepared so that supervision can continue. Confidentiality concerns are also present regarding the possibility that an employee of the software company could listen in on a session in progress. This can be mitigated by using HIPAA compliant software, which the literature notes are becoming more affordable and widespread (Rousmaniere, 2014; Rousmaniere et al., 2014).

Considerations for Cybersupervision: Maintaining the Supervisory Relationship

Coursol, Lewis, and Seymour (2016) suggest that once the cybersupervision logistics and an actual "point-to-point" connection has been created, i.e. supervisors communicating with supervisees through video conferencing software, then cybersupervision can commence much in the same way that traditional supervision does. The literature recommends that supervisors engage in a mixed cyber/traditional model to facilitate supervision, as it will increase the flexibility of and access to supervision.

As the supervision process continues, supervisors must be sure that they are adhering to not only the logistics of the cybersupervision process, but also how developmental progression of their supervisee as they move through the multiple phases of their supervision experience (Arnekrans et al., 2014; Bernard & Goodyear, 2014; Chapman et al., 2011; Rigazio-Digillio, 2016). Rigazio-Digillio (2016) noted that supervision occurs through a series of seven phases, of which phases 2, 3, 4, and 5 specifically discuss how supervisors work to build and maintain relationships with their supervisees. Supervisors can choose at what time to use certain forms of cybersupervision practices, depending on what supervisory issues are being addressed. Graf and Stebnicki (2002) suggest that supervisors need to ensure that the roles and expectations in cybersupervision are extremely structured and solid when utilizing videoconferencing. This can be done through traditional methods, cybersupervision, or a combination of both. For instance, when Melinda evaluated Steve's growth as at therapist thus far, she provided a written evaluation that Steve could review and they could discuss via email, as well as facilitated an in-person discussion via videoconferencing. As developing a standard protocol of "best practices" in cybersupervision is in its infancy, how to maintain the cybersupervision relationship is largely left to the discretion of the participants (Rousmaniere, 2014).

Platforms of Supervision: Technology

In the wake of ever-changing technology, supervisors need to be made aware of the choices available to them and whether or not they are safe to use for cybersupervision. Rousmaniere (2014) has referred to the more mechanical choices through the "toolbox" model, in which the "tools" for cybersupervision consisted of video and audio recorders. The tools used in supervision were based on momentary need; others would be left behind or not used at all. However, as technology has become more integrated with hardware and software working together, the advent of the "smart" device, the toolbox analogy no longer applies completely (Rousmaniere, 2014). Further, the toolbox analogy can be deceptive, as devices now are constantly running software programs in the foreground and background, connected to the Internet and therefore, and are never really off. The literature has made the distinction that this analogy be changed to view this 'always on' technology as that of a "technology ecosystem" (Mantovani, 1996; Rousmaniere, 2014). Given the ever-changing nature of technology today, it is important to continually update one's own knowledge about the technology being used, to explore those technologies within the context of how to maintain confidentiality and privacy when using them (Glosoff et al., 2016).

Previous scholars have posited multiple ethical and legal challenges related to using the Internet as a medium for supervision (e.g. Baltrinic et al., 2016; Bloom, 1997; Glosoff et al., 2016; Wilczenski & Coomey, 2006), with issues related to confidentiality and security commonly arising in the literature. Further, breaches in confidentiality when using technology can be technology related and/or based on human error – because of this, it is imperative that the supervisor understands how to maintain confidentiality within the context of technological use. Glosoff et al. (2016) note that the use of cybersupervision provides added layers of complexity to maintaining client and supervisee confidentiality, and that the supervisor is ultimately responsible for being aware and practicing in ways that protect client and supervisee information. The literature suggests that supervisors need to make sure all forms of communication are encrypted and HIPAA compliant. Internet connections should be done over a private server or a trusted Internet Service Provider (ISP), and/or by utilizing a Virtual Private Network (VPN; Coursol et al., 2016; Rousmaniere, 2014). All participants should also be able to connect through the VPN and have their own unique username and password. Additionally, supervisors need to consider the security of the device, the strength and structure of passwords and access points, and how to use social software and videoconferencing ethically (Rousmaniere & Kuhn, 2016). For videoconferencing, researchers recommend having a device, with Internet access, microphone, and camera either built in or standalone that can be used in conjunction. Coursol et al. (2016) lists these video-conferencing platforms as viable options: VSee, Adobe Connect; Apple

FaceTime (HIPAA Compliant), Cisco Jabber, Cisco TelePresence, Citrix WebEx, etc. Each of these applications allows real-time interactions between multiple users. Many of these platforms also have options for tele-therapy with a cybersupervision component built in. Therefore, they can be used for one or both simultaneously. For a more detailed breakdown of videoconferencing software see Rousmaniere (2014).

Advantages and Disadvantages of Cybersupervision

Cybersupervision comes with both unique advantages and limitations that set it apart from traditional supervision. In terms of logistics, cybersupervision allows for the convenience of scheduling, which can allow a more productive supervision session to occur. There is also the possibility of more effective use of time, as the supervisor can set up meetings that are convenient for all parties, and neither are forced to take extra time for travel or having to constantly work around schedule changes (Watson, 2003). Supervisees are also able to experience more favorable supervision settings/sites, as well as having more supervisors from which to learn from across many geographic locations (Stokes, 2016). This can provide supervisees the opportunity for increased access to multicultural supervision. Portability is also an advantage. Smart devices can reduce time spent traveling to a physical location allowing more time for supervision (Chapman et al., 2011; Watson, 2003).

Paperwork completion has also been helped through cybersupervision in that it provides fast and easy access to client and supervisee records. Email also has an added advantage in that it leaves a paper trail of all communication between participants, including attachments (Stebnicki & Glover, 2001). The literature has also suggested that cybersupervision can be more cost effective for supervisees in terms of travel cost, course fees, etc. This cost-effectiveness could extend to the institution through providing services to a wider range of students, including international students remotely (Chapman et al., 2011; Watson, 2003).

The literature has noted limitations in cybersupervision surrounding the expense of technology needed for cybersupervision. Even with the advent of multiple platforms for supervision available some are still costly. Cost could be a deterrent for both supervisors and supervisees who are unable to provide the necessary funds (Rousmaniere, 2014; Vaccaro & Lambie, 2007; Watson, 2003). Another limitation surrounds the need for both supervisor and supervisee to be skilled in using technology, which may not always be possible or easy to teach to either party. Inadequate training could result in confidentiality breaches when using technology (Vaccaro & Lambie, 2007). Access is unique in that it can be seen as both a limitation and an advantage; cybersupervision can provide direct supervision services to supervisees practicing in rural and/or remote areas (Chapman et al., 2011; Watson, 2003).

Although more recent literature has noted that cybersupervision is an effective means of supervising (e.g. Rousmaniere, 2014; Rousmaniere et al., 2014), Watson (2003) suggests that the lack of physical or face-to-face interaction between parties is a disadvantage of the process. Without the ability for physical interactions to take place participants may be unable to process non-verbal cues. This could lead to miscommunication and misunderstanding therefore preventing both parties from enriching and deepening their communication with each other (Bender & Dykeman, 2016; Vaccaro & Lambie, 2007). As the literature continues to develop more effective ways of cybersupervision there is one disadvantage that will impact the process, and that is not having a concrete set of guidelines in place for supervisors to ethically practice cybersupervision (Vacarro & Lambie, 2007). Because the landscape of cybersupervision is ever-evolving, it may be helpful for supervision trainings to incorporate more discussion of technology as a medium for conducting supervision.

Summary

This chapter aimed to provide an overview of cybersupervision in psychotherapy. The chapter began by providing a brief history of cybersupervision. A conceptualization of cybersupervision was identified and the cybersupervision process was discussed. Throughout the chapter, the overall importance of the supervisor being competent in supervision, technology, and the intersection between the two was noted. Cybersupervision is in its relative infancy, and if we as systemic supervisors are to consider it to a viable medium, then more research and scholarship is needed that directly addresses the issues of cybersupervision as they directly relate to our mental health professions. Perhaps, we first need to ask ourselves, "are we not examining this new practice out of fear of new technology?" If yes, then we must consider, as Rousmaniere et al. (2014) do, whether this limits our opportunities, or even pushes away new supervisors who have grown up with technology. If no, then we should see ourselves as innovators and explorers of the new frontier in technology, and to push ourselves to see the bigger picture of Internet technologies and not limit ourselves solely by geography. There are many opportunities that arise with the use of the Internet as a venue to conduct supervision. Just as Glosoff et al. (2016) state, "Instead, they [the ethical supervisor] aspire to meet the spirit of those standards by understanding the ethical principles and virtues that underlie the guidelines and to apply sound theory and research to their supervision" (34), we encourage the reader to consider how they may approach cybersupervision within the context of meeting the spirit of our professional guidelines, research, and theory.

References

AAMFT (2015). Code of Ethics. Available online at www.aamft.org/imis15/Docu ments/AAMFT%20Code_11_2012_Secured.pdf.

AAMFT (2016). Approved supervisor designation: Standards handbook. Available online at http://dx5br1z4f6n0k.cloudfront.net/imis15/Documents/Supervision/2016%20Supervision%20Forms/Jan_2014_AS_Handbook_ver_Oct_%202016.pdf.

Abbass, A., Arthey, S., Elliott, J., Fedak, T., Nowoweiski, D., Markovski, J., & Nowoweiski, S. (2011). Web-conference supervision for advanced psychotherapy training: A practical guide. *Psychotherapy*, *48*, 109–118. doi:10.1037/a0022427.

AMFTRB (2016). Teletherapy Guidelines. Available online at https://amftrb.org/wp-content/uploads/2017/05/Proposed-Teletherapy-Guidelines-DRAFT-as-of-09.12.16.pdf.

Anthony, K., & Goss, S. (2009). *Guidelines for Online Counselling and Psychotherapy including Guidelines for Online Supervision*, 3rd edition. Lutterworth: BACP.

Arnekrans, A., DuFresne, R., Neyland, L., & Rose, J. (2014, November). Inclusion of technology in supervision: ethical pitfalls and best practices. Poster presented at the All Ohio Counselors Conference, Columbus, OH.

Bacigalupe, G. (2010). Supervision 2.0: E-supervision a decade later. *Family Therapy Magazine*, January–February, 38–41.

Baltrinic, E.R., O'Hara, C., & Jencius, M. (2016). Technology-assisted supervision and cultural competencies. In Roussmaniere, T., & Renfro, E. (Eds), *Using Technology to Enhance Counselor Supervision: A Practical Handbook*. Alexandria, VA: American Counseling Association Press.

Bender, S., & Dykeman, C. (2016). Supervisees' perceptions of effective supervision: A comparison of fully synchronous cybersupervision to traditional methods. *Journal of Technology in Human Services*, *34*(4): 326–337.

Bernard, J.M., & Goodyear, R.G. (2014). *Fundamentals of Clinical Supervision*, 5th edition. Upper Saddle River, NJ: Pearson.

Bloom, J.W. (1997). NBCC webcounseling standards. *CTOnline*. Available online at www.nbcc.org/Assets/Ethics/internetCounseling.pdf.

Boyle, R., & McDowell-Burns, M. (2016). Modalities of marriage and family therapy supervision. In K. Jordan (Ed.) *Couple, Marriage, and Family Therapy Supervision*. New York: Springer Publishing Company.

CACREP (n.d.). Directory of accredited programs. Available online at www.cacrep.org/directory/#.

Carlisle, R., Hays, D., Pribesh, S., & Wood, C. (2017). Educational technology and distance supervision in counselor education. *Counselor Education & Supervision*, *56*: 33–49.

Chapman, R., Baker, S., Nassar-McMillan, S., & Gerler Jr., E. (2011). Cybersupervision: Further examination of synchronous and asynchronous modalities in counseling practicum supervision. *Counselor Education & Supervision*, *50*: 296–313.

Clingerman, T., & Bernard, J. (2004). An investigation of the use of e-mail as a supplemental modality for clinical supervision. *Counselor Education & Supervision*, *44*: 82–95.

COAMFTE (n.d.). Directory of accredited programs. Available online at http://coamfte.org/imis15/COAMFTE/Directory_of_Accredited_Programs/MFT_Training_Programs.aspx.

COAMFTE (2017). Accreditation standards: Graduate and post-graduate marriage and family therapy training programs (v. 12). Available online at http://dx5br1z4f6n0k.cloudfront.net/imis15/Documents/COAMFTE/Accreditation%20Resources/2018%20COAMFTE%20Accreditation%20Standards%20Version%2012.pdf.

Coursol, D., Lewis, J., & Seymour, J. (2016). Cybersupervision: supervision in a technological age. In S. Gross (Ed.) *Technology in Mental Health: Applications in Practice, Supervision and Training.* Springfield, IL: Charles C. Thomas.

Fialkov, C., Haddad, D., & Gagliardi, J. (2001). Face to face on the line: An invitation to learn from online supervision. *Supervision Bulletin,* Summer, 1–3.

Glosoff, H.L., Renfro-Michel, E., & Nagarajan, S. (2016). Ethical issues related to the use of technology in clinical supervision. In T. Roussmaniere, & E. Renfro-Michel (Eds), *Using Technology to Enhance Counselor Supervision: A Practical Handbook.* Alexandria, VA: American Counseling Association Press.

Graf, N.M., & Stebnicki, M.A. (2002). Using e-mail for clinical supervision in practicum: A qualitative analysis. *Journal of Rehabilitation, 68*: 41–49.

Greenwalt, B. (2001). Cybersupervision: Some ethical issues. *Supervision Bulletin,* Summer, 12–14.

Haberstroh, S., & Duffey, T. (2015). Establishing and maintaining relationships in online supervision. In T. Roussmaniere, & E. Renfro-Michel (Eds), *Using Technology to Enhance Counselor Supervision: A Practical Handbook.* Alexandria, VA: American Counseling Association Press.

Jencius, M., & Sager, D.E. (2001). The practice of marriage and family counseling in cyberspace. *The Family Journal, 9*: 295–301.

Jordan, K., & Fisher, U. (2016). History and future trends. In K. Jordan (Ed.) *Couple, Marriage, and Family Therapy Supervision.* New York: Springer Publishing Company.

Mallen, M.J., Vogel, D.L., & Rochlen, A.B. (2005). The practical aspects of online counseling: Ethics, training, technology, and competency. *Counseling Psychologist, 33*: 776–818, doi:10.1177/0011000005278625.2005.

Mantovani, G. (1996). *New Communications Environments: From Everyday to Virtual.* New York: The CRC Press.

Nagel, D.M., & Anthony, K. (2016) Using chat and instant messaging (im) to enrich counselor training and supervision. In S. Gross (Ed.), *Technology in Mental Health: Applications in Practice, Supervision and Training.* Springfield, IL: Charles C. Thomas.

Nelson, J.A., Nichter, M., & Henriksen, R. (2010). On-line supervision and face-to-face supervision in the counseling internship: An exploratory study of similarities and differences. Available online at http://counselingoutfitters.com/vistas/vistas10/Article_46.pdf.

Panos, P., Panos, A., Cox, S., Roby, J., & Matheson, K. (2002). Ethical issues concerning the use of videoconferencing to supervise international social work field practicum students. *Journal of Social Work Education, 38*(3): 421–437.

Pennington, M., Patton, R., Ray, A., & Katafiasz, H. (2017). A brief report on the ethical and legal guides for technology use in marriage and family therapy. *Journal of Marital and Family Therapy, 43*(4): 733–742, doi:10.1111/jmft.12232.

Powell, D., & Migdole, S. (2012). *Can You Hear Me Now? New Frontiers of Clinical Supervision.* Plenary presented at The Eighth International Interdisciplinary Conference on Clinical Supervision, Adelphi University, Garden City, NY.

Rees, C.S., Krabbe, M., & Monaghan, B.J. (2009). Education in cognitive-behavioural therapy for mental health professionals. *Journal of Telemedicine & Telecare, 15*: 59–63, doi:10.1258/jtt.2008.008005.

Rigazio-Digillio, S.A. (2016). MFT supervision: An overview. In K. Jordan (Ed.) *Couple, Marriage, and Family Therapy Supervision.* New York: Springer Publishing Company.

Rousmaniere, T., & Kuhn, N. (2016). Internet security of clinical supervisors. In T. Roussmaniere, & E. Renfro (Eds.), *Using Technology to Enhance Counselor Supervision: A Practical Handbook.* Alexandria, VA: American Counseling Association Press.

Rousmaniere, T. (2014). Using technology to enhance clinical supervision and training. In E. Watkins & D. Milne (Ed.) *The Wiley International Handbook of Clinical Supervision.* Hoboken, NJ: Wiley-Blackwell.

Rousmaniere, T., & Renfro-Michel, E.L. (2016). *Using Technology to Enhance Clinical Supervision.* Alexandria, VA: American Counseling Association.

Rousmaniere, T., Renfro, C., Michel, E., & Huggins, R. (2016). Regulatory and legal issues related to the use of technology in clinical supervision. In T. Roussmaniere & E. Renfro (Eds), *Using Technology to Enhance Counselor Supervision: A Practical Handbook.* Alexandria, VA: American Counseling Association Press.

Rousmaniere, T., Abbass, A., Frederickson, J., Henning, I., & Taubner, S. (2014). Videoconference for psychotherapy training and supervision: Two case examples. *American Journal of Psychotherapy, 68*(2): 231–250.

Sholomskas, D.E., Syracuse-Siewert, G., Rounsaville, B.J., Ball, S.A., Nuro, K.F., & Carroll, K.M. (2005). We don't train in vain: A dissemination trial of three strategies of training clinicians in cognitive-behavioral therapy. *Journal of Consulting and Clinical Psychology, 73*: 106–115, doi:10.1037/0022-006X.73.1.106.

Sørlie, T., Gammon, D., Bergvik, S., & Sexton, H. (1999). Psychotherapy supervision face-to-face and by videoconferencing: A comparative study. *British Journal of Psychotherapy, 15*: 452–462, doi:10.1111/j.1752-0118.1999.tb00475.x.

Stebnicki, M., & Glover, N. (2001). E-Supervision as a complementary approach to traditional face-to-face clinical supervision in rehabilitation counseling: Problems and solutions. *Rehabilitation Education, 15*(3): 283–293.

Stokes, A. (2016). Supervision in private practice. In S. Gross (Ed.) *Technology in Mental Health: Applications in Practice, Supervision and Training* (Ch. 33). Springfield, IL: Charles C. Thomas.

United States. (1996). *The Health Insurance Portability and Accountability Act (HIPAA).* Washington, DC: U.S. Dept. of Labor, Employee Benefits Security Administration.

Vaccaro, N., & Lambie, G.W. (2007). Computer-based counselor-in-training supervision: Ethical and practical implications for counselor educators and supervisors. *Counselor Education and Supervision, 47*(1): 46–58.

Watson, J.C. (2003). Computer-based supervision: Implementing computer technology into the delivery of counseling supervision. *Journal of Technology and Counseling, 3.* Retrieved from http://jtc.colstate.edu/.

Wilczenski, F., & Coomey, S. (2006). Cyber-communication: Finding its place in school counseling practice, education, and professional development. *Professional School Counseling, 9*(4): 327–331.

7 Practical Considerations for Online Individual Therapy

Haim Weinberg and Arnon Rolnick

Combine In-person (f2f) and Online Meetings

Whenever it is possible, it is highly recommended to start with an in-person meeting(s) before moving to Cyberspace. If that is not possible, consider meeting with the client in-person ASAP. In addition, schedule in advance such a meeting occasionally (twice a year?). Discuss the various experiences with the client(s).

Frequency of Meetings

Unless there are specific circumstances, there is no reason why the frequency of online meetings should be different than in-person sessions. In a way, online therapy guarantees more stable and continuous meetings with the client, as the connection can continue even when the client is away for business. As for vacations, it is important not to schedule meetings in the therapist's or patient's vacation time, although it is possible technically.

Distance from the Screen in Videoconferencing

This is an important question that not everyone pays attention to. Is it better to sit in front of the computer so that your face (and the client's face) and some of your upper torso is seen on the screen, or is it better to distance yourself from the computer and sit in an armchair so that patients will see you just as they see you in your office. The same question holds for the patient: should we instruct them to sit further from the computer so that we see their entire body, as we do in our office (providing that we don't do analysis on the couch).

There are pros and cons for each approach. Sitting close to the computer means that most of the body is invisible, enhancing the feeling that it is a disembodied environment and creating a very different experience than in f2f meetings. On the other hand, it provides a closeup and a much better recognition of facial expression. Sitting far from the computer makes it more similar to "reality", but it might mean denying and blurring the fact that online therapy is different than in-person one. We also lose the opportunity for clearly observing the expressions on the face of the people involved in the interaction.

In fact, the decision might change according to the patient's needs, and there is an option of negotiating and discussing with the patients what is the best position for them and at different times. The discussion should include the hidden meaning of the seating arrangement for the patient (e.g. shame with body parts. A need to see the eyes of the therapists). For example, if you do sensorimotor therapy online, you might suggest to the patient to move away from the screen so that you see his/her posture and work on that. If you hold the interpersonal neurobiology point of view, you want the patient to get closer so that you have a better perception of how they nonverbally express their feelings.

Need to be Keenly Focused

Online meetings are more distracting than f2f (in-person) ones, partly because there is always the possibility of intruding emails, phone calls, or other interruptions (dog barking), and partly because it is more difficult to stay focused in front of the screen. The therapist should adopt a state of mind(fullness) in which s/he is keenly focused on the patient and his/her needs. Difficulty in doing that should be considered as counter-transference and explored just as in meetings in the office. That does not mean that we ignore the need for free association or reverie.

Setting Considerations

As mentioned in the introduction, in online meetings, the therapist loses control of the setting. We suggest that the therapist makes sure that the patient holds the meetings from a quiet room, where his/her privacy is strictly kept, and not keep the meeting while driving. Remember that you have to prepare and instruct the client about the online meetings, as some of the "rules" that we therapists take for granted, are unfamiliar and might even seem strange to the client. Some people use their laptop or tablets in bed. We do not recommend conducting therapeutic meetings in a supine position.

Technological Setting

Technology becomes a significant part of the setting. Patients do not pay attention to the importance of technological requirements such as a large, immobile screen. Discard the use of smartphones to connect for the session, and explain the importance of a stable, large enough picture as an essential part of the meetings. Discuss with the patient the need for a fast internet connection. Suggest using earphones/headphones to prevent feedback loop and to improve the quality of audio conversation.

Add Items to Agreement

If you are using a written client-therapist agreement, consider adding specific items that relate to online netiquettes, such as no interruptions, guaranteeing privacy, and no distraction during the session (and/or discuss it with the client in the first session). Add information about technology risks and benefits. Mention your limited ability to remotely intervene during an emergency. Here is an example from our written agreement:

> To connect with both video and audio, unless other arrangements are made on occasion.
> To arrange for a quiet room with full privacy and no interruptions. This includes no phone calls, emails or texting during the entire session.
> To stay focused on the meeting.
> To connect from the same place each session, unless you are away and notify us of the change.

Arrange for Emergency Intervention

Whenever you start therapy with a client that lives somewhere else, check in advance the emergency contact numbers in the client's neighborhood, just in case. You might also want to consider having the name and phone number of a contact person in case of emergency. This is especially important when you treat borderline and suicidal patients.

Do not Ignore Anything that Happens on the Screen and the Room of the Client(s)

As said in the introduction, some incidents that we would not ignore if they happen in our office (e.g. bringing a cat to the session or leaving the room in the middle of the session) are easily ignored online. Like other incidents in the therapeutic field, such events clearly hide in plain sight, however, somehow many therapists forget about it when it comes to online details. Be aware of such "transparent" incidents and include them in the mutual exploration.

Technological Expertise

Therapist should acquire some technical knowledge, enough to solve simple problems, but therapists do not have to be experts. Sometimes, being helped with technological issues by patients who have more expertise, can balance the power dynamics.

Technical Instructions

Therapist should send technical instructions to the client(s) about the specific technology (e.g. use of "gallery mode" instead of "speaker view" in Zoom).

When Technology Fails

Prepare a procedure for technological failure (move to text when video freezes? call by phone?).

(Counter) Transference and Technological Difficulties

Whose "fault" is it when the connection is slow or lost? Be aware of the tendency to "blame" the other (overtly or covertly) for technological difficulties. Discuss it with the client when it happens.

Time Zones

Be aware of different time zones, and of daylight-saving time in different geographical areas, to avoid misunderstandings and missing sessions. One way to avoid mistakes is to use Google calendar or a similar application that takes into consideration the time difference.

Background Constancy

Keep a steady background for the sessions as much as possible. In Zoom, you can create a virtual background that can stay the same even when you travel. Pay attention to the background reflected on the screen and try to choose a less "noisy" one.

Cultural Sensitivity

Online, there is a higher chance that you will work with clients from another country or another culture. Learn how to become cultural sensitive and NEVER assume that the norms that you are used to in your culture are the same as the client(s)' or superior to theirs.

Camera Location

The location of the camera is crucial. It can determine whether there is more "eye to eye" contact or less, although it is never the same as in vivo. In some laptops, the camera is not located in the upper middle area, but at bottom right or left corner, resulting in a gaze that is not directed toward the communication partner, although you look straight to the face on the screen. If this is the case, consider connecting an outside camera.

Mirror

Consider the fact that seeing yourself on the screen increases your self-awareness, but also your narcisissm. Although it can help you understand how you come across to the patient, it can distarct you from payimg attention to him/her. Decide whether to turn off your "mirror" (can easily be done in Zoom), or even putting a patch on your screen to hide it.

Adding Lively Elements

Sitting in front of the screen can reduce the liveliness of the speaker. We encourage the therapist to move in the chair, use hand gestures, and sometimes even consider adding some dramatic facial expression and voice intonnation.

Legal and HIPPA Issues

In the USA, the therapist needs to be licensed to practice in the jurisdiction where the client is physically located and cannot practice across State borders. You should check the requirements for practicing psychotherapy in the country where the patient lives. While this book was being published, several States announced that they allow online therapy across borders.

HIPAA, the Health Insurance Portability and Accountability Act, sets the standard for protecting sensitive patient data. Basically, it incudes two elements: protecting clients' information under a standard set of rules, and making sure the people/companies we use to handle the information live up to the same rules. This is called "business associate agreement."

For the purpose of onilne therapy, we have to use applictions/software that is HIPPA compliant: both protection the confidentilaity and signing a business associate agreement.

Dressing Code

Even though the sessions might be conducted from home, therapists should keep the dressing code they are using in their office. The patient can appear in whatever dressing they choose, and if it's something out-standing, it is to be explored.

Section 2

Online Couple and Family Therapy

Edited by Shoshana Hellman and Arnon Rolnick

8 Introduction to the Online Couple and Family Therapy Section

Shoshana Hellman and Arnon Rolnick

We begin this section with some excerpts from a couple therapy session:

Again, they sit in front of me, the same couple and the same problems … yet something is different. The atmosphere seems to have changed a bit.

She initiated the meeting again, a little troubled, "I cannot stand it anymore."

He, as usual, disconnects, "I don't know what she wants…. I don't know what we are doing here." He does not believe in therapy.

They are in therapy for almost a year. They came because they were on the verge of divorce. Yet, I felt this is not what they really want.

"He is only absorbed in his work," she says. "he is not interested in me." She cries and is angry at the same time.

"I do not understand what she's doing," he says, his face blank. "The company in which I work is going to takeoff very shortly, and I have to invest the best of my energies there."

At first, today, there seems to be nothing new … and yet I understand them better. It is strange. I read their faces but could not feel really close.

Coming back to the meeting's content, I try to understand what has happened.

She throws down the gauntlet: "Speak to him this time"

He shrugs. "I do not know what this woman wants, she's always jealous. Once she thought I had some lover, and now she's jealous of my job. She believes I have a remote romance with the customer service girls who are in India."

And so it goes on and on … and I hear them again, summoning flames, inviting empathy, and trying to help them understand the other and see the joint dance that they returned to.

★★★★

And yet there is something different this time:

It is his facial expressions that are clearer to me today, I certainly notice the pain reflected in his face, I can see now from his mouth expression that he feels insulted. I can better hear his cracked voice, noting the creases on his forehead. He seems less indifferent to me. Even the flutter of fingers on the armrest that so characterized him suddenly disappear!

She also seems to me to be a little different. Something about her seductiveness disappears a bit, the sexuality that has always been so emphasized is suddenly missing.

I recall her usual straightening of her short skirt and this time I do not see it.

This time, too, she almost blows up the meeting, but she could not go home as usual: she was at home.

This time they appear to me as one unit. It was me facing them. I was on one screen and they were on another, thousands of miles separating us.

★★★★

Yes, after years of seeing them in my office, sitting on two leather armchairs about a meter away from me, this time I see them in remote therapy, with their faces appearing big on a 32-inch screen. Face-to-face but from afar.

The company he works for sent him for relocation in the Silicon Valley in the US. From now on, the therapy changed from co-location sessions to video conference sessions.

This time, it was hard to calm the outburst because our bodies were not there together. My breathing rate could not allow them to synchronize with their quick breathing, my relaxed and inviting sitting did not appear on the screen. I was unable to quiet them with my presence.

When we met in the same room, and I wanted to turn to one of them, I would move a little closer to the partner with my mobile chair and I would sometimes touch him or her gently to signal them to listen to the other and relax.

This time I could not do it. I had to trust my voice alone – and when that did not work, and they were shouting at each other – I did the inevitable and turned off their microphone and then they heard only me.

★★★★

Coming back to the session: All of a sudden, I see the two of them turn around in panic. Behind them there is a movement. Somebody enters the room and intrudes the session. It is their young son rubbing his eyes and telling them with a rebuke, "You make a lot of noise, so I woke up." And then he begins to cry "I do not want you to shout at each other." "Go to sleep," she orders him. The father, on the other hand, takes his son on his lap and says: "Say hi to Arnon," and I see the gentleness with which he responds to his son. I also see how they both change.

And I am left with the picture of the frightened child and the two different reactions of the parents. Maybe there is some advantage in remote therapy, I reflect when I think about the pros and cons of an online video meeting.

In this section we focus on couple and family therapy online, in particular, using video conferencing. Online therapy is referred to as tele mental health, Internet delivered, cyber psychotherapy or video conferencing. Here we focus only on video conferencing therapy. In recent years there has been an increase of online therapy provided by clinics and therapists but mostly for individuals. Even though the Internet is embedded in one's relational life, cyber issues have received limited attention by family therapy researchers and in conference workshops (Heitler and Webster 2008, Blumer et al. 2014). One of the earlier articles was written by Jenicus and Sager (2001) about the practice of Marriage and Family Counseling in cyberspace including video conferencing, addressing already then issues such as training licensure and ethical issues.

In 2014, in a content analysis of journals addressing Internet therapy by Blumer et al. (2014), they found that in terms of clinical practice, online therapy can be effective for couples, parents and families. Web based treatment services for couples and families include psycho-education, online support groups, interventions for increasing communication between couples and more. For some problems, the same outcomes show for Internet delivered interventions and face-to-face interventions. On the other hand, the content analysis points out the disadvantages which were emphasized by several other researchers as well, such as ethical concerns around confidentiality, emergency situations, credentialing of the therapist. and importance of online counseling guidelines (Blumer et al. 2014).

Ethical issues in couple and family therapy received more attention by Hertlein et al. (2014). In a survey of 226 licensed marriage and family counselors, students and supervisors, the following themes came up: confidentiality, impact on the therapeutic relationship (missing nonverbal cues and body language, diffuse boundaries) licensing and liability issues, crises situations, training and education (privacy practices and technology). The main issue noted by most participants was confidentiality. Both the ACA (American Counseling Association) code of Ethics and the AAMFT (American Association of Marriage and Family Therapy) code attend recently to the role of Internet in practice.

In an interesting article by Bagnini (2014) who is a psychodynamic couple therapist, he calls video conferencing (or tele therapy) a "fourth object" in the treatment of the couple – technology. Both the couple and the therapist are sensitive to the added burden of depending on the "technology mother" that can give so much opportunity but can also let the threesome down. Poor connection stirs up anxiety. Breaks in the line can evoke abandonment anxieties and attachment traumas. The writer views this as a temporary dissociative state in which the therapist is present but cannot be seen or heard, on the other hand the couple is together and can communicate, which can be used later for therapeutic purposes. Video conferencing can enhance projective processes and bring the couple to understand concepts of transference and countertransference. As a psychoanalyst he is interested in the unconscious dynamics conveyed in the domestic setting such as the house decor of the couple, pets that are present during the sessions etc., For him, spatial arrangements and seating arrangements symbolize intimacy concerns.

It would be interesting to have some more research about the efficacy of video conferencing therapy from the standpoint of different theoretical approaches in the field of couples and family therapy.

Other research articles focus on specific populations that could benefit from video conferencing therapy.

In some cases, video therapy for couples and families is inevitable. For example, chronic sickness that prevents couples from coming physically for therapy, couples from remote or rural areas, long distance relationships and couples and families who need support throughout deployment. Tele mental health, especially video conferencing has been shown to be an effective therapy medium especially for military couples (Farero et al., 2015). There are specific issues for these couples. Therapists must understand the military culture, and also work with the two partners who are in different locations. But, here too there is a lack of research exploring the efficacy of treating couples via video therapy.

As for long distance relationships (McCoy et al., 2013), video conferencing services are used by these couples to communicate at real time so that they are familiar with this modality. On the other hand, these couples have more unique issues such as a lack of opportunities to engage in intimacy building processes, they may experience decreased feelings of stability in their relationships, lower levels of trust and more. This would require a specific approach on the part of the therapist towards these couples. Also, in most cases both partners would not be in the same physical space, which would require the therapist to be very attentive to the nonverbal cues of both. The issue of working alliance, (or the therapeutic relationship) which is a central component of successful therapy, can be also a concern when using video conferencing. Although a few articles suggested that the working alliance in video conference is as good as in face-to-face therapy, this has not been proven in family and couple therapy.

Technical issues such as delays and distorted speech are more factors which can be considered as disadvantages, especially when working on effective communication. On the other hand, the reason these couples would look more for tele mental health options is because they cannot have the option of a local therapist. It can also solve language barrier issues instead of seeing a local therapist. Another benefit is that clients feel at times less inhibited and more open in online therapy. Since very little research was done in this area, it is hard to judge the efficacy of tele mental health especially for this population.

Germain (2010) assessed the development of a therapeutic alliance in individuals with PTSD who were treated either by videoconference therapy or face-to-face therapy. The results indicate that a therapeutic alliance can develop very well in both treatment conditions and there is no significant difference between the two. The question is whether this holds true also for couples?

The goal of this section is to present some more current research in the area of couple and family therapy using video conferencing, introduce us to the views of one of the most prominent couple therapists (Gottman) about this topic, and present a couple therapy case with its practical implications for therapists who want to utilize this modality in their work.

Trub and Magaldi present in this cluster a case of family therapy and demonstrate through this presentation four dilemmas when working with screens. The first is adopting new communication norms that therapists and clients should be aware of and decide whether and how to adopt them and help each person to find his/her voice. (for example, immediacy of responses, pace of interactions and more). The second is silence which can be difficult with a medium that privileges the verbal over the nonverbal, the incidences of frozen screen when both the therapist and the client are afraid to lose each other. The third is intimacy which can be challenged by technology. It can increase contact with people and at the same time increase loneliness. The fourth dilemma is how technology shapes identity, what is the connection of the digital self to the non-digital self. Therapists must acknowledge these dilemmas in their online therapeutic encounters.

Hertlein and Earl in their chapter discuss the client-driven barriers to couple and family therapy and the therapist-driven barriers such as alliance, not observing nonverbal clues, diffuse boundaries and training barriers. They also discuss the advantages of Internet delivered couple and family work, accessibility to rural populations, cost, ethical and legal considerations, and guidelines for implementing Internet-delivered services.

The interview with the Gottmans, who are well-known in their innovative couple therapy concepts, presents their views regarding video conferencing in couple therapy. They relate mostly to the difficulties in video conferencing which they use only after they see couples face-to-face. They feel that there is a difference between individual therapy online, and couple therapy. Physiology, and its use in therapy is an important concept in Gottman's theory and several interventions are based on research in this area. These interventions are problematic when using screens with couples. (mostly when flooding occurs). Empathy and assessing facial expressions, another important part of couple therapy, can be a difficult task, especially in the initial stage when assessing and formulating a treatment plan. According to the Gottmans there are special populations that cannot be treated online such as severe PTSD, and even long-distance couples. Technical issues can turn video conferencing to become ineffective, in particular when working on communications.

As we are couple and family therapists as well, using video conferencing in our practice, we had to cope with some of the issues described here. We will demonstrate it with another example of a couple, somewhat different from the excerpts introduced at the beginning of the introduction.

They were seen in the office for a few sessions, and then due to the therapist's traveling, they agreed to continue via video conferencing. They agreed to do it, since they themselves travelled a lot and were used to communicate this way with the extended family. Another reason was their busy schedule, which did not permit them to come to the office regularly and this way they could have their sessions from home at their convenience.

Thomas was a faculty member, American, 43 years old. His wife, a dancer, and a teacher as well, was Asian, 35 years old. They were married for two years. Thomas had a daughter from previous marriage, 7 years old, and was divorced for the last three years. His first wife was also Asian, lived in the same city and shared custody with him. Thomas would have liked full custody of the child but his second wife Ying, objected it. It was her first marriage and she felt the child was a burden and an obstacle to their relationship. She had many problems raising and getting close to this daughter who had a behavioral problem, ADHD, and some other issues. The goals of therapy were to bridge the gap between the two regarding raising the daughter, and the cultural differences between the couple. Ying felt disconnected from her own family and friends and wanted to get pregnant and raise her own child. She was much more introverted than Thomas. The approach used in therapy was solution focused therapy and CBT with some techniques from Gottman's theory. In the office face-to-face, we practiced communication skills (Gottman) and worked towards the goal of involving Ying more in the care of the daughter. When video conferencing started, the couple was satisfied because it saved them time in their busy schedule. The daughter who did not come to the clinic could be eventually part of the therapy. There was also the option of integrating the grandparents who lived in Asia and to bring them to treatment, advantages which could not have been accomplished face-to-face. When they both participated in the video conferencing I made sure they could talk to each other and not look at the camera, this was practiced in the office as well when trying some of Gottman's interventions. We also decided on a specific setting at home in terms of time and location that would guarantee privacy, and lack of external disturbances. We had several successful sessions with the couple, in which they reported improvement in the relationship and communication and less problems with the daughter. In one of the sessions, the topic of having another child emerged and Thomas expressed his dissatisfaction about them having another child. Ying became extremely upset, then silent and finally disappeared from the screen by leaving the room. We referred to her anger in the past in the face-to-face sessions as flooding and to her silence as stonewalling (according to Gottman's approach). But in the office, there was no option of disappearing completely. This exemplifies the disadvantages of video conferencing instead of face-to-face. The couple was in their own familiar home and not in the clinic which is a neutral place. It was easy to disappear from the screen, and probably this was a pattern in the relationship when fighting at home. There were not too many "warning signs" of this crisis, because of the camera. The nonverbal cues might have not been as noticeable on the screen. As a therapist who was thousands of miles away, there were not too many options. The question was whether to continue the session, ask Thomas to find her, or postpone the session to another time. How does one manage conflict or deals with a crisis situation during a video conferencing session? Despite the advantages such as the availability of the therapist, convenience for the couple, easier involvement of other members of the family in therapy, there are also the disadvantages of physical presence versus virtual.

More and more families nowadays are relocating to foreign countries, moving because of jobs or traveling for prolonged periods and are in a need of a therapist who could work with them in their own language and understand their culture. Video therapy seems a good solution for these cases.

Hopefully with growing research in this area and further development of technology we will be able to find some solutions for the disadvantages that video therapy for couples and families can present.

References

Bagnini, C. (2015) Technology stirred projective processes in couple tele therapy. In *Psychoanalysis Online 2* (pp. 186–195). London: Karnac.

Blumer, M., Hertlein, K., Smith, J., and Harrison, A. (2014) How many bytes does it take? A content analysis of cyber issues in couple and family therapy journals. *Journal of Marital and Family Therapy*, 40(1): 34–48.

Farero, A., Springer, P., Hollist, C., and Bischoff, R. (2015) Crisis management and conflict resolution: Using technology to support couples throughout deployment. *Contemporary Family Therapy*, 37(3): 281–290.

Germain, V., Marchand, A., Bouchard, S., Guay, S., and Drouin, M. (2010). Assessment of the Therapeutic Alliance in face-to-face or videoconference treatment for posttraumatic stress disorder. *CyberPsychology, Behavior & Social Networking*, 13(1): 29–35.

Hertlein, K.M., Blumer, M., and Mihaloliakos, J. (2014) Marriage and family counselors perceived ethical issues related to online therapy. *The Family Journal*, 23: 1–8.

Jencius, M., and Sager, D. E. (2001) The practice of marriage and family counseling in cyberspace. *The Family Journal*, 9(3): 295–301.

McCoy, M., Hjelmstad, L., and Stinson, M. (2013) The role of tele-mental health in therapy for couples in long-distance relationships. *Journal of Couple and Relationship Therapy*, 12: 339–358.

9 Interview with Julie and John Gottman[1]

G = Julie and John Gottman; S = Shoshana Hellman; A = Arnon Rolnick

S: So can I ask you the first question: you said you both work individually and with couples. Do you feel there is a difference using Skype with individuals and couples?

G: Yes, there is. Significant differences. First of all, with individuals, the individual is relating to you, so it's one-to-one. Though technologically it's a little bit complicated in that eye contact is not as easily made, given what computer people have, and sometimes the technology is not perfect: it will freeze, or it will do some funny stuff. And so we have to adjust to the whims of the technology. But in couples' work, I think it's much harder. And here's why: first of all, in order to see both people, they have to be sitting very close together, which is usually an unnatural positioning for them. And they're both looking at me, when many times what I want them to be doing is to be speaking with one another, they may look down or somewhere else, as they're talking.

The other thing that makes it difficult is body language. I can't read their body language well. And I think there's also something very significant about sensing.... Trying to sense what's going on between them. And it's much easier to do that when you have the actual, physical energy of the people in the room you're in, rather than on a screen that is a tiny bit fuzzy. And for some reason there's some kind of phantom in the computer so that when they're about to say something incredibly important, the screen freezes. The phantom knows when that's going to occur.... So what can you do, right? You have to wait. It's kind of like watching a really good mystery show, where you're in suspense and you don't know what they're going to say and you're dying to hear what they're going to say, it's frozen, and then it finally comes through. So you have to adjust all this. I don't think it's as efficient or as effective of course as working face-to-face.

S: And in terms of individual therapy would it be more efficient than couple?

G: Yes. So working with an individual, I mean they're looking at you as much as they can. You don't have to look at anybody else. So I'm connecting with them. But at the same time I don't know what to call it, but there's something that's very intense about face-to-face connection, body to body in the same room, where you're, you know, for lack of a better words, you're picking up energy about what's happening in the other person. And that energy for me is often very telling. I have much more intuitive sensibility when I'm working with somebody face-to-face as opposed to on the screen. But with that said, you see, the fact that I can continue a form of therapy at all from thousands of miles away – I mean I have done many Skype sessions for example with couples in Australia, and for me that's a very long distance, you know it's 10,000 miles or something. So the fact that that's even possible is really miraculous, and I'm looking forward to the steady improvement of the technology over time.

A: Do you think you must begin such therapy face-to-face and only then move to Skype sessions?

G: I will only begin in Skype sessions with individuals. That, I've done. For example, I have an individual that started with me and she lives on the east coast. So that's about 3000 miles away. And I'm seeing her regularly. But with couples, it's a different story. I think that first of all, in our couples' therapy … as you know, we do assessment. And that assessment piece is super important. It really guides everything that we do subsequently … and I also need to build a lot of trust, a lot of relationship with each person in the couple. And it's very important for me to see how do they relate to each other under normal circumstances. When you have even further alterations from the normal way that people would relate to each other, in a room, you're moving even further away from some of the difficulties they encounter in their relationship that you want to treat. And so I don't feel I get a fair enough assessment, from beginning just over technology.

S: So this actually relates to the next question, which is obviously, you have very specific principles to your approach. I know that for example, expressions are very important, the assessment is extremely important, and physiology. So how can you really integrate all these principles of your theory and still use couples' therapy on line. Can you do that when you use Skype?

G: You certainly can't if you begin with Skype. That's why I do not. I only do Skype after between 15 and 18 hours of intensive therapy. In the intensive therapy – a marathon therapy – I meet the couple for three consecutive days, five to six hours a day. So I get to know them quite well, in that time, and after that I'm willing to do Skype, when they've already made some progress. But for some people, depending on what the issues are, I'm probably not going to do much Skype, they may have to come back. For example, we treated one couple, where the gentleman was a famous person, he travelled a lot, and he had had 57 affairs in 12 years. And three of them he had fallen in love with, he had three young kids at home. And so, we got pretty far in our first marathon, but definitely they needed more, face-to-face intensive especially when you're dealing with that much intense emotions. And I'm not talking necessarily about the way that somebody might be a very passionate person or a very intense person and how they verbalize their emotions. I'm talking about the pain that is so profound, that has been caused by the other person, that the kind of support that they need and that the other person needs also, to almost be held psychologically as they're hearing the pain of their partner, and not wanting to jump off a bridge, is something that I don't feel comfortable doing over a screen. I really want to be there in-person to do that work. I guess also, that would be the same for people with severe PTSD. So, for example, I've done some work with couples with very severe PTSD, including combat. One fellow for example, who was in the Marines here and during the Iraq and Afghanistan conflict he had had 13 deployments in about 14 years. So he was barely home and he was doing very secretive, deadly, mission work. And … a young guy, he'd gone into the Marines at 18, he was now 32, and he had so much trauma he could barely see straight. And meanwhile he'd also had an affair too, abroad, which is a common problem among service people here, especially service men. And that, too, is the kind of treatment where I wouldn't feel comfortable just doing it over Skype. There's just too much agony between them and especially inside him. So when you have really severe symptoms like that, for this guy, I mean, it was terrible, very severe. Then, it's risky to do it. Especially I think in America we have a very different problem than you guys have, in Israel, in which we have almost as many suicides in the armed forces, as we have people being killed during service. The suicide rate is incredible. Because they don't get help. And so these people who are walking around, walking wounded, are just in a terrible state and high risk. That's not the kind of thing you want to treat over Skype.

S: And was this case also like a long-distance relationship? I mean did he have a relationship too?

G: Yes, this was a couples' case. He had a wife and two children at home. The wife had an affair too. And he did not talk about any of his combat experience before the treatment with his wife. Not so much because he was afraid she couldn't bear it, though that was definitely a part of it, or that she might hate him, but because he couldn't bear to think about it himself and he was already so consumed by the memories of it. At night, especially, when there was no distraction. He just couldn't bear to go down deep into it. Except that finally, he did.

S: Which brings me to ask about couples who have long-distance relationships. I wonder whether you see some of those couples and whether those are treated via Skype, because obviously that's how their relationship goes. So did you see any of those?

G: We've seen a lot of couples with long-distance relationships. But those couples come together for therapy, so they are not doing what you and Arnon and I are doing [each one of the interviewers and the interviewee were in different physical spaces] right now, where we have three different screens. They'll come together for a weekend, every couple of months or something, and during that time there'll be some treatment. Or they'll come here for an intensive. So yes, we have seen those couples, and the long distance certainly creates strain. It's a very difficult process to have intimate relationship.

A: Since what you do is not only to do the therapy but also to give suggestions to a couple how to make their marriage better, have you ever written or thought to write how to do long-distance relationship with Skype or a method like this?

G: That's a good question, Arnon. We have not, and the reason we have not is because we don't write anything unless we've done research on it. And, you know, though there have been a few long-distance couples, here and there, we haven't made a conscientious study of their relationships. Other people have, but we haven't. And we haven't tested out treatments with couples like that and we definitely haven't tested treatment over Skype. So it's not something we would write about unless we've actually conducted research.

S: Let's move from couples and long-distance relationships to family therapy. Is there any type of family therapy that you have done actually? I know that you're not doing too much family, you're doing mostly couples. Maybe just what is your opinion about family therapy. Do you think it's possible to do it via Skype?

G: I don't know. I don't do family therapy except with adult people. I've definitely done family therapy for parents and children when the children are grown and adults. And I guess the more people I think you have on a little screen, the less information you're getting for every individual. Because they're further away from you, they're more blurry, you can't see their faces unless you have multiple cameras operating, and you don't, usually. So I think you're losing a vast amount of information as opposed to doing it more closely. With younger children, depending on what you're talking about, kids would want to get up and move, they're not gonna want just sit in one place. That's hard. You can't do that either over a screen. With teenagers, it's possible but again, you'll be losing a lot of information. I think really the most you can comfortably have on the screen is two to three people. Two of them on one screen and the therapist on the other. Three? I don't know. I think it would be pretty hard.

A: I thought that one of the reasons it was important to interview you was that you do emphasize the role of the physiology and the role of the body. I was somewhat happy to see that you published a book in the interpersonal neurobiology series.

G: That's right. That was my book.

A: So if you take it into consideration that we need to "hear" the body or to sense the body or to sense the central nervous system, and I know John did a lot of work about physiology, like measuring the heart rate. I wonder where is this direction when we conduct Skype sessions. And if we do speak about Skype therapy, what do you think if I could see your heart rate now on the screen. Would that help in any way?

G: Yes, I am in favor of heart rate monitoring. A heart rate of greater than 100 beats a minute appears to be the cutoff at which most healthy hearts begin being affected by circulating adrenaline and cortisol, activating beta sympathetic nerves that increase cardiac contractility and rate, constrict arteries, and contribute to the physiological cascade of events that accompanies fight or flight and has huge consequences for cognition and affect, usually without the person's (client's and therapist's) awareness. What seems like "resistance" may be the consequences of diffuse physiological arousal.

A: Initially you suggested measuring heart rate to evaluate the level of arousal of your couple. These days there are more advanced methods to measure not only heart rate but also Heart Rate Variability. Would you consider adding such additional measures to face-to-face and online couple therapy?

G: Heart rate variability is an okay substitute for RSA (respiratory sinus arrhythmia), which can be assessed quite effectively from a spectral analysis of the area under the spectral density function of the heart period time series within the usual adult respiratory range. That computation is a better measure of vagal tone, which is what we want to sharpen in our clients (and the therapist).

G: Sure. Yes, of course, it would help. We are actually working on some technology to create therapy and track therapy including physiology over screens and it's a work in progress. Physiology plays a very important role. Heart rate of course is important, sometimes you can tell some things by respiration. And you can watch respiration through subtle movements, flesh tones for example will subtly change color with breath. Also there are tons of devices out there for heart rate, you know little pulse oximeter that can be joined through programming into different technological screens and integrated into what you're doing. So yes, that is an important thing. Sometimes I have had people on Skype, I had them purchase for 19 dollars a pulse oximeter to wear on their fingers at times, I'll ask them to do a conflict conversation. It's for themselves, what's happening, and the ones that we get have alarms built in so if their heart rate goes above a set number, usually 100bpm, that's a sign of diffuse physiological arousal, and I can hear the alarm going off and so can they, of course. So I know that they're getting flooded, and then we'll do something around that. So, there's also technology made by a company called Heartmath that I'll ask people to work with just to see whether or not that strengthens their ability to resist flooding. So, yeah, the short answer is physiology is very helpful, very important in terms of integrating that into the therapy.

S: You are doing it on Skype, from what I heard you say. So because of the alarm, because of the facilities of using it even online, you can use it actually, using Skype and doing your intervention.

G: Right. As a matter of fact there are probably ways of doing things, but you've got to have multiple cameras, that's really the secret. I was thinking about our research lab, which we just opened up again, and we've got three cameras, we've got split screen, we've got program integrating both physiology monitors and so on, into what's happening with the couple as they talk to each other. All of that is getting registered on one screen, but our focus has not been to do therapy via a screen. Our focus is doing the therapy in-person and analyzing all the data that we collect. I suppose theoretically you could set up something in a very complicated way, but the problem is the couple would have to be in a place where you've got all the equipment.... And you are somewhere else.

A: Suppose now I'm with you Julie in the same room, and you could see that I'm excited. That's one thing. And now I'll describe another situation when we are not in the same room, but you see [via some sensors] that my heart rate goes up. Theoretically, it's the same experience that you see that I'm aroused, but my feeling is that it will be a different type of right hemisphere communication. When I see you now, and I see in your face that you're trying to understand me, this information is coming from the right brain, I think. If it was with the sensors, I think you'll say "ok, Arnon's heart rate is going up, or Julie's alpha wave is going down" – it's a different type of analysis. Do you see where I'm headed to?

G: Sure. I totally do. I think, Arnon, you're making a good point, and it is what I was trying to say before, actually – not very articulately, maybe – in which when I'm sitting in the same room with you, I can sense you. As opposed to seeing an oscilloscope, say, with little waves going up and down. It creates a very different response in me. And that response guides how I intervene. So if I'm seeing signs on a screen, let's say, that your physiology is going up, I'll have a very cerebral reaction to it. If ... left and right brain stuff is not quite what it seems, so I don't tend to use that kind of language, but it's certainly a more removed response. It's an intellectualized response. Whereas when I'm in a room with you, I'm feeling it at a much deeper level. And therefore my intervention tends to be probably more powerful and more effective when I'm face-to-face with you. That's because it's coming not only from my intellect in analyzing what's going on to cause what you're feeling, but also what I'm sensing, what I'm intuiting. Just being in your presence. So, you know, can doing therapy over a screen really duplicates that? Not that I've seen.

S: There is an article of a psychoanalyst that talks about distance therapy and whether empathy can be shown on screen and can be felt as real. I want your answer because you integrate emotionally focused therapy in your approach and then you mentioned extreme cases of PTSD but what about other cases of emotions?

G: Well again, you certainly can't transmit empathy visually as well. I think in terms of the words you use, how you speak, the sound quality is much better than visual quality, as it is registered by the listener, by the receiver.

A: I'm not sure I understood.

G: What I was saying is that sound quality is transmitted much more clearly than visual quality to the receiver, in Skype.

S: So you mean to say that in Skype the sound is more important than the visual, or it's more effective?

G: No, what I'm saying is that when you compare the sound and visual of Skype, sound is certainly more finely tuned, it's more effective, than visual and here's where it comes into your question, Shoshana, which is I think you can convey some empathy through your voice, through the words of course and also through the tone, through the pacing of it, the volume of it.

G: So again to your point, I think you can express empathy. you can do a better job expressing empathy through voice, but on the screen you really lose the eye contact, the facial nuances, that convey empathy, the body movement that conveys empathy, you can't do it on a screen. So you probably lose 50% of the power of the empathy you're trying to express to the other person. And you do the best you can.

A: Speaking about empathy. Can we use facial expressions? I believe that John was one of the first researchers to use the Specific Affect Coding System (SPAFF), to code participants' behavior for specific affect from video recordings.

G: I not only used the Specific Affect Coding System (SPAFF), I invented it. So yes, it is a very effective coding system, and in the couples' arena better than Ekman's Facial Affect Coding System (FACS) in predicting longitudinal outcomes (that result is published). But FACS is fabulous. Paul Ekman has made an enormous contribution to our understanding of emotion.

A: In online therapy the camera is already there, and the picture goes directly to the computer. This can therefore be a great opportunity to show the patients their facial expressions as translated by the computer to "emotional scores." You are probably familiar with MIT/Affectiva solution which can use a simple laptop camera to assess human emotion. Would you consider adding such a non-intrusive method for couple therapy in general and online individual or couple therapy sessions?

G: I am familiar with MIT's media lab work, and automated facial coding in general. So far it's not good enough, unless misses are not counted as unreliability. Still we have to show that a particular automated facial affect matches observers by 90% or more. If anger is coded, it must be coded anger by both automated coding and observers. A serious problem is the corpus of photos used is mostly garbage. People are paid to display an emotion and that photo is accepted without questioning it. So, for example, the corpus of disgust expressions are people sticking their tongues out, instead of upper-lip raises or nose wrinkles, classic disgust expressions. Also, posed and spontaneous expressions are very different. So a lot of automated coding with a bad corpus of photos is garbage.

But, yes, I am in favor of automated coding. It would add so much. So many therapists are actually not competent in detecting emotions. I know that's a damning conclusion about therapists, but, where do they get trained? Not in graduate schools. That's sad, but it's more likely that they will get trained in projective testing than in learning how to read micro-expressions on the face.

A: Here is a broader question: Research shows that the result of Skype or online therapy is as good as face-to-face therapy and even that the therapeutic alliance is also as good. How would you explain that?

G: First of all, I want to see the research and see the measurements and how they're assessing what they're actually assessing. For example, therapeutic effectiveness, what level of therapists are they using. So you can have mediocre therapy being equal to mediocre Skype work, and so therefore they're equal. But that doesn't mean it's good therapy. So you got to look at the research more carefully. You've got to analyze what they're actually looking at, and how they're measuring it, that's very important. And, you know, typically. ... A lot of the studies will use self-report as a measurement and self-report is a terrible measurement. And there's a lot of research on that. Especially in therapy where you know the client is trying to be pleasing to the therapist, because they're grateful for whatever the therapist is giving them. And if it's part of a research study, it's typically for free. ... So you got to really look at the research, Arnon, and not necessarily take it at face value. So, the other thing I would want to see, is in terms of effectiveness, I would want to see a longitudinal follow-up. So maybe right after therapy ends they're feeling better. A year later, are they still feeling better? You know. I want to see that. So you've got to have a pretty high bar when it comes to evaluating the quality of the therapy.

A: Another question which is still related to what we spoke earlier, you are of course familiar that in some cases … there is an erotic transference either in individual therapy but also could be between the therapist and one of the partners of the couple. I wonder if you think that erotic transference would happen also in Skype therapy.

G: That's hilarious. It depends on how big the screen is and whether the client is seeing the entire body of the therapist or just the face. And I'm saying that a bit facetiously. I suppose … of course it could still happen. Because it is in fact transference. It's a transference. But it's probably not quite as likely to happen because of a variety of things. I don't know. I don't think anybody has ever measured this; it would be an interesting study, to look at pheromones of clients in therapy which in fact is largely responsible for being physically attracted to somebody. So obviously those don't transfer through Skype. Yet. Maybe it's coming. And when you're looking at just a not very well focused face you still get erotic transference from just the therapy itself really, and very little about the physical presence of the other person. I don't know. You know, it would be an interesting study. I'm sure it's possible, and I'm sure it happens, but I don't think it happens with as much frequency.

S: There's one more question that is not related at all to this. Do you know about the interventions that are online, a lot of self-help interventions online, Many therapists are using them. I know that you are using of course the assessments online. But there are also video ones. Is there a way to integrate those? Are you thinking how are those computerized interventions integrated. Obviously, I don't think it is in your approach but what do you think of these kinds of self-help video computerized interventions?

G: We're actually working on that as we speak.

A: In what way?

G: I can't go into a lot of details, but what I can say is that I do think it's possible for interventions, especially dyadic interventions to be conducted through technology. So anything that goes deep, relies on the therapist's judgement, intuition, orientation and so on, is going to be much harder. You're not going to be able to do that. But, when there are interventions that are very simple things, then I think you can give people instruction on how to do those things with one another and have them do them, hopefully successfully.

S: So you can integrate them also in your sessions, in your Skype sessions, let's say?

G: Well … we do that in our Skype sessions. We are doing that in our sessions.

A: I wonder if you are doing a group supervision via Skype.

G: Yes, we're doing tons and tons of group supervision via Skype. In fact, most of it. We have certified master-trainers who are part of our certification training. And they do group Skype meetings with small groups for consultation to direct people to get certified. So we're doing a lot of that. All over the world. It's the only way that we can actually train people through to certification, when we don't have a certified trainer in the country itself, or even, you know, in the city. So yes, most of our advanced training, in fact, is done that way. The final process. Stage 4, I guess you call it, of our training. Ok, so the first question, the future.

A: We would like your opinion about how technology affects human relationship.

G: How does technology affect relationships? The jury is still out on that. Potentially, it can create greater community. Also, it may be used to hurt people, separate people, have people rely on text instead of face-to-face interactions. It can be quite harmful. But people also said that about the telephone, and it was an unfounded worry. So I don't judge it as harmful. Like other aspects of technology, it can be used to connect people, or it can be used to distance people. I found it delightful to think about David Levy's book *Sex and Love with Robots*, because he asked the question what does it take for a human to fall in love with a machine, and the answer is not much. Some people on the planet will choose blow-up sex dolls over making love to a real person, so why not make them available to those people? Maybe it will end prostitution and sexual slavery. I think it is foolish to condemn technology without thoughtfulness. For example, in creating a virtual therapist the program Eliza (and its new incarnation woebot) a randomzied clinical trial showed it to be effective with depression. How many therapists can claim that? So Eliza may increase the competence of therapists in the long run.

G: So, what's the future? I don't think the human being will ever be replaced. I think what is the most effective is face-to-face work. I mean that's just my own prejudice. No matter how good computers get, no matter how good robots get, or robotic programming, and so on. Even with Artificial Intelligence. Everything is going towards machine learning and artificial intelligence, which I think is fabulous – I mean it's really pretty incredible. And … that's part of our work as well, some of the stuff we're integrating.

A: You give us an interesting message. On one hand I understand that you are working with some Artificial Intelligence and robotic-like interventions and at the same time you say that we still need the human touch.

G: That's right, in a nutshell.

A: Have you tried new devices like Alexa for such work?

G: In terms of therapy, my fundamental philosophy about therapy is that – and this is going to sound really cheesy or corny or very American or something. Or optimistic. But I really do believe that the therapist's love for the client is what heals the client, ultimately.

And how do you transmit love over a screen, especially building trust in the first place. Before really knowing the client well. It takes a while and I don't know if it can be done.... I don't think it can be done as effectively on a screen. I think you need real contact. I think there's something about how nature was created that is perfection on every level. And that what is natural is being-to-being contact, being-to-being communication whether it's animal-to-animal, or person-to-person. And we are animals, ultimately. So when you put a chunk of [meat] or other material between you and another human being, then what? Well, it's dehumanizing to some degree, and we're trying very very hard to negate the results of that dehumanization of connection but again I'm such a believer that what is natural is right, or best, in some ways, that it will never duplicate what is possible in person-to-person, face-to-face. So I think we are always going to need that and we need that perhaps more in the more severe cases but everybody needs it anyway. So we can move towards greater and greater mimicry of human connection and artificial intelligence is all designed ... you know, all hoping for that, in fact, when machines learn the way humans do. But is that going to really create real feelings? Well, sort of. But ultimately, human-to-human is best. In terms of couples' therapy, same thing.

A: I think that would have been a very nice way to summarize the meeting. I never met you, you never met me, and yet, our communication was as synchronized as your communication with Shoshana.

G: That's true. But, we are talking on a cerebral level, Arnon, We're not talking about deep feelings and emotions and pain and traumatic history, and ... childhood. Right? So yeah, sure, at this level you could do a lot, intellectually you could do a lot. But that's not where real healing takes place. I'm not trying to heal you, and you're not trying to heal me. We're having an intellectual conversation. And yeah, sure, you could do that.

G: I think to your point Arnon, there's so much need out there, there's huge need for so many people, to get help and especially for couples to get help, in every country that there's no way in the world there could be enough therapists face-to-face to supply the help, if ... 1% of those people even want to avail themselves to that help. So I think technology serves an incredibly important purpose in being able to reach many, many more people with at least a modicum of help, some amount of help. It's not going to be perhaps the same quality, but let's not go with "all or nothing". Let's go with what is possible. What can we give. And any help is better than ... if it's the quality, and the research backs it up, in how effective the methods are, let's give whatever we can out there, to reach as many as we can. Good enough therapy. Good enough marriage. It doesn't have to be perfect.

A: Toda Raba [thanks a lot, in Hebrew].

S: We really thank you so much for your time, we really appreciate it.

G: It was fun, it was wonderful. Thank you for reaching out to us, thank you.

Note

1 This interview was done in two stages. The first stage was with Dr. Julie Schwartz Gottman in video conferencing (Zoom). The second stage was done with Dr. John Gottman by email correspondence. We combined the two parts of the interview to this one.

10 Internet-delivered Therapy in Couple and Family Work

Katherine M. Hertlein and Ryan M. Earl

Introduction

Internet-delivered therapy is rapidly becoming a common and highly effective practice for the delivery of mental health care services, including couple and family therapy. Internet-delivered therapy is defined broadly as any professional interaction between clients, therapists, and/ or supervisors that uses the Internet and other electronic media (i.e., chatting, video calling, discussion boards, emailing, texting, websites, social network sites, etc.) (Blumer et al., 2015). Its effectiveness has been well-documented for many conditions such as eating disorders (Wagner et al., 2015), depression (Choi et al., 2014; Luxton et al., 2014; Mohr et al., 2008; Osenbach et al., 2013), anxiety disorders including OCD (Rees & Maclaine, 2015; Yuen et al., 2015), substance abuse (King et al., 2014), the mental health symptoms of individuals with physical concerns (Cosio et al., 2011; Crowe, 2017) and other issues (Maheu et al., in press; Mohr et al., 2010).

Purpose

The perception of couple and family therapists is generally one of suspicion as to the effectiveness (or perhaps appropriateness) of this form of treatment delivery for relational cases, particularly how it is perceived to damage the therapeutic relationship (Hertlein & Blumer, 2013). While much of the work examining the use of Internet-delivered therapy is focused on work with individuals, there is some evidence that Internet-delivered therapy would also be an effective treatment for practitioners conducting relational work with couples and families. The purpose of this chapter is to highlight the value of conducting couple and family therapy via Internet-delivered therapy, as well as address the misconception that face-to-face therapy is more effective than therapy conducted online.

Barriers to Internet-Delivered Services

General Client-Driven Barriers to Couple and Family Treatment

Part of what may contribute to resistance toward using Internet-delivered services include those resistances to relational treatment in general. Lack of parent engagement (as defined by treatment adherence, attendance, and compliance), for example, is a primary reason why treatment is ineffective (Baker-Ericzén et al., 2013; Staudt, 2007). Many factors related to demographic and socioeconomic status also impeded couple and family work. Children who drop out of treatment, for example, are typically older, are of an ethnic minority, and display externalizing behaviors (Oruche et al., 2014; Pellerin et al., 2010). For parents and youth, higher levels of stress, and lower levels of education are associated with dropout (Friars & Mellor, 2007; Oruche et al., 2014; Staudt, 2003). Children and families who experience that the organization from whom they are receiving services is meeting their needs are less likely to drop out (Kim et al., 2012; Staudt, 2003; Thompson et al., 2009). Drop out also may occur when therapy is cost-prohibitive (Rose et al., 2004).

These same barriers may present themselves in Internet-delivered therapy with couples and families. Despite that approximately 88% of the U.S. population is on the Internet (Internet Stats, 2016), that leaves a certain proportion of the population that is not on the Internet and perhaps others who do not have regular access, thus making it difficult to obtain therapeutic services online. These may be couples and families who perceive services to be cost-prohibitive, may have a lower level of educational attainment which may underwrite their inability to afford such services, and may also have the other characteristics described above. The limited access combined with the other factors may even increase dropout for some, as clients may perceive that to end a relationship with a therapist is as simple and clicking "Quit", particularly if that therapist is not nearby.

Therapist-Driven Barriers

Just as there are client-driven barriers contributing to the belief that Internet-delivered therapy is ineffective, clinicians (not limited to couple and family therapists) also hold some prejudices regarding Internet-delivered services (Myers & Vander Stoep, 2017). The perception for many is that Internet-delivered therapy falls short in achieving a therapeutic alliance, in the development of a proper assessment and diagnosis, does not provide adequate provisions for high-risk cases or confidentiality concerns, and lack of training opportunities. Each of these is discussed below.

Perceived Disruptions of the Alliance

Attending to the therapeutic alliance is widely regarded as a key component to conducting effective psychotherapy. Though there are no direct studies on perceived alliance and couples/families, a primary complaint from therapists (as high as 61%) is their perception that the therapeutic alliance is not developed as strongly as in-person therapeutic relationships (Hennigan & Goss, 2016; Hertlein et al., 2015). A favorable therapeutic alliance can contribute to clients' increased comfort disclosing sensitive information, responding favorably to interventions as well as to a therapist's increased ability to accurately hypothesize about a given case and/or design meaningful interventions.

Many therapists believe that conducting Internet-delivered therapy is disruptive of the joining process, interferes with structuring sessions to focus on process rather than tasks, and impedes developing and maintaining strong alliances (Hertlein, Blumer & Smith, 2014; Reese & Stone, 2005; Richardson et al., 2015; Simms et al., 2011). Research focused on the intersection of therapeutic alliance and Internet-delivered therapy, however, does not support such opinions. Consensus in the literature suggests that there are few differences, if any, between traditional therapy and Internet-delivered therapy on therapeutic alliance (Glueck, 2013; Morgan et al., 2008), regardless of presenting problem (Jenkins-Guarnieri et al., 2015) or modality (Rochlen et al., 2004). In fact, some evidence suggests therapeutic alliance may be stronger in e-therapy over face-to-face settings (Knaevelsrud & Maercker, 2006). It is unclear whether these same gains would be made in couple and family therapy. For example, journal-writing is often used as part of online therapy and has been connected to the perceived alliance (Glueck, 2013a). But in the case of relational work, the only person who may be able to submit journals would be the single account holder, impairing alliance-building with other members.

Perception of Inability to Provide Services Consistent with the Standard of Care

Another issue related to physical presence cited by 37% of those in Hennigan and Goss's (2016) study was that of not being able to properly observe the non-verbal cues and body language a client may exhibit, which could compromise an appropriate assessment and subsequent treatment strategy. Further, 28% of a sample of counselors reported concern they would not be able to intervene if their case needed serious attention and 44% cited issues around confidentiality as the barrier preventing them from engaging in this type of work (Hennigan & Goss, 2016). This is likely higher with couple and family therapists as there may be a smaller window through which to observe non-verbal cues. For example, in working with couples, one of the first things a therapist might attend to would be where the couple sits (with each other or apart), it may be impossible to use this for information gathering as there may not be enough room to sit distally when the therapist is online.

Perception of Diffuse Boundaries

There also may be a perception that the accessibility, acceptability of using the Internet via smartphones at any time (not limited to work hours), and the ease at which one can send a message may contribute to the deterioration of boundaries (Hennigan & Goss, 2016; Hertlein & Blumer, 2013) cited by 19% of counselors wary of Internet-delivered therapy. Therefore, therapists who are concerned about maintaining professional boundaries with clients may be less inclined to view the integration of technology in their practice plan as beneficial, or, at worst, may view using technology with clients as a detriment to the boundaries they want to establish. From a therapeutic lens, this means that clients can reach out to therapists to quickly share updates at any time. Clients may also believe that therapists should respond as soon as possible since they know their therapist is accessible via phone or technology. The fact that technology has the ability to allow clients to engage in this accessibility might deter therapists from including these technologies in their practice. Further, in couples and families, the therapist may receive texts or calls from independent members of the couple or family since each member has personal devices.

Training Barriers

A therapist's initial training is, more than likely, not initially in online service delivery. Therapists are typically taught how to assess, diagnose, and treat in real-time and within the physical presence of a client. The nuances of conducting online treatment are provided later and typically left up to the therapist as to whether they want to pursue additional training in this. The lack of training in this modality has been cited as a specific reason by 20% of a sample of counselors as to why they do not engage in Internet-delivered work (Hennigan & Goss, 2016). Part of the issue may be the call toward more competency-based education. A competency-based approach originated from the medical field, though it has recently been adopted by a variety of healthcare professions such as couple and family therapy, nursing, psychiatry, psychology, and social work (Halcomb et al., 2016; Kaslow, 2004; Poulin & Matis, 2015). Competency-based education was explicitly applied to the field of couple and family therapy in 2007, when a task force developed what came to be known as the Core Competencies (Nelson et al., 2007). These competencies, however, have not revolved around technology in an MFTs (Marriage and Family Therapists) practice and included areas such as case management, interventions, and admission. Blumer et al. (2015) began to apply some of the MFT core competencies to evaluate how they would include technology in a couple and family therapists' practice, and this work has been infused into the more recent (and generalized) work by Hilty et al. (2015; 2017) regarding competencies across telebehavioral health, including couple and family therapy.

Advantages to Internet-Delivered Couple and Family Work

Couple and family therapists' perceptions of Internet-delivered therapy, which drive therapists' comfortability with such practices, ultimately affect their success in working in this modality. There are, however, many advantages to using the Internet as a tool that augments the work with couples and families.

Development of Intimacy and Self-Disclosure

Like most mental health professionals, relational therapists tend to highly value intimacy within the therapeutic relationship. As a result, it is common to expect that clients are disclosing information in ways that demonstrate authenticity and contribute to the development of an honest, therapeutic relationships. Therapeutic relationships facilitated online do not result in a lesser experience for the users – merely a different one that may actually be advantageous to building intimacy. This difference can be primarily associated with the tendency for online communication to have a disinhibiting effect on clients, which can encourage therapeutic expression and self-reflection far sooner than clients might in-person (Suler, 2002). Rochlen et al. (2004) suggested that clients tend to "cut to the chase" (271) of core issues because clients no longer need to remove social "masks" that constrain intimate therapeutic relationships, especially at the beginning of therapy. In addition, early investigations on technology and therapy revealed that there may be more intimacy exchanged over video services because people felt like they could be more vulnerable since the person "wasn't really in front of them".

Increases Accessibility to Services

Therapists who participate in Internet service-delivery can provide services to varied geographical areas, regions, and populations. Rural populations are often the most logistically-difficult to provide services given the paucity of mental health providers in their areas (Gibson et al., 2011; Morland & Kloezeman, 2013; Wang et al., 2005). Even though Internet-delivered therapy can be used to reach rural populations that would otherwise not be able to access services, Internet-delivered therapy is still underutilized (Frueh, 2013). Since research suggests that couples and families in these rural populations would be likely to take advantage of mental health services if only they were available (Grubaugh et al, 2008; Harwood & L'Abate, 2009), Internet-delivered therapy can bridge the gap.

Internet-delivered therapy may also be a way for therapists and clients alike to decrease the cost of service (Flaum, 2013). For example, therapists who offer Internet-delivered therapy no longer need to rent office space, the cost of which may be prohibitive if it requires more than a 22-mile commute for the therapist (Glueck, 2013b; Modai et al., 2006; O'Reilly et al., 2007). Traveling to a physical office space may replace valuable time that could be spent seeing more clients in more geographic areas, thus generating more income (Glueck, 2013a; 2013b). The same is true for couples and families. Couples and families also benefit financially from Internet-delivered therapy in cases where there may be costs incurred from time off work, child care, travel, etc. (Glueck, 2013a). One of the most challenging aspects of couple and family work is getting everyone together at the same time. Further, even if a common hour between jobs, school activities, and extracurricular activities exists, there is still the additional time requirement of coming and going to the session. In this way, internet treatment may be the most efficient use of time for couples and families.

The Internet may also assist in treatment with Live Apart Together couples and long-distance relationships. Live Apart Together couples identify being in a relationship, but do not live together. These are distinguished from long distance relationships where the individuals are separated by large geographic distance. Individuals who identify being part of a Live Apart Together relationship may not be interested in living together because they perceive the relationship is less serious and/or is not mandated to fit in with society's norms of living together (Duncan et al., 2014). For both long-distance relationships and live apart relationships, using the Internet as a tool for treatment would increase services to these couples because they are not required to be in close proximity. In other words, therapy can accommodate their relationship configuration/physical state rather than presenting a proximity/access constraint. A clear majority (86%) of Live Apart Together couples, for example, contact each other daily via text, phone, or Internet. Likewise, couples in long-distance relationships contact each other frequently using technology and families use the Internet to connect transnationally (Bacigalupe, 2011). The benefits include that it can connect families in ways across different time zones and timelines (Treas & Gubanskaya, 2018), so long as doing so is recognized as lawful and ethical in the state(s) in which the clients reside (Caldwell et al., 2017).

Ethical and Legal Considerations

Internet-delivered services are not without ethical and legal issues. Specific to couples and families, confidentiality is a hot-button issue. First, security is often cited as a primary concern since multiple members in a relational system might have access to the therapy portal. This may include access to therapy-related items such as journals, notes, or drawings. Second, families will be encouraged to ensure that when in conversation with the therapist privately for perhaps a segregated session, the other family members may not hear the contents of that one-sided conversation. This may be difficult as the therapist cannot control the environment in which the client sits. At the same time, therapists in a physical space would also have to safeguard against this, and often do with white noise makers and other tools. The therapist working with a family online would also have to take those same precautions.

Guidelines for Implementing Internet-Delivered Services

One of the primary areas to incorporate guidelines is in the area of detailed and improved training. Hertlein and Blumer (2013) found a clear majority of licensed couple and family therapists had not received training in Internet-delivered therapy. In Hennigan and Goss's (2016) study of school counselors, the training most helpful included those specific to the student population, training on the feasibility of such delivery of services, training on the impact to the relationship, and other training such as how to specifically conduct such therapy. Internet-delivered service competencies for couple and family therapists – if adapted – would likely be shepherded by the American Association for Marriage and Family Therapy (AAMFT). AAMFT has used the term "Technology-Assisted Professional Services" and to a lesser degree, the term "Couples and Family Therapy Technology (CFTT)" practice. In the recently published set of ethical standards published by AAMFT, the relevant section is Standard VI Technology-Assisted Professional Services (2015). It suggests that members: (1) be aware of and compliant with the laws related to the delivery of technology-related practices, be sure that recommended technologies are appropriate for the recipient, transmission be secure, and be used after appropriate education, training or supervision; (2) obtain written consent for the provision of any technology-related services, including the risks, benefits, limitations, and potential issues around confidentiality and security, (3) be able to discern when services are appropriate and if so determine which kinds are most apt, and (4) participate in technology-related services only upon completion of the appropriate education, training, and/or supervision (competence first, then practice consistent with best online practices). Interestingly, the best practices for online therapy presented by AAMFT specifically do not include other forms of media. "As such, we have not addressed here the use of text messaging, email, online scheduling, or related technologies used as an adjunct to in-person treatment" (AAMFT, 2016: 1).

The latest work related to the development of competencies has been offered by Maheu et al. (in press). In this work, seven domains of competencies are offered by Maheu's interdisciplinary taskforce charged with identifying competencies for telebehavioral health. This task force carefully considered how Internet delivery would look in the cases of counseling, psychiatry, psychology, social work, nursing, and couple and family therapy. The domains include: clinical evaluation and care, virtual environment and telepresence, competencies in technology, competency in legal and regulatory issues related to technology, evidenced-based practices, mobile apps and social media, and development of a telepractice (Maheu et al., in press). Competencies in technology was defined as how well one can use the actual hardware and software involved in being able to run a practice online. In couple and family therapy, this means ensuring that the practitioner has the same practice standard for each family member, appropriate documentation, and adapting what one currently does with individuals to couples and families. Mobile health and technologies relate to the extent to which practitioners can implement appropriate apps to support clinical treatment and goals. Therapists working with couples and families via the Internet need to ensure that the interventions related to technology (including suggestions for apps) will meet the needs and abilities of couples and families. For example, giving a particular app to encourage the family to record data and send to the therapist may not be realistic for younger family members who perhaps do not have access to their own phones. Telepractice development refers to the use of technology to market one's clinical practice in appropriate ways. This means ensuring that those who have not taken training specifically how to manage the dynamics that emerge on camera with a family may wish to gain this training before advertising themselves as an Internet-delivered couple and family therapist. Further, Maheu et al. (in press) identified three levels of competency within each of these domains: novice, competent, and expert. Generally speaking, novice are those who may be students or just learning the skills competent practitioners can operate independently; expert may be those who are supervising, conducting research and/or providing training on the use of technology practice.[1]

Conclusion

Technology is not perfect, and the delivery of services via the Internet platform will continue to be met with some challenges. When trained well and used in ways that uphold the standards of care in the profession of couple and family therapy, however, the use of the internet can serve as that which can reduce disparities in access to care, increase self-disclosure, be a supportive adjunct to group processes, and provide effective service for a variety of presenting problems. Future research is needed to continue to test the efficacy of some of the Internet-delivered interventions on couples and families as we as generate data to more clearly support the evidence that Internet-therapist do not disrupt the joining or assessment process.

Note

1   The list of competencies and their descriptions is very detailed; therefore, we refer readers to Maheu et al.'s (in press) article for the specifics on this.

References

Aboujaoude, E., & Salame, W. (2016). Technology at the service of pediatric mental health: Review and assessment. *The Journal of Pediatrics, 171*: 20–24, doi:10.1016/j.jpeds.2015.12.009.

Abrams, J., Sossong, S., Schwamm, L., Barsanti, L., Carter, M., Kling, N., … Wozniak, J. (2017). Practical issues in delivery of clinician-to-patient telemental health in an academic medical center. *Harvard Review of Psychiatry, 25*(3): 135–145, doi:10.1097/HRP.0000000000000142.

American Association for Marriage and Family Therapy (2015). Revised American Association for Marriage and Family Therapy code of ethics. Available online at www.aamft.org/iMIS15/AAMFT/Content/Legal_Ethics/Code_of_Ethics.aspx.

American Association for Marriage and Family Therapy (2016). *Best Practices in the Online Practice of Couple and Family Therapy*. Washington, DC: AAMFT.

American Counseling Association (2014). Code of Ethics. Available online at www. counseling.org/resources/aca-code-of-ethics.pdf.

American Telemedicine Association Practice Guidelines for Video-based Online Mental Health Services (2013). Available online at www.americantelemed.org/docs/default-source/standards/practice-guidelines-for-video-based-online-mental-health-services.pdf?sfvrsn=6.

American Telemedicine Association Practice Guidelines for Videoconferencing-Based Telemental Health. (2009). Available online at www.americantelemed.org/docs/default-source/standards/practice-guidelines-for-videoconferencing-based-telemental-health.pdf?sfvrsn=6.

Bacigalupe, G. (2011). Is there a role for social technologies in collaborative healthcare? *Families, Systems & Health, 29*(1): 1.

Baker-Ericzén, M.J., Jenkins, M.M., & Haine-Schlagel, R. (2013). Therapist, parent, and youth perspectives of treatment barriers to family-focused community outpatient mental health services. *Journal of Child and Family Studies, 22*(6): 854–868, doi:10.1007/s10826-012-9644-7.

Barrett, M.S., Chua, W., Crits-Christoph, P., Gibbons, M.B., & Thompson, D. (2008). Early withdrawal from mental health treatment: Implications for psychotherapy practice. *Psychotherapy: Theory, Research, Practice, Training, 45*(2): 247–267, doi:10.1037/0033-3204.45.2.247.

Blumer, M., Hertlein, K.M., & VanderBosch, M. (2015). Towards the development of educational core competencies for couple and family therapy technology practices. *Contemporary Family Therapy*, *37*: 113–121.

Caldwell, B.E., Bischoff, R.J., Derrig-Palumbo, K.A., & Liebert, J.D. (2017). Best practices in the online practice of couple and family therapy. Report of the Online Therapy Workgroup presented to the Board of AAMFT. February 17.

Choi, N.G., Marti, C.N., Bruce, M.L., Hegel, M.T., Wilson, N.L., & Kunik, M.E. (2014). Six-month post-intervention depression and disability outcomes of in-home telehealth problem-solving therapy for depressed, low-income homebound older adults. *Depression and Anxiety*, *31*(8): 653–661, doi:10.1002/da.22242.

Chou, T., Bry, L., & Comer, J. (2017). Overcoming traditional barriers only to encounter new ones: Doses of caution and direction as technology-enhanced treatments begin to "go live". *Clinical Psychology-Science and Practice*, *24*(3): 241–244, doi:10.1111/cpsp.12196.

Cosio, D., Jin, L., Siddique, J., & Mohr, D.C. (2011). The effect of telephone-administered Cognitive–Behavioral therapy on quality of life among patients with multiple sclerosis. *Annals of Behavioral Medicine*, *41*(2): 227–234, doi:10.1007/s12160-010-9236-y.

Crowe, T.V. (2017). Is telemental health services a viable alternative to traditional psychotherapy for deaf individuals? *Community Mental Health Journal*, *53*(2): 154–162, doi:10.1007/s10597-016-0025-3.

Duggan, M. (2015, December) "Gaming and Gamers." Pew Research Center. Available online at http://assets.pewresearch.org/wp-content/uploads/sites/14/2015/12/PI_2015-12-15_gaming-and-gamers_FINAL.pdf.

Duncan, S., Phillips, M., Carter, J., Roseneil, S., & Stoilova, M. (2014). Practices and perceptions of living apart together, *Family Science*, *5*(1): 1–10, doi:10.1080/19424620.2014.927382.

Flaum, M. (2013). Telemental health as a solution to the widening gap between supply and demand for mental health services. In K. Myers & C.L. Turvey (Eds), *Telemental Health: Clinical, Technical, and Administrative Foundations for Evidence-based Practice* (pp. 11–25). New York: Elsevier.

Friars, P.M., & Mellor, D.J. (2007). Drop out from behavioral management training programs for ADHD: A Prospective Study. *Journal of Child and Family Studies*, *16*: 427–441, doi:10.1007/s10826-006-9096-z.

Frueh, B.C. (2015). Solving mental healthcare access problems in the twenty-first century: Mental healthcare access. *Australian Psychologist*, *50*(4): 304–306, doi:10.1111/ap.12140.

Gibson, K.L., Coulson, H., Miles, R., Kakekakekung, C., Daniels, E., & O'Donnell, S. (2011). Conversations on telemental health: Listening to remote and rural first nations communities. *Rural and Remote Health*, *11*(2): 1656.

Glueck, D. (2013a). Business aspects of telemental health in private practice. In K.M.L. Turvey (ed.), *Telemental Health: Clinical, Technical and Administrative Foundations for Evidence-Based Practice* (pp. 111–133). Oxford: Elsevier.

Glueck, D. (2013b). Establishing therapeutic rapport in telemental health. In K. Myers., & C. L. Turvey (eds). *Telemental Health: Clinical, Technical and Administrative Foundations for Evidence-Based Practice*. London, UK: Elsevier.

Grubaugh, A.L., Cain, G.D., Elhai, J.D., Patrick, S.L., & Frueh, B.C. (2008). Attitudes toward medical and mental health care delivered via telehealth applications among rural and urban primary care patients. *The Journal of Nervous and Mental Disease, 196*(2): 166–170, doi:10.1097/NMD.0b013e318162aa2d.

Halcomb, E., Stephens, M., Bryce, J., Foley, E., & Ashley, C. (2016). Nursing competency standards in primary health care: An integrative review. *Journal of Clinical Nursing, 25*(9–10), 1193–1205, doi:10.1111/jocn.13224.

Harwood, T.M., & L'Abate, L., 1928, & SpringerLink (Online service). (2010). *Self-Help in Mental Health: A Critical Review.* New York: Springer.

Hennigan, J., & Goss, S.P. (2016). UK secondary school therapists' online communication with their clients and future intentions. *Counselling and Psychotherapy Research, 16*(3): 149–160, doi:10.1002/capr.12082.

Hertlein, K.M. (2012). Digital dwelling: Technology in couple and family relationships. *Family Relations, 61*(3): 374–387, doi:10.1111/j.1741-3729.2012.00702.x.

Hertlein, K.M., & Blumer, M.L.C. (2013). *The Couple and Family Technology Framework: Intimate Relationships in a Digital Age.* New York: Routledge.

Hertlein, K.M., Blumer, M., & Mihaloliakos, J. (2015). Marriage and family therapists' perceptions of the ethical considerations of online therapy. *The Family Journal, 23*(1): 5–12.

Hertlein, K.M., Blumer, M.L., & Smith, J.M. (2014). Marriage and family therapists' use and comfort with online communication with clients. *Contemporary Family Therapy, 36*: 58–69.

Hilty, D., Maheu, M., Drude, M., Hertlein, K., Wall, P., Long, K., & Luoma, K. (2017). Telebehavioral Health, Telemental Health, e-Therapy and e-Health Competencies: The Need for an Interprofessional Framework. *Journal of Technology in Behavioral Science*, 2: 171–189.

Hilty, D., Crawford, A., Teshima, J., Chan, S., Sunderji, N., Yellowlees, P., Kramer, G., O'Neill, P., Fore, C., Luo, J., & Li, S. (2015). A framework for telepsychiatric training and ehealth: competency-based education, evaluation and implications. *International Review of Psychiatry, 27*: 569–592.

Internet Stats (2016). U.S. Usage Stats. Available online at www.internetlivestats.com/internet-users/us/.

Jenkins-Guarnieri, M.A., Pruitt, L.D., Luxton, D.D., & Johnson, K. (2015). Patient perceptions of telemental health: Systematic review of direct comparisons to in-person psychotherapeutic treatments. *Telemedicine and e-Health, 21*(8): 652–660.

Jones, A.M., Shealy, K.M., Reid-Quinones, K., Moreland, A.D., Davidson, T.M., Lopez, C.M., et al. (2014). Guidelines for establishing a telemental health program to provide evidence-based therapy for trauma-exposed children and families. *Psychological Services, 11*(4): 398–409.

Kasckow, J., Zickmund, S., Rotondi, A., Mrkva, A., Gurklis, J., Chinman, M., … Haas, G. (2014). Development of telehealth dialogues for monitoring suicidal patients with schizophrenia: Consumer feedback. *Community Mental Health Journal, 50*(3): 339–342, doi:10.1007/s10597-012-9589-8.

Kaslow, N.J. (2004). Competencies in professional psychology. *American Psychologist, 59*(8): 774–781, doi:10.1037/0003-066X.59.8.774.

Kim, H., Munson, M.R., & McKay, M.M. (2012). Engagement in mental health treatment among adolescents and young adults: A systematic review. *Child and Adolescent Social Work Journal, 29*(3): 241–266, doi:10.1007/s10560-012-0256-2.

King, V.L., Brooner, R.K., Peirce, J.M., Kolodner, K., & Kidorf, M.S. (2014). A randomized trial of Web-based videoconferencing for substance abuse counseling. *Journal of Substance Abuse Treatment, 46*(1): 36–42, doi:10.1016/j.jsat.2013.08.009.

Knaevelsrud, C., & Maercker, A. (2006). Does the quality of the working alliance predict treatment outcome in online psychotherapy for traumatized patients? *Journal of Medical Internet Research, 8*(4): 31, doi:10.2196/jmir.8.4.e31.

Leininger, M.M. (1985). *Qualitative Research Methods in Nursing.* Grune & Stratton.

Luxton, D.D., Nelson, E., & Maheu, M.M. (2016). *A Practitioner's Guide to Telemental Health: How to Conduct Legal, Ethical, and Evidence-based Telepractice,* 1st edition. American Psychological Association.

Luxton, D., Pruitt, L., O'Brien, K., Stanfill, K., Jenkins-Guarnieri, M., Johnson, K., … Gahm, G. (2014). Design and methodology of a randomized clinical trial of home-based telemental health treatment for US military personnel and veterans with depression. *Contemporary Clinical Trials, 38*(1): 134–144, doi:10.1016/j.cct.2014.04.002.

Maheu, M., Drude, K., Hertlein, K.M., Lipschutz, R., Wall, K., & Hilty, D. (in press). Telemental health, telebehavioral health, e-therapy, and e-health competencies: The need for an interdisciplinary framework. *Journal of Technology and Behavioral Sciences.*

Modai, I., Jabarin, M., Kurs, R., Barak, P., Hanan, I., & Kitain, L. (2006). Cost effectiveness, safety, and satisfaction with video telepsychiatry versus face-to-face care in ambulatory settings. *Telemedicine and e-Health, 12*: 515–520.

Mohr, D.C., Siddique, J., Ho, J., Duffecy, J., Jin, L., & Fokuo, J.K. (2010). Interest in behavioral and psychological treatments delivered face-to-face, by telephone, and by internet. *Annals of Behavioral Medicine, 40*(1): 89–98, doi:10.1007/s12160-010-9203-7.

Mohr, D.C., Vella, L., Hart, S., Heckman, T., & Simon, G. (2008). The effect of telephone-administered psychotherapy on symptoms of depression and attrition: A meta-analysis. *Clinical Psychology: Science and Practice, 15*(3): 243–253, doi:10.1111/j.1468-2850.2008.00134.x.

Morgan, R.D., Patrick, A.R., & Magaletta, P.R. (2008). Does the use of telemental health alter the treatment experience? Inmates' perceptions of telemental health versus face-to-face treatment modalities. *Journal of Consulting and Clinical Psychology, 76*(1): 158–162, doi:10.1037/0022-006X.76.1.158.

Morland, L.A., & Kloezeman, K. (2013). Rural Veterans and telemental health service delivery. In K. Myers & C. Turvey (Eds), *Telemental Health: A Comprehensive Text for Clinical Practice and Research* (pp. 223–249). Maryland Heights, MO: Elsevier.

Myers, K., & Vander Stoep, A. (2017). i-Therapy: Asynchronous telehealth expands access to mental health care and challenges tenets of the therapeutic process. *Journal of the American Academy of Child & Adolescent Psychiatry, 56*: 5–7.

Myers, K.M., & Turvey, C.L. (2013). *Telemental Health: Clinical, Technical, and Administrative Foundations for Evidence-based Practice,* 1st edition. New York: Elsevier.

Nelson, T.S., Chenail, R.J., Alexander, J.F., Crane, D.R., Johnson, S.M., & Schwallie, L. (2007). The development of core competencies for the practice of marriage and family therapy. *Journal of Marital and Family Therapy, 33*(4): 417–438, doi:10.1111/j.1752-0606.2007.00042.x.

O'Reilly, R., Hutchinson, L., Takhar, J., Fisman, M., Bishop, J., & Maddox, K. (2007). Is telepsychiatry equivalent to face-to-face psychiatry? Results from a randomized controlled equivalence trial. *Psychiatric Services, 58*(6): 836–843, doi:10.1176/ps.2007.58.6.836.

Oruche, U.M., Downs, S., Holloway, E., Draucker, C., & Aalsma, M. (2014). Barriers and facilitators to treatment participation by adolescents in a community mental health clinic. *Journal of Psychiatric and Mental Health Nursing, 21*(3): 241–248, doi:10.1111/jpm.12076.

Osenbach, J.E., O'Brien, K.M., Mishkind, M., & Smolenski, D.J. (2013). Synchronous telehealth technologies in psychotherapy for depression: A meta-analysis. *Depression and Anxiety, 30*(11): 1058–1067, doi:10.1002/da.22165.

Pellerin, K.A., Costa, N.M., Weems, C., & Dalton, R. (2010). An examination of treatment completers and non-completers at a child and adolescent community mental health clinic. *Community Mental Health Journal, 46*: 273–281, doi:10.1007/s10597-009-9285-5.

Poulin, J., & Matis, S. (2015). Social work competencies and multidimensional assessment. *The Journal of Baccalaureate Social Work, 20*(1): 117–135, doi:10.18084/1084-7219.20.1.117.

Rees, C.S., & Maclaine, E. (2015). A systematic review of Videoconference-Delivered psychological treatment for anxiety disorders. *Australian Psychologist, 50*(4): 259–264, doi:10.1111/ap.12122.

Rees, C.S., & Stone, S. (2005). Therapeutic alliance in face-to-face versus videoconferencing psychotherapy. *Professional Psychology: Research and Practice, 36*: 649–653, doi:10.1037/0735-7028.36.6.649.

Richardson, L., Reid, C., & Dziurawiec, S. (2015). "Going the extra mile": Satisfaction and alliance findings from an evaluation of videoconferencing telepsychology in rural Western Australia. *Australian Psychologist, 50*(4): 252–258, doi:10.1111/ap.12126.

Rochlen, A.B., Zack, J.S., & Speyer, C. (2004). Online therapy: Review of relevant definitions, debates, and current empirical support. *Journal of Clinical Psychology, 60*: 269–283.

Rose, L.E., Mallinson, R.K., & Walton-Moss, B. (2004). Barriers to family care in psychiatric settings. *Journal of Nursing Scholarship, 36*(1): 39–47, doi:10.1111/j.1547-5069.2004.04009.x.

Simms, D.C., Gibson, K., & O'Donnell, S. (2011). To use or not to use: Clinicians' perceptions of telemental health. *Canadian Psychology, 52*(1): 41–51.

Staudt, M. (2007). Treatment engagement with caregivers of at-risk children: Gaps in research and conceptualization. *Journal of Child and Family Studies, 16*(2): 183–196, doi:10.1007/s10826-006-9077-2.

Staudt, M.M. (2003). Helping children access and use services: A review. *Journal of Child and Family Studies, 12*: 49–60, doi:10.1023/A:1021306125491.

Suler, J. (2002). The online disinhibition effect. In *The Psychology of Cyberspace*. Available online at http://truecenterpublishing.com/psycyber/disinhibit.html.

Thompson, S.J., Bender, K., Windsor, L.C., & Flynn, P.M. (2009). Keeping families engaged: The effects of home-based family therapy enhanced with experiential activities. *Social Work Research, 33*: 121–126.

Treas, J., & Gubernskaya, Z. (2018). Did mobile phones increase adult children's maternal contact? In J. Van Hook, S. McHale, & V. King (eds), *Families and Technology* (pp. 139–151). New York: Springer.

Wagner, G., Penelo, E., Nobis, G., Mayrhofer, A., Wanner, C., Schau, J., ... Karwautz, A. (2015). Predictors for good therapeutic outcome and Drop-out in technology assisted guided Self-Help in the treatment of bulimia nervosa and bulimia like phenotype. *European Eating Disorders Review, 23*(2): 163–169, doi:10.1002/erv.2336.

Wang, P.S., Lane, M., Olfson, M., Pincus, H.A., Wells, K.B., & Kessler, R.C. (2005). Twelve-month use of mental health services in the United States: Results from the National Comorbidity Survey Replication. *Arch Gen Psychiatry, 62*(6): 629–640.

Yuen, E.K., Herbert, J.D., Forman, E.M., Goetter, E.M., Juarascio, A.S., Rabin, S., ... Bouchard, S. (2013). Acceptance based behavior therapy for social anxiety disorder through videoconferencing. *Journal of Anxiety Disorders, 27*(4): 389–397, doi:10.1016/j.janxdis.2013.03.002.

11 Digital Dialectics

Navigating Technology's Paradoxes in Online Treatment

Leora Trub and Danielle Magaldi

Introduction

The possibility of conducting therapy over a screen brings about an essential dilemma for clinicians. On the one hand, for many, clinical intuition indicates that being bodies in a room together is a therapeutic imperative for optimal treatment (e.g. Rees & Stone, 2005; Simpson & Reid, 2014). At the same time, many clinicians engage in computer-mediated treatment with positive results. Meanwhile, research continues to underscore the way that screens and ever-present digital technology can fuel disconnection and prevent intimacy (e.g. Hanlon, 2001; Przybylski & Weinstein, 2012; Turkle, 2011; 2015). Could the therapeutic dyad possibly be the sole exception to these adverse effects? Faced with these potential inconsistencies that complicate engaging in technology-mediated psychotherapy, therapists may find themselves clamoring for resolution when in fact there is something important about the dilemma itself. Indeed, finding a way to hold the different, often opposing elements of our connection to technology is necessary for creating a therapeutic experience where our patients can understand the impact of technology on their lives while also work to shape their relationship with it in a way that best serves their needs.

Functional Equivalence and Other Attempts at Resolution

One attempt at resolution is to refuse to engage with the technology at all. This position may be increasingly difficult to maintain, and moreover may prevent therapists from understanding the centrality of technology in the lives of patients, including its positive influences (Essig, 2012). Another attempt at resolution is to adopt the notion of functional equivalence, which argues that there is no difference between in-person and computer-mediated treatment. Aside from the potential dangers of maintaining the illusion of equality (Essig, 2015; Isaacs-Russell, 2015), to hold a position which negates potential differences between these two modalities runs counter to core therapeutic values, in which the therapist is open to whatever unfolds in the therapy, takes note of how a patient is experiencing all elements of therapy, and is able to recognize the limiting factors in a given modality.

This assumption may be promoted by a body of research suggesting that it is possible to develop an equally strong therapeutic alliance via a screen as in-person (Day, 1999; Glueckauf et al., 2002; Schneider, 2001). Some people even prefer treatment in this mode, allowing themselves to be more open and disclosing at a distance, or using the distance to take greater accountability and responsibility for their own treatment (Day & Schneider, 2000; Simpson & Reid, 2014). Some find it less intrusive (Simpson, 2001). This brings to light a potential conflict between meeting patients where they are at versus encouraging them to move out of their comfort zone and develop a trusting in-person relationship that may be challenging initially but may ultimately be deeply therapeutic. As Simpson (2009) notes, "a patient who fears intimacy may prefer video therapy, but may in fact benefit more from exposure to the physical closeness of face-to-face treatment" (p. 274).

Much research has emphasized the importance of matching patients to the therapeutic modality (computer-mediated versus in-person) better suited to his/her needs (Simpson, 2009; Simpson & Reid, 2014). For example, it has been noted that individuals with a history of sexual abuse who exhibit more disorganized interpersonal behaviors may require more stability and support than can be felt in computer-mediated treatment (Richardson, 2011). In short-term CBT treatments, computer mediated sessions have been promising for enhancing therapeutic engagement both in and between sessions, preventing attrition (Clough & Casey, 2015; Day & Schneider, 2002). Theoretical orientation plays into how clinicians view the computer – Zilberstein (2013) notes that cognitive behavioral therapists tend to focus on it as a tool for treatment, while psychoanalytic clinicians focus on how it might influence underlying conflicts, desires and relationships. While consistent with the general divides in theoretical orientation, she warns that this split fails to recognize the need for all contemporary clinicians to attend to both dimensions. This becomes even more important when we consider using the screen for clinical work with multiple people in family, couples, or group therapy. Thus, the current chapter considers questions about computer-mediated treatment through four essential dilemmas brought upon by the introduction of screens into contemporary living.

The Digital Third

The computer screen changes the dimensions of therapy for all dyads, regardless of theoretical orientation. We lose the opportunity to be bodies together in the same space. The therapist's body is not only a material reality but also holds symbolic meaning as a container for the supportive therapeutic holding environment (Burka, 1996). The presence of the therapist's physical body is a "carrier of meanings" (Ogden, 1994), considered so powerful it is thought to symbolize the maternal womb (Ferenczi, 1950). As Burka (1996) writes, "the physical reality of the therapist's body is measured in pounds and inches, but the psychical reality of the therapist's body cannot be seen, measured, or separated out from the physical and psychological context of a particular patient/therapist pair" (264). Patient and therapist are continuously responding to each other's bodies in both conscious and unconscious ways, sharing vital information that can only be accessed through their bodies together. The insight gained from bodies in the room together contributes inestimably to the work of therapy. This attention to physicality in therapy may not only enable discovery of what it is like for a patient to inhabit his or her particular body, but it may also explore how trauma can be stored in the body (Van der Kolk, 2015).

When a two-dimensional representation replaces the bodies of therapist and patient, we lose the subtlety of glances, smells, movements, all of which facilitate the emergence of an intersubjective dimension – what Ogden (1994) calls "the analytic third." On the screen, analyst and patient retain their individual subjectivity, but the ongoing co-created intersubjectivity is significantly altered when images replace physical bodies. In a screen-mediated session, vigilance to the technical call quality challenges the therapist's capacity to allow silence and attend to more symbolic manifestations of connection (Isaacs-Russell, 2015). The loss of silence may also cost the therapist access to reverie and fantasy – processes which enable the development of the analytic third (Isaacs-Russell, 2015). As stated by an analyst in an earlier study, "I can't hold on to the intersubjective space at all over Skype which I really find uncomfortable" (Trub & Magaldi, 2017). With the analytic third more difficult to access in computer-mediated sessions, the intersubjective space instead becomes dominated by another 'third' entity – technology. We call this the digital third.

In screen-mediated sessions, there are powerful forces at work as the digital third acts in and on the therapeutic relationship, with the potential to provoke intense transferential and countertransferential feelings (Bagnini, 2015). These feelings often go unexplored (Isaacs-Russell, 2015; Trub & Magaldi, 2017). But technology comes to hold its own intersubjective meanings – it may become an emotional barrier, a safety net, a window into the patient's world, a magic vehicle with the power to transcend time and space, and so on. But, instead of exploring these meanings to deepen treatment, psychoanalytic clinicians may unconsciously steer conversation away from feelings that they worry might be painful for the patient if the technological connection does not hold. They can then overcompensate for the emotionally flattened quality of the therapeutic interaction by hyper-focusing on the patient's words (Isaac-Russell, 2015). This privileges content over process and intersubjective meaning, which gets in the way of clinical intuition.

Regardless of theoretical orientation, therapists may worry about their ability to 'hold' (Winnicott, 1953) a patient through a screen. If the effects of the digital third go unexplored, dyads are more vulnerable to skimming the top layer of therapeutic material, leaving deeper, more difficult content and feelings untouched or avoided. Therapy then persists on a more superficial level of therapeutic engagement, where patient and therapist assess that the therapy is progressing well precisely because the therapy is not venturing into more precarious places that would require acknowledgement of the presence, risks, and impact of the digital third. Patients may sense their therapist's hesitation to either go deeper or to acknowledge the possible limitations of the medium. Similarly, they may sense the therapist's wish to protect them from these risks, or they may feel the need to protect themselves, creating the potential for collusion where therapy sidesteps fragile or regressive states (Isaacs-Russell, 2015). When a therapist instead recognizes or acknowledges the presence of the digital third in screen-mediated therapy, there is the potential to explore the joint unconscious creation of meaning between therapist and patient that arises from the use of the screen.

Four Dilemmas Impacting Treatment through the Screen

The decision to introduce screens into therapeutic spaces is about more than just introducing a new medium for conducting treatment. With the technological devices themselves come new and evolving norms, rules, and complexities about how individuals relate to one another. Moreover, much of technology's impact is paradoxical in nature, engendering simultaneous feelings of connection and disconnection; empowerment and enslavement; independence and dependence (Jarvenpaa & Lang, 2005; Turkle, 2011; Weinberg, 2014). These paradoxical effects are further complicated when bringing the phone or computer into therapy, which has its own rules of engagement. An intimate encounter between therapist and client(s), therapy is intended to be a space for thoughtful reflection, for pursuing insight, for not acting on impulse. When therapy happens over a screen, the societal shifts brought upon by the introduction of screens into our relationships come into the therapeutic encounter. In the following section, we introduce the clinical case of Nettie, an in-person treatment that included several family screen sessions, to illustrate four dilemmas that emerge when technology and psychotherapy are brought together in family therapy.

Case vignette (with identifying information modified for patient privacy)

Nettie entered treatment to address anxiety and panic attacks. Upon beginning to explore her anxiety, we came to understand that her marriage of 15 years was significantly abusive and that her fear and reluctance to recognize this was contributing to her feelings of intense anxiety and sadness. Both therapy and marital separation were considered shameful within her Filipino Catholic community, and her options felt limited. Yet the debilitating and intractable nature of Nettie's anxiety rendered her "sick" enough to override these deeply felt cultural mores and allowed her to access therapeutic services. It was important that I be the doctor, not just a therapist, to legitimize her participation in therapy for her family. As doctor and patient, we worked together to help her build a support network, including a domestic violence group. She began to find a voice for herself and her children's safety by setting limits with her husband and outlining what things she would and would not tolerate in their relationship. He could get angry but could not threaten to "bash their skulls together" when her two teenage sons were arguing. As her confidence and resolve grew, she experienced greater clarity in her desire to separate from her husband, but was afraid of her family's disapproval. At her suggestion, we had a series of online sessions that included her two older brothers, one who lived in the Philippines and the other who lived in China. Through the screen, Nettie disclosed what was happening in her marriage, describing the mistreatment she experienced and her desire to separate. We worked to reframe for her brothers that although they worried she would be financially insecure and destroy her life if she separated, Nettie instead was working to build a better, more secure, life for herself. Her brothers respected my expertise and accepted my assessment that Nettie was not acting rashly but was instead considered and thoughtful in her actions. After several sessions, her brothers reluctantly offered their acceptance, allowing her to proceed with a very difficult separation.

Dilemma 1: Adopting new communication norms. *As therapists, how do we respond to and/or integrate new norms that society has adopted around availability via technology?*

Adjusting to the new communication norm where dispersed families use technology to stay connected, Nettie and I included screens into her treatment. Initially, the screen seemed like a creative solution that increased her access to resources – both internally and externally – as she acknowledged and expressed her needs and, ultimately, garnered her family's support. Later, however, when Nettie requested to include her priest in a computer-mediated session, I wondered whether the accessibility of the screen offered too easy a solution for me to join her in facing complicated relationships, even when it ultimately might have been more therapeutic for her to face them on her own. The screen both enabled and veiled a therapeutic enactment where, like her husband, I took on the role of a powerful person speaking on her behalf. Thus, while offering a solution and giving her support, the technology allowed for the reinforcement of a problematic pattern in families rather than a disruption of it. Her need for approval along with a culture of control and domination by a powerful other, was something she wanted to speak to and work against, and yet the sessions with her brothers leveraged my expertise as a doctor instead of her feelings and thoughts, to gain her brothers' approval. For Nettie, being able to bring her brothers into our sessions by screen may have ultimately drowned out her voice – a voice she was simultaneously working so hard to develop. An essential element of family work is helping each member find their voice, recognizing the relational dynamics that make understanding each other difficult. In this case, the screen may have obscured that.

We have important decisions to make in whether and how we adopt new norms of communicating in therapy. Immediate, instant communication is now a fact of life. Yet, technology and therapy offer two very different kinds of immediacy that must not be conflated – one, the possibility and expectation of immediate contact; the other, therapeutic immediacy, is the here and now expression of feelings. As our values and expectations regarding communication change, people may trade the discovery and intimacy of therapeutic immediacy for the gratification of instantaneous contact via text messaging, Snapchat, or Skype. Family therapy by screen may have inadvertently made this trade – privileging the solving of a problem over noticing and expressing the feelings arising from bringing the family together in therapy.

Technology's effects on how we communicate is perplexing for therapy and raises questions around therapeutic expediency: technology may increase the pace of interactions, improving efficiency, while also feeding a craving for instant gratification when patience or delayed gratification may be called for. Technology may appeal to our wish for a cure-all, the proverbial magic wand of therapy, when the challenges of family relationships, psychological distress, and life changes are rarely cured, but are at best managed and explored. Increased options and accessibility generated by technology may prevent recognition and exploration of the meanings carried in our wish to solve family problems before understanding them.

Technology impinges on some foundational aspects of psychotherapy – boundaries, privacy, solitude, intimacy, and connection, just to name a few. Many therapists' increased availability to patients through technology changes the frame of the therapeutic encounter. With these new norms we may forget to consider the benefits of allowing standard therapeutic boundaries to remain – "With the possibility of video-conferencing, we may slide into thinking we didn't use it because we didn't have it, rather than considering whether not having it might be better" (Trub & Magaldi, 2017).

On the other hand, it is hard to refute the benefits of providing individual therapy to a homebound patient via the computer, or of family therapy with a patient during a crisis when family members are located around the world. Technology offers increased options for communicating, which can undoubtedly solve certain problems within family therapy. However, deciding which patients are granted increased access and which are denied, and under what circumstances, requires mindfulness that technology works against. Therapists describe feeling pressured by their patients' expectation that they can easily and quickly be reached by text or email (Trub & Magaldi, 2017). Meanwhile, even if we are thoughtful and particular about when and how we use technology to increase communication, doing so sends an implicit message that we are readily accessible and available. Texting during an emergency reminds the patient that we are only a text message away. Our wish to be the ever-present, bountiful mother, our Pavlovian response to a text chime, and our internalization of the new norm in which relationships include constant and immediate contact may muddle the observing aspect of our participant-observer role in family therapy (Hirsch & Aron, 1991). Responding to these new norms by incorporating technology into family therapy may be beneficial in humanizing the therapist, increasing access to a generation of patients for whom "in-person only" might seem old-fashioned and outdated, and signaling to patients that the therapist communicates in ways that patients do. It is enticing to be experienced as a therapist who "gets it."

At the same time, the decision to hold in-the-office in-person communication sacred may have distinct benefits. The cohort of patients growing up with screens as an ineluctable part of everyday life have a more elaborate and persistent web of social interactions than any that have come before them. Yet they feel more lonely, sad, and anxious than any prior generation (Twenge, 2017). Screens are a way family members hide from each other. Thus, we may be in a position to model communicating and building trust within an intimate relationship, that is becoming harder and harder to come by in other parts of life. While we may fear obsolescence if we resist new tech norms, in-person family therapy may be one of the remaining bastions of close, intimate, in-person encounters that allow for insight and change. Technology seems to possess endless promise. But the simplicity of the therapeutic encounter also holds invaluable possibilities.

> Dilemma 2: Silence. *Given the importance of the non-verbal domain in clinical work, what clinical challenges do we face when we communicate in a medium that privileges the verbal over the non-verbal, talking over silence?*

Silence holds deep and varied meaning in therapy: it can make space for cognitive processing, emotional attunement, or the expression of rage (Levitt, 2001); it may be an act of resistance (Reik, 1926); or by experiencing a silence that one has control over, a patient may use silence to mitigate fears of death or abandonment (Kaftal, 1980). Silence can be regressive, allowing a patient to experience an earlier or even pre-verbal phase in the therapist's presence. It can be generative, meeting a patient's needs in a particular moment (Balint, 1958; Levitt, 2001). Silence can be a space for words that cannot be spoken in families; this absence of language may express a feeling or message that cannot be expressed verbally (Sabbadini, 1991). It can enable understanding and closeness between patient and therapist (Sharpley et al., 2005).

> In Nettie's family therapy, the significant issues of connectivity, with lags and lapses that forced pauses and froze the screen at times, made silences difficult and were a harbinger of disconnectivity in already tenuous family relationships. In-person, silence was effective in offering Nettie time to think and respond. She processed her feelings slowly and then needed time to access strategies we had discussed and rehearsed to express herself. Over the screen this was more difficult, and I stepped in at times to confirm her feelings rather than allowing for silences to unfold. These moments may have unwittingly reinforced her belief that others need to decide which of her feelings are valid and worthy of acknowledgment reinforcing an unhelpful family dynamic.

Technology challenges silence. Outside of therapy, the myriad conveniences, benefits, and constant distraction offered by technology has rendered true silence a rarity, making the need for silence in therapy an even greater imperative. Our phones are now the most common way people coordinate everyday plans and activities, with therapists even relying on phones for patient scheduling. In a world of "always-on", "tethered selves" (Turkle, 2006), uninterrupted solitude is far more difficult to attain. Historically, silence in (in-person) treatment has been described with words like pregnant, heavy, reflective, or expressive (Levitt, 2001). Silences over a screen may feel quite different. When they do occur, therapists may feel more anxious than during an in-person silence because they must remain alert to the possible interruption of the digital connection. (Isaacs-Russell, 2015; Trub & Magaldi, 2017). A long pause may be quickly followed by the questions "are you still there?" or "did I lose you?". Understandably, silences over the screen may provoke a family member's deeper fear of abandonment or rejection as the therapist and family struggle to understand what is happening on a concrete as well as a symbolic level. In order for secure, reflective therapeutic engagement to be maintained in family sessions by screen, silence must be understood differently with therapists aware of what changes over the screen, what vulnerabilities may be experienced by family members within silences, and what risks are involved.

Dilemma 3: Intimacy. *What are the clinical implications of utilizing the very technology that challenges the potential for intimacy as a vehicle for increasing intimacy and authenticity?*

Digital connection is elusive – constant and instantaneous, yet somehow unsatisfying. Psychoanalyst and technology researcher Sherry Turkle has long argued that technology is the perfect antidote for someone desiring closeness while fearing intimacy, as it mediates every relational experience. "Technology is seductive when what it offers meets our human vulnerabilities. And as it turns out, we are very vulnerable indeed. We are lonely but fearful of intimacy" (Turkle, 2011: 1). This way of being in the world – connected but alone – may be becoming a norm. Based on hundreds of interviews with kids and adults about technology, Turkle (2011) notes, "As we distribute ourselves, we may abandon ourselves. Sometimes people experience no sense of having communicated after hours of connection. And they report feelings of closeness when they are paying little attention" (12). This is similar to Weinberg's (2014) conception of e-intimacy, which is often what people receive when they look for intimacy; in the absence of anything else, it becomes possible to confuse the two.

Our devices tend to hold a certain power over us, which makes it difficult to recognize when continuing to use it is no longer serving our needs. Phones tend to generate expectations of frequent contact in family relationships. While this can increase satisfaction, it also leads to over-dependence and feelings of entrapment, guilt and pressure, playing out pre-exisiting family dynamics through technology (Hall & Baym, 2012). Other have noted similarly paradoxical experiences, which can make it difficult for people to exert the optimal level of control over their use of devices (Jarvenpaa & Lang, 2005; Trub & Barbot, 2016). Indeed, the device itself can sometimes trigger the need for contact, rather than the other way around (Turkle, 2011). Ribak (2009) likened the phone to an umbilical cord based on finding that the phone's potential for connection is more meaningful than the actual conversations taking place between adult children and their parents. Technology begets an increasingly common tendency to exist in a state of "continuous partial attention" (Stone, 2014), where the act of staying only partially attentive allows us to avoid the disappointment of not being attended to fully.

What is less clear is how these experiences then play into the experience of using the very same device to communicate in family therapy. Part of what is sacred about face-to-face family sessions is knowing that a conversation will ensue, free from interruption for a set time. Aside from emergencies, it is the norm to turn phones off; we cannot be contacted. This is not true when in a computer-mediated session, as family members sit – in front of the same screen that they may use to distract or rescue themselves from family contact – and receive social media, text, or email notifications delivering news while in family sessions. Even if therapists do what is necessary to prevent the possibility of distraction, our patients may not, and thus face the potential to be contacted, taken out of the clinical moment while inadvertently orchestrating powerful family dynamics that might be ignored as technology's typical interruptions.

Such potential for distraction carries relational implications. In a study examining people's feelings about another person with whom they just had a conversation, the mere presence of a cell phone on the table negatively impacted feelings of trust and closeness towards the other individual, and reduced the extent to which individuals felt empathized with and understood (Przybylski & Weinstein, 2012). Family therapy is not immune to such negative consequences associated with the mere presence of a device in the midst of a vulnerable or meaningful conversation. Research also suggests these processes are automatic and unconscious, activating our relational schema which lie outside of our awareness (Lyons-Ruth, 1999). Thus, there may be no way to fully reverse these processes. While the presence of a mobile phone on the table is different than the use of a screen to communicate, these situations have in common the potential for being connected to individuals outside of the current conversation and with it the potential for interruption. How then, do we resolve these findings with those described earlier suggesting that the therapeutic alliance is unaffected by moving therapy to a screen?

Today, when working with families to address their difficulties around intimacy, it is crucial to attend to the medium through which our patients are conversing with family members. Our patients may describe an important "conversation they had" but fail to mention it was over text – either due to fear of judgment or because it's so normal they don't think to mention it. Similarly, we may find ourselves urging our patients to start talking right where there left off before the connection went fuzzy, to try and smooth over moments of disconnection by pushing them away and ignoring their greater impact. Feeling uncomfortable that we "dropped" a Skype call, we may ignore the moments where the therapy was untethered and the feelings that ensued for each family member. Embodying 'technological mode' during family therapy might impact communication and internal processes such that we would need to override the impulse to rationalize or ignore, making a conscious effort to talk about it and to facilitate family members discussions with each other.

> Dilemma 4: Inviting in the Digital Self. *Insofar as technology plays a role in shaping identity, how important is it to invite technologically-mediated parts of self into clinical interactions?*

How does technology shape identity? What is the 'digital self,' and what is its connection to the non-digital (analog) self? What does it mean for some members of a family to have developed digital selves while other members do not? While a full exploration of the complex interweaving of technology and self is far beyond the scope of this chapter, maintaining awareness of these questions will help prevent us from underestimating the influence of digital culture on families and unwittingly forcing our patients to check their "digital selves" at the door. As digital technology offers another arena for identity exploration and presentation, we must attend to how members of a family are using social media to express parts of themselves which may be absent in in-person interactions. This information can be useful in two main ways – first, it allows the therapist to see parts of the members of a family that might otherwise go unseen, offering the therapist a more complete picture; secondly, families can gain awareness based on constructed self-image in the digital domain to inform changes and adaptations for themselves in the world.

Therapists tend to privilege in-person interaction and may not appreciate the possibility that the Internet may be used an arena for self-exploration. Our own research has suggested that there are several reasons why therapists shy away from talking to their patients about the intricacies of the digital world, including that it engenders overwhelm (who can keep up with the latest app? And is it necessary to know that Bumble differs from other apps in forcing women to make the first move in order to understand a patient's online dating?); discomfort at interfacing with the patient's device in session (therapists prefer to have a patient describe an interaction than to read it directly on the phone); and feelings of insecurity that come with not knowing things, which sometimes exposes generational gaps. Thus, we may face a blind spot when it comes to recognizing the importance of patients' digital selves within families. And, as described earlier, digital interaction (be it texting, chatting via an app, gaming, etc.) accounts for a significant amount of interaction amongst younger members of families.

In both theory and practice, psychologists have long noted how the Internet can at times allow individuals to productively engage, explore and work through disowned parts of self, while at other times enable those parts of self to remain dissociated and disavowed (Dryer & Litmaer, 2007; Pilecki, 2017; Trub, 2016). Alongside the freedom to curate the digital self (through creation of online social media profiles, dating profiles, avatars, etc.) comes the pressure of creating an online identity that is public, on record, and open to commentary from others that is also recorded for others to see. Thus, identity exploration becomes blurred with impression management. As Christine Rosen (2007) noted, "the Delphic oracle's guidance was *know thyself*. Today, in the world of online social networks, the oracle's advice might be *show thyself*."

Online self-presentation can manifest in many ways – some attempt to create a self that is as similar to their offline characteristics as possible, some curate more ideal versions of themselves (possibly who they would wish to be), some use the opportunity to experiment with different identities (Bessière et al., 2007; Dryer & Litmaer, 2007; Koles & Nagy, 2016; Pilecki, 2017; Trub, 2016). Each of these carry different implications and may differ for different members of a family. For example, presenting digital manifestations of self in an idealized fashion can have positive and negative implications, depending on the extent to which an individual is able to embody that ideal self, and/or the extent to which it leads to further alienation or isolation. In an ethnographic study of teenage bloggers, Hodkinson (2007) notes that for some, a digital profile offered a space to explore oneself by trying on various identities without having to commit to one, while for others it facilitated a more grounded, integrated sense of identity through the support received from an online community. Discussing a teenage patient, Naso (2011) similarly described how cultivating meaningful interpersonal relationships on the platform *Second Life* (where one's avatar interacts with the avatars of others) enabled the development of previously absent compassion and empathy.

Finally, for some, the distance and anonymity of online interactions can be useful for expressing and exploring parts of the self that may be shameful and not accepted within a family (de Varela, 2015; Koles & Nagy, 2016; Trub, 2016; Trub, Revenson & Salbod, 2014). Online spaces can feel safer, leading to attenuated feelings of social anxiety related to rejection and enabling greater disclosure and interpersonal trust. Using online spaces to overcome anxiety to express oneself may be particularly helpful for members of a family who are shy or introverted (Amichai-Hamburger et al., 2002; Dunaetz et al., 2015), for people who identify with a marginalized group (Hodkinson, 2007; Pilecki, 2017), and for family members with difficulties in navigating needs for autonomy and intimacy (Jenkins-Guarnieri et al., 2012; Morey et al., 2013; Nitzburg & Farber, 2013; Trub et al., 2014; Trub, 2016).

All of these things were true for Nettie, making online interactions a place where she could be seen differently, feeling more in charge of her own story and then bringing that into her family therapy. In a similar vein, some family members may use text-based interaction to express themselves in ways they feel unable to in-person or on the phone (Trub & Barbot, in press; Reid & Reid, 2007). This was also true for Nettie who used a password protected digital diary that was stored in the cloud to safely express her terror and horror at her husband's behavior that she could not utter aloud. Afterward she would decide which entries she wanted to share, emailing me the link to access the material digitally so she could express her feelings without verbalizing them. The digital diary also represented a subversive act against her controlling husband where Nettie used technology to safely and privately present the parts of herself that she was afraid to reveal for fear of retribution from her husband.

In family therapy with young children, entering into a child's internal world, allowing oneself to be immersed in order to appreciate the child's perspective, may also include getting to know their lives with technology. Getting to know a child's gaming avatar allows the therapist access to the child's fantasies of what he/she could be without the limitations and challenges of their external and internal circumstances (Koles & Nagy, 2016). Malberg (2011) describes how getting intensely involved in gaming with her adolescent patient enabled the development of trust and playfulness in the early stages of treatment. His use of the game in therapy was also integral to the working through of traumatic experiences and the development of personal agency, which ultimately allowed for healing and psychological growth. The importance of engaging an adult's digital self is no less important, and helping family members understand the meaning it holds for each other can be an essential aspect of family dynamics now.

But paradoxically, engaging in video-conferencing may further impede a therapist's ability to engage with a person's digital self. Even in a technology-mediated treatment, we might unwittingly do this by not knowing enough about how to invite it in, and/or by implicitly or explicitly creating a therapeutic environment that is technology-free. Co-present bodies are often much more conducive to allowing a therapist to see a patient's digital self, which may involve looking at a device together with a family member during session. Unlike an in-person session, where patient and therapist can look at a screen together, it is quite challenging to show a therapist one's digital self without shifting attention away from the computer-mediated session and thereby threatening the connection. Thus, it may be an even greater challenge for the online therapist to get to know all parts of a patient, particularly those that exist in the digital realm.

Conclusion

Psychotherapy is not immune to the myriad and profound changes that technology has enacted on the way people communicate and relate to one another. With a nuanced perspective regarding the paradoxical nature of technology's impact on communication, contact, intimacy, self-expression and self-exploration, family therapists are in a position to help families explore the role of technology in their lives and relationships, so they might make more conscious choices about how they want to adopt communication inside and outside of the family, that may enhance intimacy and promote autonomy. The therapeutic encounter is unique in its deep engagement, offering opportunities for insight, awareness, and intimacy that families may not express with each other or others. When that encounter transitions to a screen, the family becomes exposed to the benefits, complexities, and risks inherent in technology's infusion in society. The therapist is then faced with a series of dilemmas rooted in the conflicts that arise when blending technology and family therapy. We highlight four of these dilemmas in this chapter – new communication norms, silence, intimacy, and inviting in the digital self. As in the case of Nettie, these and other dilemmas may be veiled in online therapeutic encounters, easy to miss or ignore unless we acknowledge how the digital third is acting upon all therapeutic encounters over a screen. Therapists may be tempted to ignore the presence of the digital third and bypass these dilemmas, achieving a sense of resolution at the expense of losing sight of dynamics impacting the therapeutic encounter. But quite simply, it is an inherent aspect of screen-mediated treatment that requires understanding. Recognizing the powerful trend to assimilate into today's technology culture is essential; being able to acknowledge the subtle complexities that arise is an initial and necessary step towards appreciating the many factors at play in computer-mediated family treatments.

References

Amichai-Hamburger, Y., Wainapel, G., & Fox, S. (2002). "On the internet no one knows I'm an introvert": Extroversion, neuroticism, and internet interaction. *CyberPsychology & Behavior, 5*(2): 125–128.

Bagnini, C. (2015). Technology-stirred projective processes in couple teletherapy. *Psychoanalysis Online, 2*: 185–193.

Balint, M. (1958). The three areas of mind. *The international Journal of Psychoanalysis, 39*: 328–340.

Bessière, K., Seay, A.F., & Kiesler, S. (2007). The ideal elf: Identity exploration in World of Warcraft. *Cyberpsychology & Behavior, 10*(4): 530–535.

Burka, J.B. (1996). The therapist's body in reality and fantasy: A perspective from an overweight therapist. In B. Gerson (Ed.), *The Therapist as a Person: Life Crises, Life Choices, Life Experiences and their Effects on Treatment* (pp. 255–276). Hillsdale, NJ: The Analytic Press.

Clough, B.A., & Casey, L.M. (2015). The smart therapist: A look to the future of smartphones and mHealth technologies in psychotherapy. *Professional Psychology: Research and Practice, 46*(3): 147–153.

Day, S.X. (1999). Psychotherapy using distance technology: A comparison of face-to-face, video, and audio treatments (Doctoral dissertation, University of Illinois at Urbana–Champaign). *Digital Dissertations.*

Day, S.X., & Schneider, P. (2000). The subjective experiences of therapists in face-to-face, video, and audio sessions. In J.W. Bloom & G.R. Walz (Eds), *Cybercounseling and Cyberlearning: Strategies and Resources for the Millennium* (pp. 203–218). Alexandria, VA: American Counseling Association.

Day, S.X., & Schneider, P.L. (2002). Psychotherapy using distance technology: A comparison of face-to-face, video, and audio treatment. *Journal of Counseling Psychology, 49*(4): 499–503.

de Varela, Y. (2015). Cyberspace as potential space. In J.S. Scharff (Ed.), *Psychoanalysis Online 2: Impact of Technology on Development, Training, and Therapy* (pp. 233–238). London: Karnac Books Ltd.

Dryer, J.A., & Litmaer, R.M. (2007). Cyber-sex as twilight zone between virtual reality and virtual fantasy: Creative play space or destructive addiction? *Psychoanalytic Review, 94*(1): 39–61.

Dunaetz, D.R., Lisk, T.C., & Shin, M.M. (2015). Personality, gender, and age as predictors of media richness preference. *Advances in Multimedia*, 2015(7): 1–9.

Essig, T. (2012). Psychoanalysis lost and found in our culture of simulation and enhancement. P*sychoanalytic Inquiry*, *32*: 438–452.

Essig, T. (2015a). The "Full training illusion" and the myth of functional equivalence. *Division of Psychoanalysis*, *2*. Available online at http://internationalpsychoa nalysis.net/wp-content/uploads/2015/05/RoundRobin2Essig2015FINAL. pagestpdel.pdf.

Ferenczi, S. (1950). Silence is golden. In J.A. Suttie (Ed. & Trans.), *Further Contributions to the Theory and Technique of Psychoanalysis* (pp. 250–252). London: Hogarth Press.

Glueckauf, R.L., Fritz, S.P., Ecklund-Johnson, E.P., Liss, H.J., Dages, P., & Carney, P. (2002). Videoconferencing-based family counseling for rural teenagers with Epilepsy: Phase 1 Findings. *Rehabilitation Psychology*, *47*(1): 49–72.

Hall, J.A., & Baym, N.K. (2012). Calling and texting (too much): Mobile maintenance expectations, (over) dependence, entrapment, and friendship satisfaction. *New Media & Society*, *14*(2): 316–331.

Hanlon, J. (2001). Disembodied intimacies: Identity and relationship on the internet. *Psychoanalytic Psychology*, *18*(3): 556–562.

Hodkinson, P. (2007). Interactive online journals and individualization. *New Media & Society*, *9*(4): 625–650.

Hirsch, I., & Aron, L. (1991). Participant-observation, perspectivism and countertransference. In H. Siegel, L. Barbanel, I. Hirsch, J. Lasky, H. Silverman, & S. Warshaw (Eds) *Psychoanalytic Reflections on Current Issues* (pp. 78–95). New York: New York University Press.

Isaacs-Russell, G. (2015). *Screen Relations: The Limits of Computer-mediated Psychoanalysis and Psychotherapy*. London: Karnac Books Ltd.

Jarvenpaa, S.L., & Lang, K.R. (2005). Managing the paradoxes of mobile technology. *Information Systems Management*, *22*(4): 7–23.

Jenkins-Guarnieri, M.A., Wright, S.L., & Hudiburgh, L.M. (2012). The relationships among attachment style, personality traits, interpersonal competency, and Facebook use. *Journal of Applied Developmental Psychology*, *33*(6): 294–301.

Kaftal, E. (1980). Clinical manifestations of death imagery. *Issues in Ego Psychology*, *3*(1): 7–12.

Koles, B., & Nagy, P. (2016). Avatars as transitional objects: The impact of avatars and digital objects on adolescent gamers. *Journal of Gaming & Virtual Worlds*, *8*(3): 279–296.

Levitt, H.M. (2001). Sounds of silence in psychotherapy: The categorization of clients' pauses. *Psychotherapy Research*, *11*(3): 295–309.

Lyons-Ruth, K. (1999). The two-person unconscious: Intersubjective dialogue, enactive relational representation, and the emergence of new forms of relational organization. *Psychoanalytic Inquiry*, *19*(4): 576–617.

Malberg, N.T. (2011). From blood elf to angry young man: An atypical analysis or simply the use of a new facilitating object? *Journal of Infant, Child and Adolescent Psychotherapy*, *10*(4): 392−401.

Morey, J.N., Gentzler, A.L., Creasy, B., Oberhauser, A.M., & Westerman, D. (2013). Young adults' use of communication technology within their romantic relationships and associations with attachment style. *Computers in Human Behavior*, *29*(4): 1771–1778.

Naso, R.C. (2011). Role-playing games: Bridge or barrier to object relationships in socially-isolated teens? *Division/Review, 1*(2): 27–30.

Nitzburg, G.C., & Farber, B.A. (2013). Putting up emotional (Facebook) walls? Attachment status and emerging adults' experiences of social networking sites. *Journal of Clinical Psychology, 69*(11): 1183–1190.

Ogden, T.H. (1994). The analytical third: Working with intersubjective clinical facts. *Int. J. Psycho-Anal, 75*(1): 3–20.

Pilecki, A. (2017). Screen images: Transitional and defensive internet use LGBTQ adolescents and adults. In J.S. Scharff (Ed.), *Psychoanalysis Online 3* (pp. 153–168). London: Karnac Books Ltd.

Przybylski, A.K., & Weinstein, N. (2012). Can you connect with me now? How the presence of mobile communication technology influences face-to-face conversation quality. *Journal of Social and Personal Relationships, 30*(3): 237–246.

Rees, C.S., & Stone, S. (2005). Therapeutic alliance in face-to-face versus videoconferenced psychotherapy. *Professional Psychology: Research and Practice, 36*(6): 649–653.

Reid, D.J., & Reid, F.J.M. (2007). Text or talk? Social anxiety, loneliness, and divergent preferences for cell phone use. *CyberPsychology & Behavior, 10*(3): 424–435.

Reik, T. (1926). The psychological meaning of silence. *Psychoanalytic Review, 55*(2): 172–186.

Ribak, R. (2009). Remote control, umbilical cord and beyond: The mobile phone as a transitional object. *British Journal of Developmental Psychology, 27*(1): 183–196.

Richardson, L. (2011). *"Can you see what I am saying?": An action-research, mixed methods evaluation of telepsychology in rural Western Australia* (Doctoral dissertation, Murdoch University).

Rosen, C. (2007). Virtual friendship and the new narcissism. *The New Atlantis* (17): 15–31.

Sabbadini, A. (1991). Listening to silence. *British Journal of Psychotherapy, 7*(4): 406–415.

Schneider, P.L. (2001). A comparison of outcome variables in psychotherapy: Distance technology versus face-to-face. Available online at www.telehealth.net /articles/litreview.html.

Sharpley, C.F., Munro, D.M., & Elly, M.J. (2005). Silence and rapport during initial interviews. *Counselling Psychology Quarterly, 18*(2): 149–159.

Simpson, S. (2001). The provision of a psychology service to Shetland via teleconferencing: Patient/therapist satisfaction and ability to develop a therapeutic alliance. *Journal of Telemedicine and Telecare, 7*(1): 34–36.

Simpson, S. (2009). Psychotherapy via videoconferencing: A review. *British Journal of Guidance & Counselling, 37*(3): 271–286.

Simpson, S.G., & Reid, C.L. (2014). Therapeutic alliance in videoconferencing psychotherapy: A review. *Australian Journal of Rural Health, 22*(6): 280–299.

Stone, L. (2014). Continuous Partial Attention. Available online at https://lindastone.net/qa/continuous-partial-attention/.

Trub, L. (2016). A portrait of the self in the digital age: Attachment, splitting, and self-concealment in online and offline self-presentation. *Psychoanalytic Psychology, 34*(1): 78–86.

Trub, L., & Barbot, B. (2016). The paradox of phone attachment: Development and validation of the Young Adult Attachment to Phone Scale (YAPS). *Computers in Human Behavior, 64*, 663–672.

Trub, L. & Barbot, B. (in press) Texting – Great Escape or Path to Self-Expression? Development and Validation of the Messaging Motivations Questionnaire. *Measurement and Evaluation in Counseling and Development.*

Trub, L., & Magaldi, D. (2017). Left to our own devices. *Psychoanalytic Perspectives, 14*(2): 219–236.

Trub, L., Revenson, T.A., & Salbod, S. (2014). Getting close from far away: Mediators of the association between attachment and blogging behavior. *Computers in Human Behavior, 41*: 245–252.

Turkle, S. (2006). 10 Always-on/always-on-you: The tethered self. In J. Katz (Ed.) *Handbook of Mobile Communication Studies* (pp. 121–128). Cambridge, MA: MIT Press.

Turkle, S. (2011). *Alone Together: Why We Expect More from Technology and Less from Ourselves.* New York, NY: Basic Books.

Turkle, S. (2015). *Reclaiming Conversation: The Power of Talk in a Digital Age.* New York: Penguin Press.

Twenge, J.M. (2017). Have smartphones destroyed a generation. *The Atlantic.* Available online at www.theatlantic.com/magazine/archive/2017/09/has-the-smartphone-destroyed-a-generation/534198/.

Van der Kolk, B.A. (2015). *The Body Keeps the Score: Brain, Mind, and Body in the Healing of Trauma.* New York: Penguin Books.

Weinberg, H. (2014). *The Paradox of Internet Groups: Alone in the Presence of Others.* New York: Karnac Books.

Winnicott, D.W. (1953). Transitional objects and transitional phenomena: A study of the first not-me possession. *Int. J. Psycho-Anal., 34*: 89–97.

Zilberstein, K. (2013). Technology, relationships and culture: Clinical and theoretical implications. *Clinical Social Work Journal, 43*(2): 151–158.

12 Practical Considerations for Online Couple and Family Therapy

Arnon Rolnick and Shoshana Hellman

There are specific issues for couple therapy and use of video therapy. Here are some tips for the practitioners:

Seating Arrangements: Should the Couple use the same Computer and Camera or should they use Separate Computers?

Most approaches consider the seating arrangement as very important: On the one hand, we want the couple to talk to each other. On the other hand, we want the couple, as a unit, to face the therapist as well. Apparently, the school of thought in couple and family therapy determines the seating arrangement online.

Imago relations therapy puts a significant emphasis on sharing and active listening, so the couple should actually face each other. Hence one should consider using two different computers according to this approach. The Gottman method emphasizes assessment of facial expressions, as a way to perceive the emotional aspects of the interaction. Sue Johnson's EFT (Emotional Focus Therapy) emphasizes being together in front of the therapist and still be able to talk to each other. Thus, the couple should use one computer and camera. However, it might reduce the therapist's ability to notice the facial expression of each partner.

In general, video therapy enables the therapist to observe the couple's faces in a very detailed way. Each of the partners sees the therapist's face in detail as well. Therefore, there is a unique advantage in sitting close to the camera. However, as mentioned in the general practical instructions, sitting like this prevents perceiving the body expressions

Ellyn Bader and Peter Pearson suggest that the way the couple chooses to sit, might give the therapist some information about their intimacy. So, the online therapist should wait and see what type of seating arrangement the couple chooses.

These are all important considerations, and the therapists should choose their preferences according to the specific situation and the stage of therapy.

Who Does the Therapist Refer To?

In an in-person setting, where everyone is in same room, it's very clear to whom the therapist is referring. The therapist's head and body face either one partner or the other. Using video, the therapist should be aware that the couple cannot perceive where he or she is heading, so the therapist should find ways to indicate it, sometimes simply by mentioning the name of the person s/he is addressing.

Setting

Since the couple is sitting in their own premises doing video therapy, it is important to define the specific environment where therapy is going to take place. It is also important to keep the consistency of the same place. The therapist should note the spatial arrangement of the space where video therapy is taking place. Sometimes the specific objects in that space can have significance for the couple. Even a presence of a pet can be significant. The same holds true for the therapist who is not using his private office for the video therapy.

Should Couple and Family Therapy start Face–to–Face and then Continue with Video Conferencing, or Is It Just as Efficient to do it Only via Video Conferencing?

During intake, when assessment is important, in-person meetings are highly recommended, but if it is not possible then the first meeting should be arranged so that the partners are sitting together and seen on one screen, since the purpose is to assess the problems of the couple and their togetherness. In subsequent meetings there might be an advantage for each partner to use a different computer.

The possibility of one partner sitting with the therapist and one partner sitting in a remote place using video conferencing, is not recommended, due to the fact that it might be perceived as a coalition between the therapist and that partner.

Individual Meetings

There is a long debate whether couple therapists should see the partners individually.

According to the Gottman approach, the intake includes individual meetings as well, in which it is important to keep privacy conditions. The other partner or any other family member should not be in vicinity of the meeting, and it should be clarified for the online meeting. Other approaches do not encourage individual meetings in couple therapy.

Conflict Situations

In treatment, especially in situations of conflict, it is important that the therapist should intervene actively and make sure that each of the partners gets his or her turn to speak separately. Bader and Peterson emphasize the need for the therapist to take a leadership role in couple therapy and to refuse to allow the session to begin with anger and hostility. While in the same physical space the therapist can use some cues (like physically approaching one partner with his/her chair, as Sue Johnson's suggests, or slightly touching the other). This cannot be done in video therapy. The therapist and clients can agree ahead of time to certain cues (visual or auditory) that the therapist can use during conflict. There are even some situations where people sit apart in which the therapist can use the mute button for some members of the family when another member is talking.

Real Life and Crisis Situations

The fact that therapy can be conducted at the couple's premises, opens the opportunity for the couple to demonstrate real life situations and crises even more than in the therapist's office, and allows the therapist to intervene while seeing these real-life situations. However, in extreme cases (e.g. when violence or real threat is involved), the therapist should prepare in advance someone in the couple's neighborhood to intervene.

Emotional Flooding

Emotional flooding is an important factor in the assessment and the treatment of a couple. Usually, couple therapists use verbal and nonverbal cues to assess it. The Gottman method uses technical tools such as a pulse oximeter for each of the partners. In video therapy these technological means can be easier to use and implement. For example, in video therapy one can share the results on the screen or even see them on the screen in real time, while being measured. (pulse, heart rate), which cannot be done in face-to-face therapy.

However, we should take into consideration that it might be difficult to control such flooding from a distance as there is no physical proximity that might help in preventing escalation and even acting out of one of the partners.

One way to overcome this, is to make sure that both the therapist and the clients are aware of community resources in the proximity (geographical area) of the clients, especially in crisis situations. Another way is to teach strategies such as relaxation techniques or meditation to cope with these situations.

The Rhythm of the Session

In in-person therapy silence is a common technique and the therapist has many other nonverbal possibilities. In video therapy, blurred or slow speech, delays in speech or silences can be interpreted as technical issues, therefore it is important to keep a certain rhythm and refrain from too many silences, which could be interpreted at times as technical difficulties.

Recording of Sessions

Recording the couple therapy sessions is common in many couple therapy schools and is in fact built-in for training couple therapists, and for receiving feedback and supervision. The use of recording in assessment and therapy is one of the important factors in Gottman's theory. The video recording can help the therapist in assessing the couple, and in some cases could be used by the couple during treatment while teaching them new skills. Recording the sessions online is much simpler and easier than in the office setting.

The accessibility of using computers and video cameras in remote therapy can help couples and the therapist to intervene in conflict situations at home. If the couple uses the camera in such situations and shares it with the therapist live, the therapist can intervene immediately without having to demonstrate or talk about these situations in the office.

Long-distance Relationships

The prevalence of long-distance relationships in the modern era emphasizes the necessity of online distance therapy, as this is one of the major means that a couple in such relationship is using to communicate. In these cases, online therapy is the only way to use for couple therapy since the partners are not living in the same geographical locations.

Family Therapy

When dealing with children in family therapy via video conferencing, the therapist should remember that children need real physical presence of a therapist while participating in therapy. It is hard also to keep children's attention for longer periods of time, especially online. These are considerations before therapy involves children, but of course every child can be different.

Section 3

Online Group Therapy

Edited by Haim Weinberg

13 Introduction to the Online Group Therapy Section

Haim Weinberg

We are "social animals," wired for social interactions. This is one of the reasons why it is only natural to use groups to help people. Group psychotherapy has been an important treatment modality for many years, with its long history extending back to Freud's writing about group psychology. The great need for psychological support and for the treatment of many soldiers suffering from "shell shock" during the Second World War led to an increased focus on group treatment. Bion and Foulkes developed their group theoretical approaches in the UK, while on the opposite side of the ocean Kurt Lewin applied his concept of a field of forces, to groups, which led to the development of sensitivity groups (T-groups) at the National Training Laboratories (NTL). In the seventies of the previous century, encounter groups in the USA spread like wildfire, fulfilling the need for connection in an alienated society. Yalom was one of the advocates of group therapy and his book *The Theory and Practice of Group Psychotherapy* became well-known to most psychotherapists.

Over the past decades, the focus of group studies has shifted from an emphasis on process research to an examination of outcome studies. Research confirms that the therapeutic outcome of group therapy is at least equal to individual therapy. Studies found out that group therapy appears to be effective overall (Burlingame et al., 2003), and as effective as individual therapy for many problems (Barlow, 2011; Bernard et al., 2008; Burlingame et al., 2004; Oei, Raylu, & Casey, 2010). However, strange enough, despite its evidence-based validity, interest in group therapy seems to decay in the past decades in most Western countries, and less therapists are using it, especially in their private practice.

One of the reasons for this situation is the difficulty in gathering enough people to start a group. In private practice you need a relatively large pool of patients from which to recruit a group. It is not easy to find the time and space where all the group members can meet together, and by the time the therapist has interviewed the last candidate, the first interviewee (with whom the therapist has met months ago), has already dropped. Many groups do not start because of these practical considerations. Even after the therapist had overcome all these technical difficulties and the group started, there are restrictions that might prevent a participant from coming to a meeting: traffic jams, illness, work travel, etc. Group instability can decrease the sense of safety and causes feelings of frustration, rejection and less engagement in the group process.

As emphasized more than once in this book, the Internet can make therapy more accessible to people, so it can probably help overcoming some of the above problems. A larger pool of candidates (not only from the therapist's geographical area) and more continuity and stability of participation (less absences) can guarantee a smoother group process. However, although remote therapy exists from the fifties of the previous century (mostly by phone, see the review in the introduction to the individual section of this book), the use of remote group therapy has rarely been experimented. Perhaps one of the reasons is that in a group phone session it is not easy to identify the speaker. Weinberg (2001) pointed out the importance of group dynamics on the Internet (in online forums) already at the beginning of the twenty-first century. Online group therapy using videoconference has only started lately, probably due to the development of better applications for video connection. It took some time for video programs to find good technical solutions for multi-participants. As far as we know, this is the first book that reviews in depth the use of the Internet for group therapy.

Although technical solutions exist already, remotely managing a group of participants is not a trivial thing. As emphasized in the introduction for this book, the disembodied interaction poses difficulties, but there are many other difficulties as well. For example, the group participants cannot identify who each member is looking at. Especially important is the inability to locate the gaze of the group leader. Hearing all the group members talking at the same time is also problematic. It's an art to be learned.

This section can be of importance not only to group therapists, but also to family therapists who work with families spread around the globe, where the grandparents, parents and grown up children each live in a different place. It can also be relevant to organizational consultants, as online team meetings, with team members working in different continents, became a norm in organizations. Many times, the process aspect is neglected in those meetings. As process is highlighted in group therapy, it is recommended for organization consultants to read this section as well.

Let us start with a vignette.

In a therapy group, a group member brought her cat to one of the sessions. She did not ask the permission of the group leader or the other members and behaved as if it is natural and an accepted norm to bring pets into the group. None of the group members commented on the presence of the cat, until the group leader asked her whether she would like to say something about this boundary violation. She did not see it as a boundary violation at all and was actually angry at the group leader for bringing it to discussion. Most of the group members thought that the therapist is making too much fuss about the presence of the lovely creature and claimed that it does not create any disturbance and distraction and does not interfere with the group process.

I assume that most readers who are familiar with group therapy, the importance of boundaries and the group agreement, would find this member's behavior strange, and would interpret the group's obliviousness as a clear resistance. But what if I told you that this was an online group using a Zoom application for a video conference meeting, and that the presence of the cat was revealed towards the middle of the session when its beautiful furry tail appeared in front of the camera as he jumped and started walking on the table? Would it still be a boundary violation? Would it still be a group resistance?

This short example shows that although online groups using video look very similar to in-person groups, where all the participants and the therapist are in the same room, we clearly relate to them differently, at least in some respects. The important question is how different online groups (especially those who use video conferencing) are from groups where all the participants and the leader are in the same room. This question has implications to the theory of groups therapy: Should the group therapist lead those groups differently than when leading groups in his/her office? The goal of this section is to explore these similarities and differences and to present different online applications of online therapy groups.

As of today, online group therapy is done either through text, e.g. using Google groups or listserv forums, or through video, using applications such as Zoom or Skype. The text format allows for synchronic groups (in chat rooms, where all the group members are online at the same time), or asynchronic ones (in forums, where there are no time boundaries and people send and read messages whenever they have the time). Online forums have their own dynamics, which were fully described in Weinberg's book (2014) *Alone in the Presence of Virtual Others*. He saw forums as large groups disguised as small groups and pointed out to the massive projections that can occur in only text-based communication. He hypothesized that there are unconscious assumptions and beliefs that impact people's behavior online ("the Internet unconscious") and emphasized the importance of the group leader's presence in such boundless virtual groups (a topic that almost every book about online therapy refers to). He also claimed that intimacy in such online groups is different from intimacy f2f and termed it E-ntimacy.

As video communication quality through the computer improved dramatically since around 2010, the video conference option for group therapy (and online therapy in general) has become more and more popular and widespread, probably because it became much more similar to "reality". In fact, it is f2f, just not in-person. However, while articles (and some research) about online individual therapy using video started appearing, I have not seen articles about online groups using video. One of the purposes of this section is to fill this gap, although the section is not limited to using video in groups.

This section includes an interview with Molyn Leszcz, who wrote with Yalom the fifth edition of *The Theory and Practice of Group Psychotherapy* (2005). In this interview, Molyn Leszcz and I discuss many of the aspects later summarized in my chapter that is also included in this section. Worth mentioning is the question that Leszcz discusses about cohesion and how it is impacted in Zoom groups. Cohesion is one of Yalom's therapeutic factors and it is found in research as correlated with positive outcome in group therapy. In a way it replaces the therapeutic alliance factor that is correlated with outcome in individual therapy. Highlighting this concept, wondering how cohesive an online group becomes, and suggesting how the online group leader can enhance this factor, might be crucial to the success of the group.

Many of the topics raised in this interview are developed further in Haim Weinberg's chapter. The issue of the disembodied group usually preoccupies the attention of the writers about online therapy. Knowing that people's physical presence regulates one another's emotions (according to the IPBN approach), it is questionable whether this regulation can occur online. However, Weinberg suggests ways to increase the impact of the online group therapist's presence to compensate for the absence of the body. He also draws the attention of the readers to how much we ignore important events that happen in the background in online groups (see the case of the cat at the beginning of this introduction). Last but not least, he focuses on the fact that the therapist is not controlling the setting as in-person groups, and wonders what it means for the dynamic administration of the group.

Another chapter is this section is written by Raúl and Lara Vaimberg. They describe two different kinds of online groups. The first is a three years long-term therapy group using an Internet forum. As this group developed from a previous in-person one, it was easy to compare between the f2f and the online text-based one. The second group used online video games to treat children and adolescents diagnosed with Autism Spectrum Disorders. The game helped these children to learn how to collaborate with others.

This section also includes practical considerations for online groups, as we included in any other section of the book.

So what is the bottom line about online group therapy? Let me summarize it through another vignette.

In an online group a member talked about a distressful event but asked the group not to worry about him or ask him to talk more about it, as he is okay. The group members were torn between their wish to respect this member's request and between their care for him, feeling that perhaps he is in denial and does need their help. The group felt stuck, and the member sensed it. Finally, he told the group leader: "You cannot see it online, but I am staring at you, wanting you to find a way out of this impasse". It helped the group leader intervene, supporting the group to discuss their dilemma.

Conclusion: Online groups pose some challenges, but there are creative ways of overcoming these challenges …

References

Barlow, S.H. (2011). Evidence bases for group practice. In R.K. Conyne (Ed.), *The Oxford Handbook of Group Counseling* (pp. 207–230). Oxford: Oxford University Press.

Bernard, H., Burlingame, G., Flores, P., Greene, L., Joyce, A., Kobos, J.C., et al. (2008). Clinical practice guidelines for group psychotherapy. *International Journal of Group Psychotherapy, 58*: 455–542.

Burlingame, G., Fuhriman, A., & Mosier, J. (2003). The differential effectiveness of group psychotherapy: A meta-analytical perspective. *Group Dynamics: Theory, Research and Practice, 7*: 3–12.

Burlingame, G.M., MacKenzie, K.R., & Strauss, B. (2004). Small group treatment: Evidence for effectiveness and mechanisms of change. In M.J. Lambert (Ed.), *Bergin & Garfield's Handbook of Psychotherapy and Behavior Change*, 5th edn (pp. 647–696). New Jersey: Wiley.

Oei, T.P., & Dingle, G. (2008). The effectiveness of group cognitive behaviour therapy for unipolar depressive disorders. *Journal of Affective Disorders, 107*: 5–21.

Oei, T.P., Raylu N., & Casey L.M. (2010). Effectiveness of group and individual formats of a combined motivational interviewing and cognitive behavioral treatment program for problem gambling: a randomized controlled trial. *Behavioral Cognitive Psychotherapy, 38*(2): 233–238.

Weinberg, H. (2001). Group process and group phenomena on the Internet. *International Journal of Group Psychotherapy, 51*(3): 361–379.

Weinberg, H. (2014). *The Paradox of Internet Groups: Alone in the Presence of Virtual Others*. London: Karnac.

14 Interview with Molyn Leszcz

M = Molyn Leszcz; H = Haim Weinberg

H: If you ask me what is one of my conclusions, after doing many online groups and after reading what is written and talking with many colleagues, one thing is that although it resembles face-to-face groups, it is not exactly the same. And the difficulty – because it resembles so much – that most of the therapists ignore the tiny differences, or what looks like tiny differences. And I think this is a mistake.

M: We know that if you are using the group as a setting for an intervention, the process dimensions kind of fade into the background. But if you are using the group as an agent more for the treatment, then the process variables move much more into the foreground.

H: That's a great sentence. And actually it helps me a lot because one of the difficulties of moving to online therapy is that the setting changes. What you said is actually helping me understand that yes, there might be a problem, but the question is whether we focus on processes or the setting. Say more about that, because I think that this is fundamental and so important.

M: Sure. You may know that I'm focused a lot on the concept of being an evidence-based practitioner. In the work that we're talking about, in regards to using the Internet, as a vehicle to deliver face-to-face group therapy, the same things that matter – plus matter in the Internet – so, attention to cohesion is critically important. We don't know yet how cohesion is impacted by a Zoom group as opposed to a face-to-face group. In some ways, there are advantages to the Internet, because there may be more willingness to take risks on the part of the patient, especially when they are texting a response. There's a kind of subliminal space … we're face-to-face, but it's a little different than if we are actually in the same room. Because all you can see of me is my face. You don't know what else I'm doing. And all I can see of you is your face and … so, we have to be that much more attentive to what is not being communicated manifestly. Using the group as an agent – to come back to my earlier comment – part of why group therapy struggles, is that in the hands of many people, the group is used as a setting to deliver an intervention. Which is fine, if what you are aiming to do is a psychoeducational group, or support group, or learning how to cope with chemotherapy. I think there is great utility and value in that. But if you are looking at this as a vehicle in which the group itself, the processes of the group are intending to facilitate self-awareness, inter-personal learning, self-understanding, then attention to process becomes critically important. By "process" I mean in essence, "why is this happening in this way, at this point in time". For me, that's a simple way to remember what is happening, who is saying what to whom, what is being said, who is not speaking. What is not being said. And why specifically is this happening in this way at this point in time. And how does this relate to the two key elements that we know predict better outcome in group therapy: development of cohesion, and the manifes-tations of empathy.

H: And all these elements of the process and the here-and-now, are not different between online and face-to-face.

M: I would hazard to guess that they are at least the same, plus.

H: Can you say more about the plus?

M: When I do a group in my hospital I am embedded in a particular kind of social, cultural environment. if I feel supported in my work, if I feel my work is valued, if my work is respected, if I work in an environ-ment where people are compassionate in their delivery of healthcare – that influences me. By working in an environment where I feel a sense of inequity or lack of attention to social justice – that also impacts me. And when you're doing an Internet group, a Zoom group, then you're open to all of the other forces that surround that dynamic. There are people in different locations. You may have people from different countries. So the larger forces may even make it more complicated.

H: So this is a plus … usually we add the cultural, social component – maybe even the social unconscious issue – clearer when you do a group that's from many cultures and from all over the world.

M: Right. I would suggest that the more we can make a Zoom group like a face-to-face group and take advantage of the additional properties, the more effective we will make it. so: preparation, selection, a formulation – all are very, very effective.

H: I agree. Going back to the therapeutic factors that you mentioned before, I think that regarding text groups – [forums] – there is already enough evidence that there is developing cohesion … but I think that you are right that there is not enough research and evidence about Zoom or video conference groups. Am I right?

M: I would say so. I mean this is your work; you know this better than anybody. I haven't found a lot about [online] face-to-face. Most of the work that I've found has been about more traditional Internet groups.

You're saying that there isn't much right now, face-to-face, using Zoom as a platform.

H: Yes. There isn't much. And that's why in this book we want to focus more on video conferencing, whether couples or groups or individuals – we hope it will complete and add to the literature.

M: Yeah, I think that would be very important. There's another variable to talk about, which is … many of the people who are seeking treatment now, in their 20s and 30s are much more comfortable with the Internet, than people in their 40s and 50s. there's a generational phenomenon as well. Things we might have felt were barriers to engagement are not going to be barriers to engagement for people of a different generation.

H: You might be right. And probably people from a younger generation do it more easily. Maybe even benefit more from that. But let's also talk about the disadvantage for the younger generation. Doesn't it mean that … I'm playing the devil's advocate.... Doesn't it mean that we support a culture of being there all the time, quick fix, not delaying gratification, by our providing online therapy? What do you think, what do you say about that?

M: I think those are good questions. I think there are ethical considerations with regard to unintended consequences to offering Internet group therapy. For example, how do you deal with a crisis? How do you deal with a situation where one becomes acutely distressed? And they are 400 miles away. What kind of contract must be established to safety. What I don't know about, but have curiosity about is … we know so many people who are engaged with a kind of surreal life. A virtual life and not a real life. So is a Zoom group bringing people closer together – which we hope – or is it fostering this kind of idea that "I don't have to leave my house. I can access the world sitting in my chair". And, on the one hand, I mean a lot of people I see are socially anxious and depressed and on the one hand this is a way for them to access treatment that they might not have access to otherwise, but is it not an inadvertent reinforcement of the idea that they can actually really control their exposure, and not be out in the world at all, at large.

H: You're pointing out to what I wrote in my book *The Internet Paradox* – that it's a paradox. Also actually Sherry Turkle wrote about it in her book *Alone Together* … so it's a paradox and maybe, what you said at the beginning, it means that in the session we need to pay attention more than usual to questions of boundaries. And to keeping the setting very clear. Like the agreement that you mentioned. Adding a section about online ethics or norms or rules. And also establishing what we do in crisis.

Something else I would like us to discuss: one of the main questions is what happens in the disembodied environment. Something is missing, which is the body. Anything you can say about that. What are your thoughts?

M: It requires the group leader on a Zoom group to have an extra degree of caution and an extra degree of humility. Because the inference that you are making that what you see tells the story is gonna be that much more limited. Because you're only able to see a piece. If you're sitting in a room you can … a skilled group therapist can scan the room pretty quickly. I think it's a different skill to scan a computer, with 8 faces on it.

H: So you lose something … I think it's also in the eye to eye contact. It's another paradox: although you see the person much more closely than you see him or her in the group – you can focus more on the facial expressions, actually you cannot have an eye to eye contact.

M: And if you're focusing intently on one person, your vision is gonna be obscured with regards to other people on the same time. I would imagine. I know it's hard to take in everything that's happening in a group when you're in the same room. And body posture … I am not as attuned as I should be to the role of body posture but I enjoyed, for example, Pat Ogden's talk at the AGPA about sensori–motor perspective.

H: So what you actually say is that you might lose something by focusing on one person, lose some attention to the group as a whole.

M: Yeah. I'm imagining that. I would think that everything we do gives us something and takes away something. So the issue here is to be aware of what this gives us and to be mindful of what it takes away. What it gives is access. What it gives is connection to a larger group forces. What it takes away is the potential to really examine someone's totalistic expression of what they're feeling. You can see my face but you can't see my hands. And that's just you and me. If there are eight other people on the screen it becomes that much more complicated.

H: You're right. It's so interesting, I have a process training group of therapists from the US and at one meeting they said that they don't see the whole body. And then what they did, they showed the leg [and] the shoes, to complete the entire body picture.

M: That's a concrete enactment. It still doesn't make it possible, in an ongoing way. But these people wouldn't be in this process group with you, without the Internet. So again, we have to look at what it brings, and what it obstructs.

H: So, talking about the difference between the concrete and non-concrete, it's not only not seeing the whole body, it's the ability to sense exactly what's going on. Somehow there is some disconnection I think, because … through the mediation of the computer. Do you agree?

M: I agree. I certainly have felt that when I've done teaching through Zoom. When you get variation in the technology, in people's Internet, in people's wifi, it can be a distraction just from logistics.

H: I agree it's a distraction, but maybe we can also use it. For example, when there is a disruption, when there is a break in the communication, what do you do with that? Many times, you blame the other: "Your Internet is not strong enough." So you can use it and say: "Ok, what did you feel? Some people might even be triggered by that. It's more in one-on-one but you can use it in the group.

M: That's an illustration, Haim, of how you can take advantage of everything that happens, if you are alive to the process in the here and now. In my group in the hospital, there was a fire alarm. And it was quite loud, and so it led to a discussion about Are we safe? Can we trust Molyn's determination that we are safe. We haven't heard a fire alarm before, at this time of the evening. What does it mean? And so it opens up issues around authority, around trust, around safety. It's all potential material for our work. And the Internet is gonna open up some new avenues. And a skilled group therapist, who is comfortable with technology, I think can probably manage the process of that, in the same way that he would manage the process of doing a group in out of the ordinary situation or circumstance. But you have to know what to be thinking about and what is manifest and what is latent.

H: Yeah that's another good sentence. And maybe that brings us back to what you said, that as long as you focus on the process and not ignoring things that happened that are not exactly like the regular face-to-face, then you can go deeper and you can work well even online. In my online group contract it's written, because the group member control the setting in their house, then I ask to have a private room, with the door closed, with no interruption, and no distractions, no looking at emails or iPhone. It goes without saying, but we don't do it in our regular contract, because I'm taking care of the group's room. And in one of the sessions, suddenly there was a cat on the table. First we saw only its tail and then (the rest). What do you do with that? Because you don't have it in the office. Rarely would people bring their cats. So I had to talk about it. It's actually not exactly according to the contract. We need to pay attention to things like that. Most of the therapists simply ignore it.

M: We know that many therapists in their face-to-face groups also ignore important elements of the process. And aren't as attuned empathically as they need to be. So the person whose cat comes into the group – what does it mean? Did the person make the decision that the cat … if I close the door the cat will drive me crazy, scratching to get in, and I'll be distracted. Or, if I bring the cat in, I will feel comforted and be able to take some bigger risks because I will have my pet with me. Or is the person using the cat as a way to create a bit of a barrier to be not alone so there's two of them against everyone else. There's a dozen ways to make sense of it. And sometimes a cat is just a cat.

H: So what you say, actually, is that we simply need to explore and not ignore. And there are therapists who will not explore even in face-to-face, in the same room, they might be in greater danger of ignoring while online, because it's kind of in the background, we don't think about it enough.

M: I bet you there isn't a group therapist who hasn't had the experience of a member of his/her group falling asleep. Especially in an evening group. How do you deal with that? Do you ignore it? Do you, as a group leader, speak to it? Do you, as a group leader, ask how come no one is addressing this? I had this happen in my group recently – it also speaks to the intersubjectivity of our work. Because this is a young father, came to the group, and fell asleep. You can see him struggling to stay awake. So … no one spoke to it, until I said: you know, how come no one is speaking to this? And then he apologized. And someone said to him: this is rude of you to fall asleep. And someone else said: we need to find out why, it's not typical [of him] to fall asleep. And he said he had to take his daughter to emergency in the middle of the night before. And he struggled, he didn't get much sleep, and he decided that he would still come to the group. So, is he to be criticized for falling asleep, or is he to be commended for making an extra effort to come. and so it was a kind of useful elaboration about "We need to understand everything from as many sides as possible." And there will be that much more in a Zoom group because you're gonna be in ten houses.

H: So I take what you say in two directions. One – again – things happen also in a non-Internet group. And some people will ignore them even in a non-Internet group. And the other: we might need to be more alert in online groups because it's so easy to ignore something. As if it's part of the set…. Maybe you'll try to bring up more things?

M: For me, questions that I have are in the ethical domain: how do you ensure privacy? How do you ensure confidentiality? How do you ensure that no one is making a videotape? I know you have a contract for someone who becomes extremely distressed or suicidal, what are the terms of that contract? If somebody is across the ocean. And the other thing is, from a jurisdictional perspective, are you licensed to be doing this? If you're in Massachusetts, and you have a Zoom group with somebody from a state where you're not licensed, I would say you're exposed to law suit … there's a vulnerability.

H: Yes, all these things should be considered, and maybe written in the agreement. Let me ask a question: one of the things that we say about groups is that the fact that we arrange the chairs in a circle has some deep mystical meaning: the womb, the container, whatever you want. Here, on Zoom, we don't see it in a circle, we see squares, do you think that it has some impact?

M: It's a good question. Again, I think we need to understand cohesion in those kinds of groups. Are there particular layouts that are better or worse. The contract that you referenced I'm sure is helpful in promoting cohesion. I would think a contract is even more important in this kind of group than a face-to-face group. I'm sure you have experience as well: in face-to-face groups people will sign the contract and forget what's in the contract. They'd say "That really does?" It's a good question. When you do a group and someone is missing. Do you leave the chair in or take it out?

H: That's a good point. I leave the chair in, and the presence of the person is there. Actually, online I did not think of doing that. I don't know how to do it.

M: For me it's less of an issue because I pull the chair out if somebody is missing.

Just last week my group spent some time looking at the relationship I have with my co-therapist. She's a resident, and people said "We noticed that you never sit beside one another." So we discussed the fact that we try to be able to see one another in the group and as a way of facilitating our communication. That was a great interest to members of the group. So I would imagine that when you're doing an Internet group, you're doing it by yourself.

H: Usually. But I did a process group for my students in Singapore and in Israel with my co-leader in Israel and what happened was that we felt that we lost something in sensing where the other co-leader is. Usually, when you are working a lot with a co-leader you sense one another, you just have to look at the other to warn him or her … you know what I'm talking about. We lost it online.

M: So let me ask you this question: knowing this is work that you do and that you enjoy. Do you think everyone, every group therapist should anticipate that they should or could do this kind of group work? Or are there some who are better at it and some who should stick to face-to-face?

H: That's a great question that I haven't thought about. First of all, let's begin with the fact that I think that you do need some specific training to make the transition from the circle to the screen. Like for the transition from individual therapy to becoming a group therapist you need a specific training. I think that you need to add some training about groups online. Meaning, understating the difficulties, being aware of all those tiny things that are not so tiny and all that. Now, I don't think everyone should, for sure, and I also don't think everyone could. You need to feel comfortable with online communication because some of what Foulkes called "dynamic administration," online, is the ease of solving technical problems. It's difficult, when you feel you don't know what to do when you hear an echo or something like that. So first of all you need to feel comfortable with technical things. And also feel comfortable in the environment, not just the technology – feel comfortable with the online environment. Some people don't like the online communication. So that's one thing that I can think about immediately. What do you think?

M: I think that a person to do this kind of work needs that kind of technological security. Because the group requires your full attention. And if your attention is split because you're worrying about the technology, you're not gonna be present in the room, that you need to be. I think you need to be even more present doing a Zoom group than a face-to-face group because, I would imagine … this is an assumption, that in a face-to-face group I would frequently say "You know, I noticed earlier tonight there was a moment of distress on your face that we didn't have a chance to talk about then, but I want to come back to it now." I don't know how easy it would be to do that in a Zoom group. I would think that *I* would miss more cues.

H: I think that you introduced one of the main questions, which is the question of presence: what does it mean to be present? And how to be present online. For me, this is the crucial question in online therapy, whether individual or groups. What does it mean to be present, and how do we make our presence clear online. I think that you said it, I just repeat what you said: we need to put more emphasis, we need to make more effort, we need to find a better way of being present than [with] a group that is in the same room. Do you agree with that?

M: Yes, I think that the demands on the group leader would be greater online, than face-to-face, because there is more that is not directly accessible.

H: Yes. I think that we covered most of the important things.

15 Online Group Therapy

In Search of a New Theory?

Haim Weinberg

New Ideas – New Concepts

When Foulkes (1964), the founder of group analysis, probably the most practiced modality of group therapy in Europe, Israel, the United Kingdom, and Australia, started working with groups, he understood that moving from the couch to the circle (as the title of John Schlapobersky's book about groups from 2016 goes), is not just a shift in technique, but involves a change of theory, using new concepts. Scholz (2011) writes: "Like Freud, Foulkes innovation was first a methodological one: He changed the setting – from the couch to the circle, from the rule of free association to that of free discussion. Foulkes was very much aware of the fact that changing the setting required a change in theory. He had to integrate into his theoretical thinking the fact that in his groups, unconscious material was communicated and understood" (268). Moving from the couch to the screen, or from the circle to the screen when talking about groups, involves no less a dramatic change in the setting and the technique. Shouldn't such a change require a change in theory, then?

Actually, most group therapy theoreticians faced the same dilemma in establishing their school of thought. The question of creating a new theory involves the dilemma of using new concepts. Usually, inventing a new theory means creating new terms, in order to be clear that we are not talking about the same theory and same concepts of the old one. Most of the psychodynamic group theoreticians made a mistake by using concepts such as transference and resistance for group therapy as well, thus confusing the reader that assumes that we are talking about the same phenomena as in individual therapy. Some, like Rutan, Stone and Shay (2014) do emphasize that groups allow for multi-transferences and show a horizontal one in addition to the vertical one we see in individual therapy, however they still use the same concept of transference. Foulkes himself struggled with this dilemma and finally distinguished between Transference towards the therapist (with capital T) and transference towards other participants (with a small t). In fact, only Foulkes and Yalom seem to consider this important question, as Foulkes used the new terms of mirroring, resonance and exchange to describe the main mechanisms of change in the group, and Yalom (1970) used concepts such as cohesion and universality to describe some of the therapeutic factors in the group. Yalom's concept of cohesion proved especially fruitful, as research showed that in groups, the therapeutic alliance is replaced by the group cohesion, so that while in individual therapy the alliance with the therapist is highly correlated with positive outcomes (Safran and Segal, 1990), in groups – the group cohesion is the factor highly correlated with these results (Yalom and Leszsz, 2005).

So, which new concepts shall we use for online relationships and groups? As mentioned in the introduction to this book, *E-ntimacy* is one example of a phenomenon that is different online from the regular intimacy we encounter in face-to-face (f2f) interactions. Intimacy is commonly related to concepts such as love, closeness, self-disclosure, support, bonding, attachment, and sexuality. It can be defined as an exchange that involves sharing what is personal and private (Prager, 1995). Moving to online interactions results in new ways to experience and actualize intimacy, since physical proximity disappears, and privacy is questionable. This concept online and the difference from f2f interaction can be better understood in the group section, by being acquainted with the dynamics of Large Groups. In large psychodynamics process-oriented groups (above 30–40 members), in which the participants cannot be seated in one small circle, people lose the ability to connect intimately and to see one another's faces, and the intimate quality of the usual small therapy groups is lost (see Weinberg and Schneider, 2003; Weinberg and Weishut, 2012). However, people can still feel connected to the Large Group and its members, though not necessarily to specific members. This intimacy is based more on confluence and belonging than on the "into-me-you-see" popular version of intimacy. Weinberg (2014) identified large group processes on Internet forums such as Google groups, and described those forums as large groups disguised as small groups, so it is only natural to assume that the intimacy created online has similarities with the one constructed in large groups.

Weinberg's (2014) conclusion about online intimacy (*E-ntimacy*) is:

> "Psychoanalysis is about what two people can say to each other if they agree not to have sex" (Bersani & Phillips, 2008, p. 1). The psycho-analytic/psychotherapeutic setting allows for an intimacy that is not exactly the same as the intimacy created when two people are not bound to the therapeutic rules. *E-ntimacy is about what people can say to each other if they agree not to have a body*. It is not an impersonal intimacy, it is a different kind of intimacy. In fact, it challenges the Western cultural norms of independence, as always-on connection is sensed as a more collaborative self.

(147)

If this is the case, we can assume that when we do group therapy through Internet forums (using only text), we face and should take into consideration Large Group phenomena, such as feeling lost in Cyberspace and some threats to identity and one's subjectivity (Turquet, 1975), and that people sense *E-ntimacy*, not intimacy.

Wondering whether a new theory about online group therapy is needed, we should not only use new concepts, but also suggest what works in online groups, and explore whether it is the same as in f2f groups. Yalom's famous therapeutic factors (1970), enhancing change in every psychotherapy group, might not all function in online groups. Indeed, Weinberg and Raufman, in Weinberg's book (2014) about the dynamics on Internet forums, summarize the evidence from both research and personal experience that an Internet forum can become cohesive, and that universality is a common factor on Cyberspace. Catharsis, Instillation of Hope, Imparting Information and Altruism were also found in studies to be helpful in Internet support groups. However, the corrective recapitulation of the primary family, might not work for everyone. In addition, they identified that two other factors, typical of the Large Group, such as representation of society and the struggle for power exist on the Internet as well.

In contrast to Internet forums, there is no reason to believe that any of those therapeutic factors would not work in online groups using video, however, it might take more time for the group to develop a sense of belonging and cohesion, so change might take more time online. On the other hand, just as it happens in text-based forums, universality and existential factors are strengthened online. The possibility of expanding human limitations beyond time and space, rising above the restrictions of physical existence, to create a disembodied interaction, and allowing an experience that crosses boundaries, is very powerful. If we see the group as a social microcosm (Yalom and Leszsz, 2005), online there is a greater chance to gather people from different cultures, so diversity is prominent and many times the group becomes a concrete representation of society, a factor identified by Weinberg and Weishut (2012) as typical to large groups.

Transference to the group-as-a-whole is one of the important factors distinguishing individual therapy from a group setting. In f2f groups, in addition to the regular transference and countertransference towards the therapist (the group leader in the case of the group), people experience also the horizontal transference toward one another (the Foulksian small t transference, as mentioned above), but also transference (and counter-transference, by the therapist) towards the entire group. Does this element appear online? As said earlier, both in text-based forums and in video group setting, we lose the circle form of the f2f group. This might make it more difficult to experience the group-as-a-whole, and we might have to rely solely on our imagination. However, actually, the group-as-a-whole is another abstract concept, and we always use our imagination to perceive the group as an entity. Weinberg (2016) included online groups as an example of "impossible groups that thrive and flourish in leaking containers," as Cyberspace is a huge, boundless, unlimited container, which threatens the sense of safety, privacy and confidentiality. He claimed that these groups succeed due to the secure presence of the group conductor, holding the reflective space in his/her mind, and the group members having a fantasized invisible group in their mind. It might take more time and become more complicated to do so online, but it is still possible.

Setting and Dynamic Administration

In the introduction to this book, we mentioned that one of the unnoticed differences between in-person (f2f) therapy and online one, is the fact that in online therapy the therapist lost control over the setting. We clarified that although it seems like a subtle change, it has a huge influence on the session, due to the impact of the setting on therapeutic processes. In group therapy this change has a specific meaning and emphasis.

Foulkes focused on the importance of the "dynamic administration." The conductor takes charge of the administration of the group's setting and translates "external material" brought within these boundaries, where appropriate, as matter pertaining to the dynamic flow of communication "here and now." This is why Foulkes (1975: Chapter 6) calls this task, which includes attending to events at and beyond the boundaries of the group, ever in the service of the group's better understanding of its experience, "dynamic administration." This concept conveys the message that administrating the group, taking care of its environment and even physical setting, carries a deep dynamic meaning. Administrative functions provide the group with a sense of safety and continuity, and enhance a dynamic flow of communication. Therapists tend not to pay attention to the impact of their physical actions on their patients, because they usually focus on psychological processes. However, actions such as arranging the group seating in a circle, with sufficient comfortable chairs (all of them similar to one another), with enough (but not too much) space between them – are crucial for a healthy group function. Symbolically, the group analyst is acting like a maternal figure creating a holding environment for the group.

In small f2f groups the holding function of the group leader is similar to the work of the blue-collar worker. The leader provides the basic conditions for making the environment comfortable. The group members should be free of worries about the physical environment in order to be able to work on their psychological issues. How does the group leader achieve this function on the Internet (both in forums and in video setting)? In the simplest form, holding occurs by being available to quickly respond to technical questions and solving technological difficulties. We need to remember that many adults participating in virtual communication still feel anxious when they enter this unknown country and behave like immigrants who do not know the norms and language, who depend on their children's competence and skills navigating in this scary land. Of course, younger participants who were born into the Internet era might not need this leader's technical help.

Conducting group therapy through the Internet imposes severe challenges for this dynamic administration. If we conduct it by text messages, in an asynchronic forum (such as Google Groups, or a text application such as WhatsApp), we have no way of creating this physical holding environment. Those Internet groups, text-based, resemble more a boundless, new, unsafe and unknown environment, especially for those inexperienced with technology. However, sometimes, the mere fact that the group therapist can handle technical difficulties, or even just subscribes the members to the forum, makes the members feel that someone is taking care of them. When we move to a group video setting, which requires even more technological skills, the technical assistance of the therapist is no less important. This does not mean that the group therapist should be an IT expert, but that s/he should certainly be more experienced in overcoming technical difficulties than the average group member. In a way, the group therapist should compensate for the loss of the control on the setting by developing suitable online administrative functions.

Add to these considerations the fact, mentioned above, that the online group loses its classical format of people sitting in a circle. In a f2f group, when the group therapist arranges the chairs for the group in a circle (at least in private practice), this closed circular form, with its archaic associations of a womb, conveys the unconscious meaning of a perfect maternal container. Most of the group therapy theories cherish the availability of such a safe and good-enough container in order to work through deep unconscious psychological group processes. Moving from the physical reality to cyberspace tears this container apart. In text-based groups, no circle is evident at all. In video-conferencing groups (e.g. using Zoom application), group members are shown on the screen in boxes, one besides, above and below the other, with no specific order. Actually, we do not even have the same order on all the screens, as each computer is generating a different group composition.

The fact that group members decide from where they connect to the meeting, allows them to control the background and actually "decorate" the meeting room in any way they choose. Some connect to the group from their office and some from their home. Sometimes they unconsciously choose a picture in the background that has an unconscious meaning and sometimes they deliberately think in advance about the background and "choreograph" their environment to make a specific impression. The group leader should be aware of the decoration and explore its meaning when appropriate. In one of my groups, a woman constantly chose to connect from a room with a huge picture of a general on a horse hanging behind her. After some time, the group members mentioned the picture and one of them said that it has a powerful impression on him. "Indeed, that was the impression I wanted to create," replied the woman.

Another topic mentioned in the introduction is the fact that many boundary crossings or even violations that therapists would not ignore when the patients are in their office, become transparent and ignored when it happens online. In a video group session, where there are many people on the screen, this obliviousness is even stronger, and the group usually joins the silence about the boundary crossing. Fortunately, when group therapists do notice that something is happening "in the background," they can recruit the group to work it through, and do not have to carry the burden of processing the event alone. The following group vignette is a good example of such a case:

In an online group using video conferencing, one of the participants, Sima, that had missed the previous session, appeared on the screen sitting in the back seat of a car, probably a cab, using her iPhone to connect to the group. The group members wondered what happened to her that she had been absent last time, but nobody mentioned the fact that she is in a car with someone else driving it. After a while, when the group leader saw that the group continues to ignore the situation, he wondered aloud whether he is the only one that noticed that Sima is on her iPhone in a car, and how do people feel about it.

One group member, Nora, said that she doesn't feel safe and she is worried about confidentiality, to which Sima replied that it is okay because she does not know the driver, so she feels free to talk about anything she wants. This response enraged some group members who felt that she does not consider their privacy. Another member, Fiona, was concerned that Sima will not be able to emotionally connect with the group while her attention would be on the road. Hella, on the other hand, expressed her sympathy with Sima, saying how glad she is that Sima did not want to miss this group session as well, and made the effort to connect despite her not being at home. Sima was touched by this empathic response and acknowledged that she wanted to eat the cake and have it all: drive to an important business meeting and still not miss the group. She asked the group what they think she should do. Nora said that she still feels unsafe and wanted Sima to leave the session and come back next time, connecting from home. David joined her, saying that Sima violated the rules and the agreement they all have made entering the group.

After a lengthy discussion, the group leader decided that a decision should be made: He suggested that Sima leave the group session and welcomed her to join next session and discuss it. Sima became rageful, shouted that the group and its leader act like machines, in a nonhuman way, and that she doesn't want to be there anymore. She disconnected her iPhone and disappeared. The group continued to process their feelings for the rest of the session, shifting between people expressing anger at Sima and the group leader (who should have intervened earlier, in their opinion), and between people fearing that they will be rejected if they deviated from some group norms. The group leader encouraged them to express their feelings, saying how important it is to allow different opinions and attitudes, and that safety is about the freedom to discuss difficult issues no less than setting boundaries.

The next meeting Sima showed up as usual, in her home, to the relief of everyone (including the group leader). After they expressed this relief and wanted to move forward, the group leader suggested discussing the dramatic events from last meeting. Following some conversation, Sima thanked everyone for the previous meeting, saying that she thought a lot about what has happened and her strong emotional reaction. She brought memories of rejection by her family of origin and peers. Other members who had felt rejected through their life, joined her. These two meetings became a turning point for the group and increased the ability of the members to express differences and to feel safe in opening up.

In order to deal with the fact that the group members determine most of the group setting and to gain back some control over the "dynamic administration," the group therapist should instruct the members in advance how to create the suitable environment for which they should take responsibility. This should be done partly in the preparation meeting-(s). It goes without saying that although some group members live thousands of miles away, the group therapist should never give up a screening and preparation meeting with the group candidates, just as the standard practice of in-person therapy, even though it has to be done online. In that preview meeting, the group therapist checks the suitability of the member for group therapy in general, and the specific group in particular, prepares the candidate for the group meetings, and educates him or her about the conditions that the group member should keep in order to maintain safety and confidentiality. The group agreement (which should be also sent to the candidate as a document) should include a specific paragraph about online "etiquettes" in order to adjust to the fact that the therapist does not control the group members' environments any more. Here are some sentences from my online group using a video setting: "The group members agree to connect with both video and audio, unless other arrangements are made on occasion. To arrange for a quiet room with full privacy and no interruptions. This includes no phone calls, emails or texting during the entire session. To stay focused on the group interactions. To connect from the same place each session, unless you are away and notify us of the change."

As said in the introduction to this book, in online therapy we need to overcome the media barrier and find ways to be present despite the mediated communication, causing disconnection and distraction. It requires special attention from the group therapist to stay connected in the session and be attentive to all the group members. However, sometimes these technological obstacles obscure other difficulties in close relationship, and we can easily fall into the trap of "blaming" the online modality for members' difficulties to be in touch and connect emotionally with one another.

Another group vignette:

Karin joined an online process group led by the author after participating in an intensive workshop he was leading in a professional conference. In that workshop she was very impressed by the group leader's skills and felt that he understood her deeply. She perceived him as giving her special attention and being very attuned to her. However, a few months after she had joined the weekly online group she felt very disappointed. She did not feel as special as she felt in the intensive f2f workshop and she thought that she does not draw the leader's attention as she expected. She said something about losing his attention in the group, but the topic was not explored much further.

A few weeks later she wrote an email to the group leader, letting him know that she considers leaving the group. She blamed it on the fact that it is an online group and that she cannot build the connection she is used to create in a group meeting in-person. She wrote that the online format did not work very well for her. She added that there is something about not being in the same physical space at the same time that presents a barrier to the group process for her.

The group leader suggested that she will bring this issue for discussion in the group, sticking to the common practice of in-person groups that everything relevant to the group process that is discussed outside the group, should be brought back to the group, especially when someone considers termination. She agreed and in the next online group session she told the group that she does not think that the online format suits her. As usual with such announcements, people's reactions varied between expressing sorrow and sadness and between being irritated. They did not suggest exploring her motives further. Eventually, the group leader asked whether it means that they agree with her that the online modality does not allow for "real" connection. This intervention helped the discussion to deepen, and one member suggested that perhaps there are other issues that block her ability to connect. The group leader reminded her how disappointed she was about not getting enough attention from him and wondered whether it was more meaningful than she had allowed herself to imagine or experience.

After the conversation began to move away from this dialogue between Karin and the leader, Nina said, "Karin, I can see that the connection between you and Haim (the group therapist) is important to you right now, and I want you to have that. I want to do whatever I can to help you have it." Karin became tearful and was deeply touched by this sacrifice. She remembered that in her family of origin, her youngest sister always received her father's full attention and she painfully longed for him to pay attention for her as well. She was shocked that this group "sister" of her did not play the role she had expected. All the group members were touched by Nina's generosity. When the group leader asked Nina whether she can reflect on her motivation, Nina understood that Karin was her "sister," too, that in fact, at that point in time, Nina's father was battling the end stages of cancer, and Nina desperately wanted her own sister to receive the validation of her relationship with their father. Nina had the opportunity to realize the painful impact of her sister's longing to be validated by their father.

We can see in this vignette how easy it can be to accept the member's arguments about the impossibility of "real" online connection as the only truth, and ignore the important exploration of other barriers. When we do remember to do so, the results might be reconnecting and very satisfying.

The Disembodied Group

Creating a holding environment (Winnicott, 1960) is one of the main tasks of the group therapist. The group members need to feel securely held by a maternal container (Rutan, Stone and Shay, 2014). Maintaining the group's external boundaries is one way of holding the group and making the members feel protected, and we have discussed above the difficulty of doing it online. Another way of holding the group is through the leader's gaze. Just like the mother's mirroring, looking at the infant with glittering eyes, making him or her feel accepted, worthy and even admired, the group therapist looks at every group member, sustaining his/her gaze, encouraging the member to speak out or making them feel appreciated for what they said. This look is essential in fulfilling the need of group members for mirroring, as Kohut (1971) reminds us in individual therapy. Of course, members of the group can also get approval and satisfy their mirroring transference needs by looking at one another. This important gaze is clearly lacking in online groups. Even if the group therapist tries deliberately to look at a specific member in video meetings, this member will not be able to perceive that.

The gaze is only one aspect in the important presence of the body in therapy in general, and group therapy in particular. The interpersonal neurobiological (IPNB) perspective enabled clinicians in understanding interpersonal aspects of brain functions, and especially in developing models of the social brain (Badenoch, 2008; Cozolino, 2006). It has been applied successfully to group therapy (see a special issue on this topic of the *International Journal of Group Psychotherapy*, edited by Susan Gantt and Paul Cox, 2010). Integration between the body, the limbic system, and the neocortex is necessary for wellbeing. As Siegel writes: "Integration is seen to be the heart of health. Transformative experiences recruit the sharing of information and energy flow within relationships to actively move the synaptically stuck brain to fire off in new ways—ones that are now shaped toward integration" (2010: 484). In the IPNB approach, much emphasis is put on the emotional regulative impact that the physical and emotional presence of the group therapist has on different group members (and sometimes the regulation that group members exert on one another). In Cyberspace all this seems to be lost, and the question is whether anything can replace it. My answer is that the there are other ways for the group therapist to become present and compensate for the "loss of the body."

The Group Therapist's Presence

One of the ways to overcome "the media barrier" is by a more intensive use of the therapist's self (compared to groups that meet in-person). Most of the time this can be achieved by a certain self-disclosure of the group therapist. The traditional psychoanalytic approach discards disclosing of personal details of the (group) therapist's life and history, and recommends that the therapist remains a blank screen, mostly in order to allow for projections and the development of pure transference. Yalom and Leszsz (2005) distinguish between two kinds of self-disclosure, one regarding the personal life of the therapist (information from the there-and-then), and the other is about the therapist's feelings in the group (which is actually emphasizing the here-and-now). They recommend that the group thera- pist will practice transparency of the second kind and they claim that the therapist who judiciously uses his or her own person increases the therapeutic power of the group. Such a transparency can become a model for group members to reveal their feelings toward one another. Of course, this use of self should be executed cautiously, always bearing in mind that the end goal is the benefit of the group members and not the relief for the group therapist. Online, this transparency can become a very useful tool to show group members how to overcome the difficulty that the screen imposes. It might be easier for intersubjectively-informed self psychologists, who stress therapist attunement and empathy, than for conservative therapists. Although this recommendation can be applied to online individual therapy as well, it is especially applicable in groups therapy because unlike individual psychotherapy, in the group setting the therapist is not the sole object of patients' transference projections (Durkin and Glatzer, 1997).

Cohen and Schermer (2001) provide some directions when to use trans- parency in the group: "The therapist's self disclosure is likely to be an effective element of the total therapeutic process insofar as: (1) the group's develop- mental level has prepared members to contain the disclosure without it being a 'shock to the system' (Rachman, 1990), (2) the act of disclosure is perceived as spontaneous and appropriate to the group's ongoing discursive content, and (3) the therapist's disclosure clearly, even if implicitly, accords legitimacy to the member behavior to which it is 'responsive'" (Bacal, 1998). In short, I recommend that the group therapist discloses positive attitudes toward group members, only when the group reaches advanced stages (see Berman and Weinberg, 1998).

Especially powerful and connecting are the group therapist's interven- tions in which he or she takes responsibility for mistakes s/he has made in approaching some group members. When the therapist notices some subtle expression of dissatisfaction of a group member (say, by a facial expression that in an online video meeting can be noticed more easily because of the close-up posture), reflects on his or her intervention, checks with the participant and acknowledges the mistake, it usually has a strong impact on the member and the entire group. For many group members, it creates a corrective experience as a contrast to parents who never admitted or acknowledged their mistakes. Apparently, many people who still carry scars from their parents' insensitive attitude towards them in childhood, hold the fantasy that their parents will ask for their forgiveness. When the group therapist notices the hurt online and acknowledges the mistake, it is especially impressive because it overcomes the "screen barrier" and helps the group members feel that they can also stay sensitive and compassionate despite the limitations of online connection.

Here is an example:

In an online group using video conferencing, one of the group members, Sheila, requested feedback from the group, saying that she is usually satisfied with her life, happy and easy going, wondering whether she is denying something. Some group members said that they find it hard to believe that she is always content. Summarizing their responses, the group leader suggested to Sheila that her limited range of emotions is perceived superficial to the group members. The leader noticed that some group members' facial expressions online seemed shocked or irritated (but not Sheila's). After some reflection, he got back to Sheila and said that he wanted to correct his previous intervention, because it might have been understood as if Sheila is superficial, which was not the therapist's intention. He corrected himself by telling Sheila that when she only expresses joy and never any sign of irritation, dissatisfaction or any negative emotions, it makes it difficult for him, the group leader, to get closer to Sheila. She had a strong emotional reaction to this intervention and later on it became clear how much her parents did not allow for any emotional strong reaction, and never acknowledged that they had made mistakes.

In this example the group leader's intervention combined both elements recommended above: Acknowledging a mistake and being transparent. The online component intensified the power of this intervention for both Sheila and the other group members.

In Summary

Online groups present a special challenge for the group therapist, greater than in online individual therapy, mostly because of the many factors involved that include the different members and the group-as-a-whole dynamics. The dilemma of staying present, focused and attuned is intensified, and the fact that the group therapist does not control the setting, thus posing obstacles to the "dynamic administration," makes the group leading even more challenging. However, with enough awareness of the obstacles, trying not to ignore the subtle background events and decoration, and finding ways to stay connected, the group can thrive and become no less successful than in in-person group, although sometimes in a slower pace. If we want to go online, we need to be aware of the similarities and differences pointed out in this chapter. We might need new concepts, and it might be essential to go through specific training (only after being experienced enough in leading group in-person). As for the question of whether a new theory is need, group therapy online might not be the same as when it is done f2f – but it is not that different.

References

Bacal, H. (1998). Notes on optimal responsiveness in the group process. In H. Harwood & M. Pines, (Eds) *Self Experiences in Group: Intersubjective and Self Psychological Pathways to Human Understanding* (pp. 175–180). London and Philadelphia: Jessica Kingsley and Taylor & Francis.

Badenoch, B. (2008). *Being a Brain-wise Therapist: A Practical Guide to Interpersonal Neurobiology*. New York: Norton.

Berman, A., & Weinberg, H. (1998). The advanced stage therapy group. *International Journal of Group Psychotherapy*, 48(4): 499–518.

Bersani, L., & Phillips, A. (2008). *Intimacies*. Chicago: The University of Chicago Press.

Cohen, B.D., & Schermer, V.L. (2001). Therapist self disclosure in group psychotherapy from an intersubjective and self psychological standpoint. *Group*, 25(1–2).

Cozolino, L. (2006). *The Neuroscience of Human Relationships: Attachment and the Developing Social Brain*. New York: Norton.

Durkin, H.E., & Glatzer, H.T. (1997). Transference neurosis in group psychotherapy: The concept and the reality. *International Journal of Group Psychotherapy*, 47: 183–199.

Foulkes, S.H. (1964). *Therapeutic Group Analysis*. London: George Allen and Unwin.

Gantt, S., & Cox, P. (2010) Introduction to the special issue: Neurobiology and building interpersonal systems: Groups, couples, and beyond. *International Journal of Group Psychotherapy*, 60(4): 455–460.

Kohut, H. (1971). *The Analysis of the Self: A Systematic Approach to the Psychoanalytic Treatment of Narcissistic Personality Disorders*. New York: International Universities Press.

Prager, K.J. (1995). *The Psychology of Intimacy*. New York: The Guilford Press.

Rachman, A.W. (1990). Judicious self-disclosure in group analysis. *Group*, 14(3): 132–144.

Rutan, S.J., Stone, N.W., & Shay, J.J. (2014). *Psychodynamic Group Psychotherapy*, 5th edition. New York: Guilford Press.

Safran, J.D., & Segal, Z.V. (1990). *Interpersonal Process in Cognitive Therapy*. New York: Basic Books.

Schlapobersky, J.R. (2016) *From the Couch to the Circle: Group-analytic Psychotherapy in Practice*. London: Routledge.

Scholz, R. (2011). The foundation matrix and the social unconscious. In E. Hopper & H. Weinberg (Eds) *The Social Unconscious in Persons, Groups and Societies, Volume 1: Mainly Theory* (pp. 265–285). London: Karnac.

Siegel, D.J. (2010) Commentary on "integrating interpersonal neurobiology with group psychotherapy": Reflections on mind, brain, and relationships in group psychotherapy. *International Journal of Group Psychotherapy*, 60(4): 483–485.

Turquet, P. (1975). Threats to identity in the large group. In L. Kreeger (Ed.), *The Large Group: Dynamics and Therapy* (pp. 87–144). London: Karnac.

Weinberg, H. (2014). *The Paradox of Internet Groups: Alone in the Presence of Virtual Others*. London: Karnac.

Weinberg, H. (2016). Impossible groups that flourish in leaking containers: Challenging group analytic theory. *Group Analysis*, 49(4): 330–349.

Weinberg, H., & Schneider, S. (2003). Introduction: Background, structure and dynamics of the large group. In S. Schneider & H. Weinberg (Eds) *The Large Group Revisited: The Herd, Primal Horde, Crowds and Masses*. London: Jessica Kingsley.

Weinberg, H., & Weishut, D.J.N. (2012). The large group: Dynamics, social implications and therapeutic value. In J.L. Kleinberg, (ed.) *The Wiley-Blackwell Handbook of Group Psychotherapy* (pp. 457–479). New York: Wiley-Blackwell.

Winnicott, D.W. (1960). The theory of parent–child relationship. *International Journal of Psychoanalysis, 4*: 585–595.

Yalom, I.D. (1970). *The Theory and Practice of Group Psychotherapy*, 1st edition. New York: Basic Books.

Yalom, I.D., & Leszsz, M. (2005). *The Theory & Practice of Group Psychotherapy*, 5th edition. New York: Basic Books.

16 Transformations Through the Technological Mirror

Raúl Vaimberg and Lara Vaimberg

Introduction

In recent decades, there has been a breakthrough in technological developments leading to significant changes in our minds as well as our ways of understanding our grouping forms and social life.

The global village idea (McLuhan, 1967), together with the psychoanalytic reading that explains the origin of culture in totemic societies (Freud, 1913), allow us to have a vision of these micro and macro sociological changes. According to this theory, current society would be like a globalized village in which the organizing totem of these small primitive groups is replaced by modern technology.

Life on the screens (Turkle, 1995) is a significant part of our contemporary world, on two opposite extremes: the fears that every new sociocultural advance generates, that leads us to imagine a hyper connected world but in solitude; and a modality of hybrid virtual-f2f functionality. This functionality allows, especially for today's young people, simultaneous connections in both virtual and f2f (face-to-face) spaces, in an unlocalized and global matrix relationship and with access to an unprecedented digitized memory capacity in the entirety of our civilization's development.

In the field of online group psychotherapy, we can count on this enormous described potential, but we must also consider the effects that psychopathologies can produce in the use and meaning that is given to these technologies.

We define online group psychotherapy as a psychological procedure that considers the same objectives as f2f group psychotherapy and uses different online communication devices as instruments to connect the group.

In this chapter we will discuss the similarities and differences between online and f2f group psychotherapy. We will elaborate on some preliminary theoretical ideas on technology and mental apparatus, as well as the basics of online psychotherapy with its essential components. We will examine the possible applications in virtual, f2f and mixed environments and how they adapt to the psychopathological characteristics of group participants.

Finally, we will present two studies: A three-year work of a technology-mediated psychotherapy group and a case on the use of video games in the group approach of children and adolescents diagnosed with Autism Spectrum Disorders (ASD).

Mental Apparatus and Technology

We think that the development and systematization of methods of technology-mediated group approaches could produce fundamental changes in the mismatch between demands and offers existing in the public and private mental health systems.

These new virtual spaces, which together are called "cyberspace", are built through the network connection made possible by Information and Communication Technologies (ICT). According to their different applications in mental health, they can be classified as follows (Vaimberg, 2005):

1. In primary health, as a means for the promotion and prevention of mental health.
2. In secondary and tertiary prevention, as a means for intervention in mental health problems.
3. As a vehicle to improve public systems and mental health management.
4. As a tool for the training of mental health agents.

The relationship with technology can be perceived as a prosthesis within the mental apparatus representation. In *the narcissistic relationship type*, the other (Figure 16.1, in dark gray) exists only as a part of oneself (the other is included within oneself). In *the support relationship type* a part of the self generates an extension to meet the other, now experienced as something external to the self. In *the technological prosthesis relationship type* the black segments represent technology as an extension of the self, which mediates the relationship with the other, affecting the sensoperceptive apparatus in general. It's a type of inter-objective relationship that influences and is influenced by intersubjectivity (Figure 16.1).

The third model of relationship, technological prosthesis type, could well represent the virtual environment's matrix in a normal person, this interconnection of different technological prosthesis, allows digitalization and communication of the self with the virtual other.

There are people who can develop psychological distress and social deterioration symptoms caused by the amount and quality of Internet connection. These addictive relationships tend to coincide with other pathologies and especially with social isolation.

The Myth of Narcissus and the Technological Mirror

The myth of Narcissus represents the eternal dilemma between self-love and love for others. Psychic life begins with a fusion experience that leads

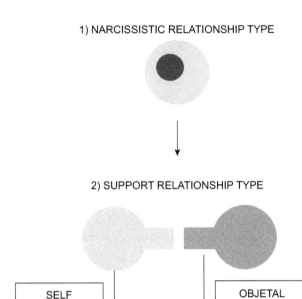

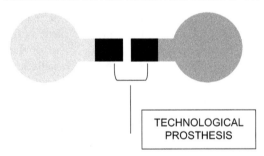

Figure 16.1 Narcissistic, support and technological prosthesis relationships

to the fantasy that there is only one body and psyche for two people. When the mother–child relationship is "good enough" (Winnicott, 1979), a progressive differentiation develops in the young child's psychic structuring between his own body and the first representation of the external body that is the maternal body.

In technology-mediated relationships, if the personality structure has narcissistic characteristics, it is more likely that it cannot establish an intersubjective communication, since the other will only be a reflection of itself or the self will only be a reflection of the other, an echo.

This conceptualization explains a series of Internet communication pathologies. By not seeing the other's image, as well as the body elements that intervene in communication (especially touch and smell), the narcissistic relationship is enhanced. In addition, the distance established by written communication, asynchronic in time, produces a dislocation in space that facilitates the other's discrimination. We are facing a 'technological mirror' that will reflect a different image to that of the Narcissus pond. In cases of online communication by videoconference, in addition to being able to see the members of the group, the image of oneself is reflected on the screen, which may influence the characteristics of online group communication.

The 'technological mirror' is formed by a variety of technological artifacts interconnected through electronic networks, capable of recognizing, memorizing and hypertextualizing. Several texts and images can appear on the screen simultaneously, allowing the participant to make their own edition or an active and personal interpretation of the hypertext. The richness or poverty of the technological mirror and the connection characteristics between the virtual and f2f mirrors will strengthen the narcissistic positioning or facilitate the intersubjective constructions.

Online Psychotherapy Bases

Techno-social Structure and Psychopathologic Structure

Online interventions are more effective if there is an adequate adjustment between the technical and social characteristics of the virtual communication and the characteristics of a person's psychopathological structure or groups connected to a specific techno-social device.

The individual's personality structure, connected to the network, produces different subjective experiences with which the individual perceives itself and the relationship with the other in virtual environments. These subjective experiences determine different ways of moving through the interface between virtual and f2f, online-offline environments. For example, in a group of neurotic patients (see case 1 below) patients with paranoid characteristics have great difficulty to communicate effectively in the virtual space, the unerasability and unchangeability of the intervention is found threatening, and they find it easier to communicate in the f2f space. The opposite occurs in patients with phobic characteristics, who usually express themselves more freely in the virtual space, becoming anxious in direct contact.

In another example, in a group of patients diagnosed with ASD (see case 2 below) who work in person through a virtual reality platform, relationship difficulties with their companions are moderated in the online space and can be helped more easily. The contact within the virtual space is more concrete and protected than that of the f2f space. For example, in one session, one of the members in a virtual game lost the thread of the activity online and did not respond to his colleagues requesting his attention.

The therapeutic team can work on the need for isolation and the children's communication, using their experiences through the game, while taking into account their character. This gives them a useful distance to address personal issues indirectly through a game they like.

Virtual and f2f Relationship

As much as possible, we prefer to mix virtual and f2f frames, since they strengthen the benefits and reduce risks. We can consider the advantages and disadvantages of each of these environments (see Table 16.1).

Use of the Characteristics of Online Communication

The computer screen stands as a transitional space, resulting in a diversity of projections determined by the connected participants personality characteristics, as well as those of the online connected groups. We can develop the following online communication's general aspects:

1. *Immersion.* In psychoanalytic terms, the virtual space can be considered an extension of the intrapsychic space. It can be experienced as a transitional space between the self and the other, which is partly oneself and partly the other. This feature allows us to have the experience of being inside the screen.
2. *Disinhibition effect, screen effect.* When a person separates his actions from his real world and his identity, he feels less vulnerable, as well as a decrease in responsibility for the effects of taken actions. There is an operational dissociation between the person and the character that is represented in a certain scenario.
3. *Non-specific space.* The extension of the global village in cyberspace is one of the greatest potential characteristics. This can connect people with geographical limitations or disabilities. In technology-mediated group psychotherapies, group cohesion is especially favored by this communication characteristic.
4. *Timeless time.* In all types of online communication there is a delay from seconds to minutes or days between a message and its response, a time that is effectively different from f2f communication. This time gap generates a space for reflection and delay that might be beneficial. The possibility of editing text, image and sound allows to alter the story's temporal sequence of lived events.
5. *Fragmentation of the self.* In modalities that use asynchronous textual communication such as forums, it is possible to project fears or problems but in a fragmented way. This fragmentation might mean new protective or enriching defensive aspects of the self or the lifting of repression and expression of aggressive, destructive and disintegrating aspects of the internal world.

Table 16.1 Virtual, f2f and mixed environments. Advantages and disadvantages.

	F2f environment	Virtual environment	Alternating virtual and face-to-face environment
Advantages	Synchronous and multisensory perception facilitates the intensity and quality of communication. Shared emotional experience as well as collective phenomena is made possible.	Time and space boundaries do not exist, facilitating meetings. It has a large memory capacity. The 'disinhibition' effect or 'screen effect' allows people to express and recognize their fears or conflicts. The delayed time between the message and its response can be beneficial for reflection, the expression of ideas and feelings, and the possibility of researching oneself.	The continuous virtual space created by online meetings between f2f sessions allows the interaction to extend beyond the space–time of the f2f session, facilitating group cohesion and therapeutic alliance. As a result of the permanent rotation between virtual and f2f environments, a space for elaboration and reflection is created. The psychic fragmentation experience★ is eased by the mixed modality of online/offline communication.
Disadvantages	In certain psychopathological structures, such as borderline, direct presence can promote too intense and threatening transference. There are major complications related to f2f meetings in terms of schedules, absences and relocation.	The virtual communication structure allows erroneous interpretations of the meaning of what has been said, including massive projections. The experience of permanent presence created by the virtual forum can generate the emergence of paranoid defensive mechanisms and control experiences or merging fantasies. Passivity and silence are more difficult to interpret or to contain in the virtual forum. The 'disinhibition' or 'screen effect' allows the expression of violent or perverse aspects.	Possibility of splits between the f2f and the virtual experience. Those members who do not actively participate in the virtual space may feel alienated in f2f sessions.

Note: ★We consider the existence of three organizations or matrices of the self: integrated (neurotic syndromes), fragmented (border syndromes) and fused (psychotic syndromes). By psychic fragmentation we understand a state in which the self appears divided into different fragments. The depth and breadth of the crack that exists between these fragments will determine a greater or lesser tendency to recognize the different constituent parts of the self. In the border disorders this psychic fragmentation will produce identity alteration symptomatology, however in the neuroses, it will allow anguish attenuation and the possibility of resolving situations by parts, to later integrate them again with some transformation in their interior.

3.4 The Role of the Online Psychotherapist

The online psychotherapist should follow the rules established by the professional code, paying special attention to ethical issues related to network confidentiality and guaranteeing necessary professional accreditations. Given the special characteristics of the communication dynamics and the psychotherapeutic processes that are produced online, a specific theoretical-technical training is required that includes the characteristics of online therapy and the online therapist's role.

Different Environments and their Applications

In the study of online psychotherapy groups, we will describe three fundamental aspects: modality, interconnectivity and synchronicity. In these groups, we have access to different modalities: textual, hypertextual, online virtual reality platforms, collective creation platforms and videoconference.[1] All these modalities can be used in a uni-user or multiuser formats or in multigroup network structures and also in synchronous, asynchronous or mixed modes.

Throughout 15 years of experience we witnessed the evolution of communication modalities from textuality and asynchronicity to moving images and synchronicity. In the past, multi-user videoconferencing communication could only be used for a short time and with some technical difficulties. We have learned to differentiate the applications of the different techno-social tolls according to the particular characteristics of the people's psychopathology and of the treated groups.

As can be observed in Table 16.2, the textual and hypertextual modalities of online communication, due to the absence of non-verbal language, often generate frequent difficulties in the field of message interpretation, meaning that the severity of psychopathology increases. In contrast, environments that use preverbal resources, such as collective creation platforms, facilitate communication processes in pathologies where deeper regressive states occur.

In the neurotic pathologies, with a greater development of transitional space and creative capacity, textual communication can facilitate the unveiling of hidden contents. Videoconferencing is very useful in individual and family interventions but still has technical deficiencies in the approach of small and medium groups. Finally, virtual reality platforms are useful in the treatment of specific focused symptoms such as certain phobic disorders and are significantly helpful in different groups of children and adolescents.

Case Studies

In this section we will describe two research studies carried out in online psychotherapy groups. The first one lasted three years and consisted of a virtual group combined with an f2f psychotherapy group of neurotic

Table 16.2 Types of virtual modality and their adaptation to different psychopathological
structures. (XX: better adapted, X: less adapted.)

Modality	Neurosis	Personality disorders	Psychosis
Textual	XX	XX	X
Hypertextual	XX	XX	X
Video conference	XX	XX	–
Virtual reality	X Specific symptoms xx	X	XX
Collective creation platforms	X	XX	XX

Note: XX = better adapted; X = less adaptated

patients. The experience was carried out through an asynchronous textual online forum combined with a monthly session of four hours f2f. The second vignette was conducted in a group of adolescent patients diagnosed with Autism Spectrum Disorders (ASD) using virtual reality platforms.

Case 1 Friday Group

The Friday group worked for a couple of years in a classic format of weekly two-hour f2f sessions. Then, about 15 years ago, due to the new dynamics that daily and work life acquired, group absence had increased, and this affected achieving the group task. In one of those sessions, because I was late to the start of the group session beginning, they began to send messages to my mobile phone. This accidental event raised the idea that we could have the session online.

The idea was initially taken as a joke but slowly it started to acquire consistency and the group raised the possibility of holding a closed text forum for its participants. Everyone was enthusiastic about the project, one of its members (computer engineer) offered to build the platform and we decided to modify the structure by changing the f2f sessions to a four-hour monthly session in addition to the online forum, and to explore how the new online space worked. An asynchronous text forum was organized, open 24 hours a day, seven days a week, including holidays.

At first the feeling of entering an unknown and innovative terrain generated great enthusiasm, a new way of communication was being created. Little by little, new possibilities and difficulties offered by the forum were experienced. Once the f2f session arrived, a great deal of work had been done during the month, this produced a quick and intense start of the session. In the online forum, dreams were analyzed collectively, conflicting situations occurred during the month and even weekends, discussions and misunderstandings created, some days, a very high message circulation. New leaderships were appearing, some coincided with those of the f2f space but others were really new. We detected that some members participated more in one environment and others handled both in a similar way. The elaboration of this topic led to interesting discoveries about subjective experiences that the physical and virtual environment generated in each member. For example, the record of the written word was extremely disturbing for some participants, probably because of the permanence of what was said and the impossibility to modify or erase this information; others experienced the effects of virtual absence intensely, reacting strongly to periods of silence or response delay to some of the sent messages. The virtual presence sometimes generated feelings of idealized encounter, related to the fantasy of permanent unions in bonds that can last eternally. This experience continued for five years, three years for this study and two more years until the group finished its task.

Therapeutic Macro and Microprocesses Study in an Online Psychotherapy Group Using Text

Many classical socio-psychological principles of group dynamics can be applied to the understanding and improvement of these online groups, such as issues related to leadership, communication patterns, cohesion, the unconscious and the group mind, vital experience and collective creativity (Weinberg, 2014). However, the special psychological characteristics of 'cyberspace' determine that online groups dynamics can also be very different (Suler, 2000). We point out characteristics provided by text and hypertext communication, the greater equality of communication possibilities and the opportunity to alter or hide the participants identity.

The group consisted of eight participants, half of them male and half female, diagnosed with neurosis. This research work produced a doctoral thesis (Vaimberg, 2010).

Research Design

In this research, we used a mixed-method design, based on systematic observation; the qualitative data collected in the initial observation phase is transformed into quantitative data and subsequently interpreted qualitatively.

Material produced by the psychotherapy group was digitally self-registered in a textual and asynchronic online forum, which worked for three years, seven days a week and 24 hours a day. About 500 text pages, approximately 300,000 words.

CREATION OF AN INDIRECT OBSERVATION INSTRUMENT

An indirect observation non-standard instrument was elaborated *ad hoc*, based on the theoretical framework and produced text. The data analysis obtained criteria for the following themes: degree of presence, relationship to the other, emotionality, capacity for thought, positivity and realism. Based on each of these criteria, a system of categories was created (see Table 16.3).

The instrument was structured, for each dimension, in the form of rating scale. In the central positions of each dimension there are categories that describe mental states of equilibrium, while progressively moving from the center, in the extreme positions, to mental states that represent excesses or defects.

The results show that at the beginning the group moved cyclically between centered and extreme positions, creating crisis along the lifetime of the group. As the process evolved, both group and individual processes showed a tendency toward centralization and balance.

Table 16.3 Description of the PSICAT.G instrument. Studied dimensions

DA. Degree of presence	From overpresence experience to abandonment: A scale in which one extreme represents exhaustive control of the other, in the middle a balanced relational distance and ends with the feeling of non-existence of the other or extreme loneliness.
DB. Relationship to the other	From overidentification with others to isolation in the self: A scale that goes from fusion with the other, through a balance between self-love and love for the other, to the other extreme of melancholy identification feeling and self-absorption.
DC. Emotionality	From hyper-emotionality to alexithymia: The experience of hyperthymia and emotional lability, through states of emotional balance and ending with emotional coldness, alexithymia or psychosomatic diseases.
DE. Capacity for thought	From hyperrationality to irrational action: On one pole, the capacity for abstraction and rationalizing tendencies, going through a balance between thinking and acting, and reaching impulsive anger and violence situations or suicidal actions.
DF. Positivity	From hypomanic positivity to depressive pessimism: Great optimism or euphoria, going through balanced assessments of the positive and negative aspects of the self and relationships with others and reaching situations of life dissatisfaction, anhedonia and apathy.
DG. Realism	From hyperrealism to derealization: From adaptation to reality, through situations of modulation between reality and fantasy, and reaching immersions in a world of fantasy, delirium or hallucination.

A qualitative interpretation of the results was performed, detecting different macro and micro therapeutic processes. Therapeutic macroprocesses (across long time periods) showed a marked tendency to develop in phases partly conditioned by the following contextual characteristics: 1) the frame; 2) group task objectives; and 3) the extragroup reality characteristics. Therapeutic microprocesses were collected from the analysis of short and continuous group text sequences.

THERAPEUTIC MACROPROCESSES

Therapeutic macroprocesses are understood as the study of the therapeutic transformations observed along prolonged sequences of group interaction, such as a month or in phases of group dynamics. There are several authors who describe the phases through which a psychotherapy group goes through (Lewin, Tuckman, Pichon Rivière) We describe 5 phases (Vaimberg, 2012) existing similarities and some differences with online psychotherapy.[2] In these macroprocesses we analyze the different communicational leaderships as well as the development of the emotional and intersubjective states of the group.

We also analyzed the position in which every member is located within the network, based on one's attributions and the different relationships that were established.

THERAPEUTIC MICROPROCESSES

Therapeutic microprocesses study the moments of therapeutic transformation observed in short sequences or in hidden patterns of group interaction. The systematic study of these microprocesses allows us to visualize more clearly the brief constellations of group interaction phenomena and intersections of emotional experiences that affect the production of subjectivity transformations.

Case 1 Conclusions

ONLINE PSYCHOTHERAPY GROUP BENEFITS AND RISKS

The creation of a continuous virtual space between f2f group sessions, allowed group interaction to extend beyond the space-time of the f2f session, clearly facilitating group cohesion. From the permanent transfer between both virtual and f2f environments, an elaboration space arose around both spaces that facilitated the discrimination and stabilization process of intersubjective relations.

The forum's communication structure, through written language, sometimes created erroneous interpretations of the meaning of what was said and the possibility that these would be anchored in the virtual space. We found out that passivity and silence are more difficult to interpret in the forum.

Regarding the benefits and risks of online group psychotherapy, we can conclude that the fluctuation of virtual and f2f therapeutic environments offers a series of benefits that outnumber the risks observed, providing new therapeutic possibilities, reducing their respective risks and generating new problems that require the development of innovative solutions.

CHARACTERISTICS OF GROUP DYNAMICS

The personality structure characteristics of the individual connected to the network, determine the different subjective experiences in virtual environments, as well as different ways of acting in virtual and f2f, online-offline environments.

The experience of psychic fragmentation, emerging as one of the online communication characteristics, was lessened by the mixed modality of the communication system employed online-offline. Despite this, we collected sufficient qualitative data to affirm the existence of this psyche fragmentation characteristic. We also observed that the incidence of this phenomenon in different participants had favorable effects on the therapeutic process or generated new difficulties and that the predominance different tendencies was related to the previous personality structure of each subject. For example, a group participant, frequently experienced situations of confusion and conflict with his f2f group companions, due to a marked use of projective identification mechanisms. In the online text group, he was able to develop a capacity for literary creation through metaphors and narrations that referred to experiences of his internal world and the internal world of his peers. The temporal space distance provided by the online device had a beneficial effect on his intersubjective group experience.

Cyberspace is constituted as a special space in a transition between the inside and the outside (transitional space), with a physical support made of electronic devices connected in a network that make possible an intersubjective experience among the people connected to the network at a certain moment.

Regarding the group macroprocess, the detailed study of centered categories/extreme categories made it possible to detect the existence of group macroprocesses of cyclical characteristics, each group phase having specific characteristics.

Finally, we think that the group process in general is characterized by evolving crises as the group dynamics progresses through new problems and conflicts.[3] The group process works like a spiral, with each phase working on similar issues but on a deeper level.

ANALYSIS OF THERAPEUTIC TRANSFORMATION MECHANISMS

We detected the existence of specific therapeutic processes and micro-processes in online group psychotherapies when considering moments of transformation or individual or group insight. We detected 74 moments of therapeutic transformation that we studied by interpreting the micropro-cesses that allowed these transformations. These studies showed character-istics of category centralization in the different studied dimensions.

Finally, we would like to emphasize that we consider that the possibi-lities offered by online group psychotherapy in terms of the development of group psychotherapeutic processes are sufficiently demonstrated. We used specialized software in this research and found out that it helps in exploring therapeutic processes and microprocesses. It can support clinical research and deepen the methods of therapeutic processes evaluation.

Case 2: Video Games in the Group Approach of Children and Adolescents Diagnosed with ASD

In the case below, the use of virtual reality platforms in the group treatment of children diagnosed with ASD is addressed. The group consisted of four children between the ages of 11 and 14 and two therapists: a psychologist and an educator with experience in the use of video games.

The group basically worked with the Minecraft video game (see Figure 16.2), which all participants knew before starting therapy. This is an online construction game, a fiction planet where collective constructions can be produced. According to Vaimberg (2012), solitary games, in which one competes with oneself, can keep a young person connected to the computer in an absolute narcissistic withdrawal. Online games encourage virtualized contact with the other. The type of spontaneous choice of computer games that people perform depends on the different needs of the individual connected to the network.

The choice of the game is determined, in part, by the interests of the group participants. It is important to work with a virtual support that fulfills these essential characteristics: 1) facilitating interaction between participants; 2) allowing group participants to decide freely about their act and having an open story; and 3) there is a task to be carried out, creative or collective in nature, encouraging the establishing of common objectives.

From this perspective, virtual reality is presented as a transitional space that allows the transfer of representations and emotions that come from factual reality and that affect the psychic reality. The screen, then, is structured as a place for staging situations from the participants internal world, the interactions that take place between them and where situations that occur in the screen's virtual space can be elaborated later in the f2f space.

Figure 16.2 Minecraft video game screenshot

General Objectives of the ASD and Virtual Reality Groups

Firstly, we create a space for group participation where we can work on the relationship and communication difficulties that follow the pathology. A mixed space for play and reflection, and necessarily f2f in this type of pathology, where in the same session both f2f and virtual spaces are used.

Secondly, we seek to use the transitional space of the screen as a place to travel between the f2f group world with all the limitations that these pathologies produce, and a virtual reality world in which to explore and elaborate the children's fantasies, ghosts, difficulties and abilities. The screen not only constitutes a space of representation but also a protected environment free of physical contact and direct gaze of the other.

Finally, it is important to create a playful space in which group activity can be associated with moments of enjoyment. Often this activity is carried out alone at home, but this time it is different. We have witnessed cases of children diagnosed with ASD in which the videogame is not only practiced in a solitary and abusive way but also creating a restricted or obsessive interest, becoming abnormal due to its intensity and perseverance.

Session Structure

Case sessions had a duration of one and a half hour with a weekly frequency and consisted of five fundamental stages that were varying in duration and importance during the course of the group.

In the first stage (f2f) we discussed with the group members the structure of the session, recorded the important moments and reminded the patients at what point the previous session had ended.

In a second stage (online) we played a short videogame that worked as a warm-up for the activity. The game was chosen by the therapeutic team to facilitate a certain atmosphere for the rest of the session. Games were initially collaborative and with pleasant themes to facilitate group cohesion and friendly attitudes in the participants. As the group progressed, competitive games were added that produced more intense sensations and emotions and aroused some of the individual or relational conflicts that were being worked on.

In the third stage (f2f) there was a short dialogue about what had happened in the warming-up and we proceeded to set group objectives for the Minecraft space and reach some agreements, if necessary. This space needed more intervention of the therapeutic team at the beginning of the group, as well as at the beginning of certain creative projects.

In a fourth stage (VR) the activity was carried out with Minecraft, which was mainly based on cooperative building construction projects that could last from a single session to two months. In this space, both group members and the therapist-educator participated in the game. However, the therapist-psychologist remained as a participant observer during game time. The group could progress from simple building individual constructions in the game's 'easy mode' to more difficult game levels such as having difficulties in obtaining construction resources in 'survival mode'.

In a final stage the group elaborated on what happened in the session. At the beginning, it was very difficult for the children to participate, as they were still immersed in the game and very frustrated by the end of the activity. Little by little they became more willing to talk about what happened and to close the session.

Group Specific Objectives

Specific individual and group objectives were established. The first had to do mainly with observation and intervention on the role of participants in the group and their emotional reactions before specific situations of the activity.

For group objectives, we established a group identity and a sense of belonging, as well as adapting the task to the needs, limitations and characteristics of each individual.

Therapists' Roles

In this group, we differentiated two roles in the therapeutic team that facilitated the transition between virtual and f2f realities. The first is the therapist-psychologist role, leading the reflection spaces (first, third and fifth session stages). When the game started, the therapist-psychologist remained outside the virtual activity observing and interpreting the participants verbal interactions, body postures and emotional states.

The second role of the therapist-educator: providing information to the group regarding what happened in the game in the stages for reflection. He guided the playing time (second and fourth session stages), participating in it and proposing or generating concrete situations as agreed with the therapist-psychologist.

It is worth noting the essential coordination between therapists that nourishes both spaces. Thus, for example, when the group could not say goodbye temporarily to one of its members, who was absent during several sessions followed by a hospitalization period, the following proposal was made by the therapeutic team:

The therapist-psychologist discussed the situation even though the participants tried to avoid it, some feeling very sorry for the partner's absence and others not being able to perceive this change in the dynamics of the group. It was decided to use the game facilitating a situation in which the participants had to build a room for each group member within a castle of fear project. The group decided to jointly build a room for the child who is absent. During building the collective construction the therapist-psychologist commented on participants' attitudes and verbalized what these attitudes imply for the absent child and for those present in the group. In a later stage the group assessed their attempt to repair the vacuum left by the partner's absence.

Conclusion

As a final conclusion, we can say that life and psychotherapy are currently being developed in virtual and f2f environments. We need original theories and techniques to understand and intervene on the new forms of mental functioning that occur for all ages and psychopathologies.

Communication mediated by technologies and the new mind architectures have developed a universe that incites us to different understandings of the intersubjective phenomena and the development of new psychotherapeutic intervention methodologies. In the two cases presented, we believe we have made progress in the field of online group psychotherapies in neurotic patients and in children diagnosed with ASD. There is a world of possibilities to continue investigating.

Notes

1 *Hypertextual*: environment created from written words, voice files, image files and hyperlinks between them. *Virtual reality platforms*: they allow an interactive experience from the artificial simulation of an environment. *Collective creation platforms*: they allow creative works online through words, images and sounds, in small, medium or large groups.
2 1. Formation: elaboration of fusional and paranoid anxieties that allow initiating idealization processes. 2. Idealized group cohesion: Group consciousness as a whole. Experimentation of identification, dependence and counterdependence phenomena. Experimentation of passivity and submission to authority

relationships. 3. Real group cohesion: experience in the group of intrapsychic and intersubjective conflicts, expansion of discrimination and differentiation capacities. Creation of subgroups and exclusion experience elaboration. 4. Group maturity: deepening of nuclear conflicts. Attempts of psychic and intersubjective transformation. Development of potentialities and acceptance of limitations. 5. End of the group: Elaboration of experiences of mourning, separation and farewell, closure and future projects.

3 For example, in the group formation stage, if we analyze dimension B: "From overidentification with others to isolation in the self". Successive crises of decentered, of isolation or overidentification states are observed, evolving into intersubjective states centered on a balance between love for oneself and love for others. Subsequently, new crises are repeated, although in different ways in each phase of the group.

References

Freud, S. (1913). *Tótem y tabú y otras obras*, en vol. XIII, O.C. Buenos Aires: Amorrortu editores.

Freud, S. (1914). *Introducción al narcisismo*, en vol. XIV, O.C. Buenos Aires: Amorrortu editores.

McLuhan, M. (1967). *The Medium is the Message*. UK: Penguin Books.

Suler, J.R. (2000). Psychotherapy in cyberspace: A 5-Dimensional Model of Online and Computer-Mediated Psychotherapy. *CyberPsychology & Behavior, 3*(2). doi:10.1089/109493100315996.

Turkle, S. (1995). *Life on the Screen: Identity in the Age of the Internet*. New York: Simon and Schuster.

Vaimberg, R. (2005). Psicoanálisis y Sociedad de la información. *Intercambios, 14*: 63–71.

Vaimberg, R. (2010). *Psicoterapias tecnológicamente mediadas (PTM). Estudio de procesos y microprocesos terapéuticos a partir de participación online*. Tesis doctoral, Facultad de Psicología, Universidad de Barcelona.

Vaimberg, R. (2012). *Psicoterapia de Grupo. Psicoterapia de Grupo online*. Barcelona: Octaedro.

Vaimberg, R. (2015). *Psicoterapia de grupo y psicodrama. Teoría y Técnica*. Barcelona: Octaedro.

Weinberg, H. (2014). *The Paradox of Internet Groups: Alone in the Presence of Others*. London: Karnac.

Winnicott, D.W. (1971). *Playing and Reality*. London: Tavistock Publications.

17 Practical Considerations for Online Group Therapy

Haim Weinberg

Screening and Preparing Group Members

In therapy groups, it is highly recommended to have an online pre-group meeting with each group member, just as we do f2f. This meeting is for screening, preparing and bonding with the group member. Use it to explain technical issues and online etiquette (even if you have a written agreement) as well.

Group Agreement

As recommended in the general practical considerations, don't forget to add items that relate to online etiquette in the group agreement. Most of the additional items mentioned in that section can stay the same as for individual therapy, except that the item:

> To stay focused on the meeting.

should be replaced by:

> To stay focused on the group interactions.

Outside the Group Contact

In therapy groups we recommend group members not to socialize outside the group. Online, outside the group contact can be done through emails as well, so remember to mention the recommendation for not having out of the group relationships, even online.

Confidentiality

Be careful not to send the email addresses or phone numbers of the group members to one another.

Technical Explanations

Remember that your technical expertise can become a holding environment for the group members, so learn well the application you use for the group meetings. Send the members technical explanations about the use of application (e.g. Zoom) before the beginning of the group, and learn how to solve simple technical problems (e.g., audio is not connecting).

Specific Instructions for Text-based Communication (emails, forums, Google groups)

1. Be aware that text-based communication is susceptible to massive projections.
2. An Internet text group is a Large Group disguised as a small group. Be prepared for Large Group dynamics as well as small group.
3. Intimacy is replaced by E-ntimacy (Weinberg, 2014), which is less based on I-thou self-disclosure.

Specific Instructions for Video Conference Groups (Zoom)

1. Remember that in online groups the group leader is not controlling the setting, and instruct group members about the proper environment.
2. Do not ignore events and stimuli that seem part of the background (a cat entering the screen?) and include them in the process.
3. Technical difficulties and communication failure are part of the dynamics. Include them in the exploration.
4. In Zoom: For groups – Gallery view is better than Speaker view because you can see all the group members on the screen.
5. In Zoom: Teach the group members how to hide their own video, or put a patch on your screen where your face is showing, in case they are distracted by their own reflection.
6. In Zoom: Do not encourage using chat function during the group meeting, as it takes away the attention of the members and can become a kind of outside the group communication if the exchange is private.
7. Connecting from a smart phone is not recommended as you cannot see all the group members on the screen. Use a tablet or laptop.
8. Instruct group members not to connect from a car, even when they are not driving, as you cannot guarantee confidentiality and privacy, and the member cannot stay focused.

The Group Leader's Presence

The main obstacle in online video groups is how to create a presence. Find ways to increase your presence. Appropriate self-disclosure related to the here-and-now (feelings towards the members) is one possibility. Identifying an emotional state of a member from non-verbal communication is another. Acknowledging and accepting responsibility for mistakes is very powerful.

Centrality of the Group Leader

Be aware that online group leaders tend to be more in the center. Do your best to avoid a "star-shaped" communication structure (when you are in the center of communication) and remember to encourage group members' interactions.

Training for Online Groups

Just as we need training in the shift from individual to group, we need specific training to move from f2f groups to online groups. It is not always the same.

The Optimal Model for a Time Limited Group:

Start with an intensive two to three days' f2f group experience (marathon group), continue with a weekly session of 90 minutes and end with another two to three f2f intensive groups.

When Some of the Group Members are in the Same Room

The specific setting in which one group member is online and the other members are in the same room, is not recommended (at least not as a constant solution). It easily creates the dynamics of competition and envy, as it takes more efforts for the member online to stay connected or needs more attention from the group leader to include him/her.

Section 4

Online Organizational Consultancy

Edited by Rakefet Keret-Karavani and Arnon Rolnick

18 Introduction to the Online Organizational Consultancy Section

Rakefet Keret-Karavani and Arnon Rolnick

Alex was frustrated and confused. What has just happened with this bunch of guys? Ten minutes ago he was pleased with the way he had succeeded in running the meeting, specifically managing the new allocation of assignments. Having people from three very different cultures in his team, in five locations around the world, was one difficulty. His boss clarified that he will not tolerate any more delays in the project, since the customer complained directly to the general manager.

During the last two months the project team worked more or less well. His people were very skilled and experienced, and he assigned a mentor to the two promising "freshmen" he recruited. They had very efficient weekly videoconference meetings. This was a huge step forward from the audioconference meetings they used to have, although at times there were Internet breakdowns in two of the locations. Still he could see everyone and felt much more in control. The people said it was nice to see faces and get to know each other.

The meetings were dedicated to reports on planning vs. execution. They shared data. If there were problems, they discussed it. It is not as if they had big issues, just little moments such as when someone was silent when other team member complained "someone" had not delivered his report on time – and everyone knew who it was. Or that time when the three Dutch team members were very keen on understanding how come that the data they had sent everyone for the project's sheets, rarely got the technical input needed form others as well. It developed to a little conflict, but Alex stopped it by saying that from now on he will take the responsibility and make sure others will fill in the input as well. So there were no "dramas". At least that was what he thought until now. Maybe he shouldn't have led the meeting from his home, when the only quiet room was the one with slow Internet connection. It took some time to upload the data sheets, and he couldn't see all faces when he re-assigned tasks and emphasized the time pressure. The two team leaders started asking him questions. At some point one of them argued about who should get task number 3, and the other one got quiet and looked distant. The technical problems that the argumentative team leader (and two other participants) faced, were not helping with the communication flow.

In the past he could use this look of his to convey the message: "This has to be done. No arguments," or putting his hand on the shoulder of the speaker, actually communicating: "I'm here. I'm with you." No longer. So, he ended the meeting before time, saying it's impossible to continue with all the disruptions, and he will see them next week. Of course, he didn't have the coffee corner to get the "after meeting chat," and sense what people thought of the meeting, and how they felt. Maybe it's time for a co-location meeting.

Well … at least shortening the meeting got him some extra time to complete his presentation for tomorrow.

The first few questions coming up from this scenario might be:

- What "entered" the meeting and brought it to its frustrating end?
- What part was affected by purely management? What was the technology part? Other factors?
- What could have been anticipated and managed, and how should we deal with the unexpected?

We will probably find that organizational, managerial and technological factors, mix together with cultural and other diversities, played a role and shaped the meeting the way it was.

Having said that, before anything else, every meeting is about people, their relationships and communication. Bernard Shaw once said: "The single biggest problem in communication, is the illusion that it has taken place." We can assume Shaw was referring to the common reality he knew in the first half of the twentieth century: people communicating with each other in the same physical room. No technology mediation. Rarely with people from different cultures.

Chris Argyris, one of the founders of organizational development (O.D.) theory and practice, wrote a lot about the challenges people face in the communication process. According to Argyris (1990: 87) one strategy for understanding one's subjective mental models and assumptions is to become cognizant of one's "ladder of inference", a common mental pathway. The ladder has multiple stages, each has an effect on the way one perceives and interprets the other's intentions and behaviors. Indeed, it illuminate how much the communication process is prone to misunderstandings. Obviously when adding to the process elements such as technology as a go-between, rich diversity, organizational context and more, it becomes even more challenging.

The section of articles in the online organizational section was written by colleagues with years of experience dealing with these challenges.

The objectives of this section are to:

1. Explore the nature of organizational videoconference meetings, through sharing experience and suggesting theories to analyze the processes involved.
2. Offer guiding rules for effective videoconference meeting.

The section includes two theoretical chapters, each written from a different theoretical angle, and different leadership role perspectives. The first chapter presents a managerial point of view, the second and third ones display external consultant stance. We believe that the various angles can deepen the readers' understanding of the phenomena and enable a better application of the guiding rules.

This section's introduction presents a few concepts that aim to serve as an organizing frame of work to the chapters' content.

From our experience we grouped four key contexts which influence the organizational videoconference meeting, and which are dealt with through all three of the following chapters:

1. The broad *virtual* context that brings in a lot of diversities.
2. The *technology* context that makes distant communication possible, and yet impacts it in various ways.
3. The *videoconference* context, the medium characteristics and it's paradox nature.
4. The *organizational* context.

Virtual Context

Business today is dynamic, global, ever-changing, fast-paced. *New York Times* expert Thomas Friedman (2016) talks about the increasing/accelerating rate of change: Acceleration of the pace of improving and perfecting technology (for example, Moore's Law[1]) and no less amazing – globalization, which turns the world into a small village. While Friedman focuses on how those changes affect the external world, we would like to focus on our inner and interpersonal world.

As a result, one of the major changes over the last two decades in how work is conducted, has been the growth of virtual teams (Hassell & Cotton, 2017).

Virtual teams are based on individuals collaborating in geographically dispersed work groups and who may reside in different time zones and countries (Lauring, 2013). Hassell & Cotton (2017) quote a recent survey which found that 46% of organizations utilize virtual teams (Minton-Eversole, 2012), and the use of these teams is expected to grow (Dobson, 2011, p. 3).

While virtual teams hold the promise of increased organizational flexibility and resource utilization, there are challenges as well.

Chudoba, Lu, Watson-Manheim and Wynn (2013) claim that in lifting some barriers to collaboration, the technology simultaneously exposes a presumed structure that no longer applies but lingers as a model in the minds (Hammer & Champy, 1993), and opens the possibility of less cohesion in the work environment. As Scott and Timmerman (1999) note, "the very technologies that provide … [workers] with the freedom and flexibility they desire, also allow them to be further removed from key aspects of the organization" (241). Watson-Manheim et al. (2002) refer to these barriers as discontinuities. They suggest that discontinuities draw attention to underlying process issues and potential problems created by hidden boundaries. Drawing from the literature on virtuality, they identified six discontinuities – geography, temporal, cultural, work practices, organization, and technology – that captured distinctive aspects of the virtual teaming environment.

In addition to the discontinuities, virtual teams tend to focus more on task aspects, and place less attention on social-emotional aspects (Powell, Piccoli, & Ives, 2004 in Hassell & Cotton, 2017). This focus leads to lack of unplanned opportunities for interaction, relationships, group cohesion and trust which are less developed in virtual teams than traditional ones (Hassell & Cotton, 2017).

So, the rational-task orientation in business organizations places a challenge for the work with the social-emotional aspects, yet they are the cornerstone of relationships and effective communication. The opportunity for such discussions is mostly during specific organizational development initiatives like team building, leadership workshops etc. It is very common to hear participants in such process meetings saying: "What happens here is great and important, but back in the office it's another world." What they actually say is that it's not easy to develop social–emotional discourse in the daily routine, even when it's needed.

The need for team cohesion and trust is even more significant in light of the business surrounding. A report by Deloitte (2017) points out that the rapid pace of today's work environment and the need for speed, forces employees to work faster. Therefore, employees have to collaborate more effectively to get their jobs done.

In Chapter 20 of this volume, Jensen and Dennis elaborate on these points and suggest the Gestalt approach as a framework to effectively communicate.

Nuela Dent in Chapter 21 shares with us the challenges of working with groups from different spaces, cultures and time zones, from a consulting perspective. Dent uses the systems psychodynamic approach to explain phenomena in the various groups. The consultant working with the approach attempts to inquire beyond the obvious to reach the underlying dynamics in groups and organizations.

Adizes, a well-known name in the organizational world, developed a very structured methodology called "organizational therapy" aimed to improve teamwork when facing challenging times. Discipline and rules make communication flow easily and clarity is created. The work is done both in co-located room and videoconference, each has its own advantages. He is interviewed for this section.

In sum, comparing organizational communication between co-located teams and virtual ones, two interesting points pop up simultaneously:

- The starting point of virtual communication is based on various *discontinuities* the participants inherently bring into the meeting, creating challenging barriers.
- The fast pace and collaboration needed from the employees, and complex nature of the work require the most clear and fluent communication we can get. Ideally, when all team members *share the same understanding* of the tasks at hand, it's easier to collaborate fast and get qualitative results.

In other words, on the one hand we have inherent communication barriers, on the other hand we have the critical need for a mutual and flowing communication process. We acutely need continuity in a discontinuous situation.

Technology Context

Guo, D'ambra, Turner, and Zhang (2009) claim that we should distinguish between the technology channels, and understand their varied nature. Computer-mediated technologies differ quite considerably in the degree to which they transmit social context cues (Straus & McGrath, 1994). Social context cues play a vital role in the reduction of ambiguity, which in turn has important social consequences for guiding the degree of intimacy and the quality of team meetings (Martin & Tom, 2003). Thus, when we discuss virtual teams, we must be aware that virtual teams may operate in the context of different types of communication technologies and that the type of communication technologies implemented may have a significant impact on team interaction (Driskell & Radtke, 2003).

According to media richness theory (Daft & Lengel, 1986, Daft, Lengel, & Trevino, 1987), and social presence theory (Short, Williams & Christie 1976), media differ in the extent to which a team:

    (a) can overcome various communication constraints of time, location, permanence, distribution, and distance.

(b) transmit the social, symbolic, and nonverbal cues of human communication.

(c) convey equivocal information.

(Rice 1993)

The researcher concludes that social context cues are important for team members to regulate interaction, express inform action, monitor feedback from others, and create a sense of common ground and shared understanding (Guo et al., 2009).

In addition to the social context cues, rich information includes nonverbal, immediate feedback, therefore reducing ambiguity and uncertainty in communication (Pearroja et al., 2013).

Empirical evidence has shown that verbal and non-verbal cues help to regulate the flow of conversation, facilitate turn taking, provide immediate feedback, and convey subtle meanings, which are important for team coordination (Montoya-Weiss, Massey, & Song, 2001 in Pearroja et al., 2013).

Whatever media the team is using, Brown, Poole and Rodgers (2004) claim that "participants' degree of acceptance of new technology is an additional factor in effective collaboration" (130). They suggest that factors such as perceived ease-of-use, control over technology, and computer anxiety, vary among participants and influence the dynamics. Therefore, technology itself is subjected to trust/distrust when working virtually.

In Chapter 20 Jensen and Dennis argue that technology amplifies the heuristics which is embedded in the human way of thinking. In turn, technology-mediated human interaction makes us prone to even a quicker judgment and automotive behavior.

Dent in Chapter 21 adds a perspective and relates to technology not only as a mediator but as a subject of itself. She refers to Bion's basic assumptions and claims that participants may relate to technology in a fight/flight mentality, dependency mentality or any other basic assumption. For example, technology is to "be blamed" for the people inability to speak on relationship issues.

Videoconference

What characterizes videoconference as a medium? How does it affect the meeting's course and outcomes?

Synchronous video-conferencing systems allow team members separated by geographical distances to interact in an approximation of face-to-face interaction through audio and video communication capabilities (Guo et al., 2009).

Webcams are used widely since Apple, Microsoft and Logitech started selling them in 2003. In 2005, the first high definition videoconferencing systems were introduced (Olson et al., 2014).

We choose to add this specific section about video conferencing in organizations as we believe that organizations that will use the video meetings wisely will have an enhanced performance and better effectiveness. Moreover, as part of our psychological view of organizational behavior, we believe that visual face-to-face encounters can enhance teams' coordination and cooperation.

We partly base these assumptions on Forbes (and Zoom) Report on video conferencing characteristics and their effect in the workplace, see the survey conducted in 2017 by Forbes Insights and Zoom global (www.forbes.com/forbes-insights/our-work/the-connected-culture).

Although video chat is a channel most similar to face-to-face, it still lacks nonverbal cues such as eye gaze and body gestures (Fullwood, 2007 in Shin et al., 2017). For example, research on non-verbal behaviors has often discussed the importance of eye contact to signal turn-taking intentions that help the smooth flow of conversations (Duncan, 1972 in Shin et al., 2017) and to deliver intimacy (Mehrabian, 1969 in Shin et al., 2017).

In all three chapters in this section these video conferencing characteristics and their effect on the meeting's course, are widely discussed.

We would like to note a few more points that impact the participants and the process taking place, as we have experienced in our work.

Smoothness and spontaneous level of the conversation is a subject of other situations occurring in video conference:

- In most cases the screen default shows the participant own image, not the natural mode when we are meeting with others. Seeing oneself frequently increases self-awareness (sometimes embarrassment as well), which may result in a restrained behavior or enhanced one.
- As for now, people can talk only one at a time, since talking stimulatingly sounds like a noise. Therefore, unless the conversation is regulated by turns/hand raising, one is "taking a risk" of a clash when trying to talk.
- When technological faults, such as Internet disconnections, image freeze etc., happen, participants are often concerned that they will not be heard/seen well, and may think twice before talking.

These situations, among others, may cause some hesitation to "jump" into the conversation spontaneously. At the same time, these very situations forces people to better plan and control their behavior. Thus, for task-oriented meeting with non-native English speakers as well as with impulsive participants, this regulated pace is often effective.

One more aspect to consider is the way participants are distributed. We will explore this issue when discussing the organizational context, but for now we will assume that *each participant sits individually in a separate location.* We believe that this will become the most frequent pattern, following globalization trend, technology constant improvements and more.

- Since the participant is in front of the screen, it provides an easy access to whatever the Internet has to offer. This is both a great advantage if any materials needed to be pulled for the discussion, and yet places a constant temptation for multi-tasking and distraction.
- Sitting in one's home/office/etc. on one hand is *convenient* (for all the known reasons), yet at the same time can be *inconvenient* since it forces the participant to be responsible for suitable physical and technology conditions.

The last item leads us to consider videoconferencing in a wider sense, as a medium with an inherited paradoxical nature:

> Participants can feel *excluded* and disconnect since their presence is *remote*, and yet the *proximity* of seeing facial expression has a *connecting* and *including* quality.
>
> Participants might feel that it is easy to "*hide*" and do some other staff outside the camera zone, or on the screen (emails etc.). Actually, seeing closely everyone's faces makes it easy to reveal when the participants' attention is diverted.
>
> They might sense the screen as a *barrier* to getting to know the others. Yet the background seen on the participant's image oftentimes is part of the home/office, and can serve as a *catalyst* for a more personal flavored small talk, and ease the way for building relationships.

Looking at the managerial aspects, the paradox plays a role as well. For example, the picture on the screen does not reflect the traditional status signs such as: everyone is gathering in the boss's office, or the boss sitting at the head of the table in the meeting room. The manager cannot entirely ensure proper meeting's conditions, as it depends on various variables (e.g. Internet connections, participants' equipment). The flat screen actually echoes the lean organization and minimal hierarchy of current organizations. At the same time, the manager has control over the "mute" button of each participant, a very strong management tool. The person who hosts the meeting room (mostly the manager) is the one who can record the session, hence has control over the information, it's maintenance and sharing options.

In a routine videoconference meeting, peoples' attention and energy are focused on a task. If they do sense some of what we just described, it is mostly not discussed since it's not considered as relevant or important for the results. Oftentimes ambivalence is awakened toward the manager/a colleague/a situation etc., but the participant cannot articulate the actual reason. Yet, the manifestation of the paradox resides in the meeting.

The Organizational Context

We will use the definition of Doolen, Hacker and Van Aken (2003) for organizational context as "the management processes, organizational

culture and organizational systems that exist within a parent organization" (287).

We refer to two aspects: *organizational culture*, and the videoconference
screen display as a representation of dispersed locations participating. We
consider the final image we see on the screen as the result of both
management processes and organizational systems.

Nguyen and Mohamed (2011) bring Schein's definition to organizational
culture, as consisting of two layers of concepts: visible and invisible characteristics. The visible layer means external buildings, clothing, behavior modes,
regulations, stories, myths, languages and rites. The invisible layer means
common values, norms, faith and assumptions. Organizational culture, in
addition to the capability to integrate daily activities of employees to reach the
planned goals, can also help organizations adapt well to the external environment for rapid and appropriate responses (Nguyen & Mohamed, 2011).

In Chapter 21 Dent describes, in one of the case studies, how she noticed
"a double handling of information, storing documents in both digital and
electronic form; speaking to a lack of trust or confidence in the technology"
(p. 249). Indeed, the organizational assumption toward technology is evident,
affects the teamwork and is reflected in the consultation process as well.
"They need technology to support their work as a team, but the organization
provides technological systems which are limited in their capability and
consequently impact the team's capacity to work together" (p. 248).

For Adizes in Chapter 19, discipline is the key for effective work. He
noticed how technology forces participants to speak one at the time, in
contrast to the co-located meetings.

We can see how different a videoconference meeting looks like in an
established organization, where it is obvious that everyone turns on the
camera, connects on time and sits in a quiet space, as oppose to an
informal start-up where the manager will not force "camera on", being
late is not handled and meeting can be taken from a coffee place.

We related earlier to the distribution of participants' location as a factor.
When participants sit together, the organizational context impose itself on
the dynamics and has an impact.

Dent describes it well:

> In the location where I was, the manager and team leader were present
> and participants seemed less able to "play".... This seemed harder to do
> when people were with others in their reporting line. Or it could have
> been related to being in the same location as the researcher.
>
> (pp. 248–249)

Adizes adds an angle and claims that as a consultant, it's easier for him to
establish authority when he sits alone and appears on the big screen of the
different meeting rooms people are gathered.

We would like to stress another aspect. As for now, when we look at the screen of a common videoconference meeting, we often see the co-located team members sitting together, therefore each image on the screen represents a site/office. Due to the medium, what actually is created is a visual vivid reflection of the organizational distribution.

It doesn't matter what organization we are dealing with, this image will always have a meaning other than just a location. It might be the representation of the power relation between headquarter vs. field office, the distribution of projects done by the different sites, the minority/majority status of certain cultures in the team, etc. Where does the manager sit? How many people sit with him? If some sit individually, how do they feel and behave?

A group sitting together creates a certain dynamic which affects the meeting's flow, content and more. A few groups sitting in different rooms obviously create multiple dynamics. Since the groups interact, we can only imagine the variety of the inter-groups dynamic that produces "the group as a whole" behavior and results. Hence when the use of videoconference is in that setting, it structures the team's behavior and illuminates visually some organizational elements as well.

Getting back to our manager Alex from the beginning of the introduction, we believe that organizations will benefit a lot from training whoever is leading a videoconference meeting on a regular basis. It is not a simple "copy-paste" of co-location meetings. It is a vital management practice with its special features.

We will funnel our practical considerations as a summary, at the end of the section.

Note

1 Moore's Law is the observation made by Intel co-founder Gordon Moore that the number of transistors on a chip doubles every year while the costs are halved. The extension of Moore's law is that computers, machines that run on computers and computing power all become smaller and faster with time, as transistors on integrated circuits become more efficient.

References

Argyris, C. (1990). *Overcoming Organizational Defenses: Facilitating Organizational Learning*. Needham Heights, MA: Allyn & Bacon.

Brown, H.G., Poole, M.S., and Rodgers, T.L. (2004). Interpersonal traits, complementarity, and trust in virtual collaboration. *Journal of Management Information Systems*, 20(4): 115–137, doi: 10.1080/07421222.2004.11045785

Chudoba, K.M., Lu, M., Watson-Manheim, M.B., and Wynn, E. (2005). How virtual are we? Measuring virtuality and understanding its impact in a global organization. *Information Systems Journal*, 15(4): 279–306, doi:10.1111/j.1365-2575.2005.00200.

Daft, R.L., and Lengel R.H. (1986). Organizational information requirements, media richness and structural design. Management Science, *32*(5): pp. 554–571. Available online at www.jstor.org/stable/2631846?seq=1&cid=pdf-reference #references_tab_contents.

Daft, R.L., Lengel, R. H., and Trevino, L. K. (1987). Message equivocality, media selection, and manager performance: Implications for information systems. *Management Information Systems Quarterly, 11*(3): 355–366, doi:10.2307/248682.

Deloitte (2017). The digital workplace: Think, share, do. Transform your employee experience. Available online at www2.deloitte.com/content/dam/Deloitte/mx/ Documents/human-capital/The_digital_workplace.pdf.

Dobson, S. (2011). Virtual teams expected to Grow: Survey. *Canadian HR Reporter.*

Doolen, Toni L., Hacker, Marla E., & Van Aken, Eileen M. (2003) The impact of organizational context on work team effectiveness: A study of production team. *IEEE Transactions on Engineering Management, 50*(3): 285–296, doi: 10.1109/ TEM.2003.817296.

Driskell, J.E., and Radtke, P.H. (2003). Virtual teams: Effects of technological mediation on team performance. *Group Dynamics: Theory, Research, and Practice*, 7(4): 297–323, doi:10.1037/1089-2699.7.4.297

Forbes Insights (2017). *The Connected Culture: Unleashing the Power of Video in Everyday Collaboration.* Available online at www.forbes.com/forbes-insights/our-work/the-connected-culture.

Friedman, T.L. (2016). *Thank You for Being Late: An Optimist's Guide to Thriving in the Age of Accelerations.* New York: Farrar, Straus and Giroux.

Guo, Z., D'ambra, J., Turner, T., and Zhang, H. (2009). Improving the effectiveness of virtual teams: A comparison of video-conferencing and face-to-face communication in China. *IEEE Transactions on Professional Communication, 52*(1): 1–16, doi: 10.1109/TPC.2008.2012284.

Hammer, M., and Champy, J. (1993) *Reengineering the Corporation.* New York: Harper Business.

Hassell, M.D., and Cotton, J.L. (2017). Some things are better left unseen: Toward more effective communication and team performance in video-mediated interactions. *Computers in Human Behavior, 73*: 200–208, doi:10.1016/j. chb.2017.03.039.

Kirkman, B.L., Cordery, J.L., Mathieu, J., Rosen, B., and Kukenberger, M. (2013) Global organizational communities of practice: The effects of nationality diversity, psychological safety, and media richness on community performance. *Human Relations, 66*(3): 333–362, doi:10.1177/0018726712464076.

Klitmuller, A., and Lauring, J. (2013). When global virtual teams share knowledge: Media richness, cultural difference and language commonality. *Journal of World Business, 48*: 398–406, doi:10.1016/j.jwb.2012.07.023.

Lauring, J. (2013). International Diversity Management: Global Ideals and Local Responses. *British Journal of Management, 24*(2): 211–224, doi:10.1111/j.1467-8551.2011.00798.x.

Martin, T., and Tom, P. (2003). Social cues and impression formation in CMC. *Journal of Communication, 53*(4): 676–693, doi:10.1111/j.1460-2466.2003.tb02917.x.

Minton-Eversole, T. (2012). Virtual teams used most by global organizations, survey says. *Society for Human Resource Management.* Available online at www. shrm.org/hrdisciplines/orgempdev/articles/pages/virtualteamsusedmostbygloba lorganizations,surveysays.aspx.

Nguyen, H.N. and Mohamed, S. (2011). Leadership behaviors, organizational culture and knowledge management practices: An empirical investigation. *Journal of Management Development*, *30*(2): 206–221, doi:10.1108/02621711111105786.

Olson, J.D., Appunn, F.D., McAllister, C.A., Walters, K.K., and Grinnell, L. (2014). Webcams and virtual teams: An impact model. *Team Performance Management*, *20*(3/4): 148–177, doi:10.1108/TPM-05-2013-0013.

Pearroja, V., Orengo, V., Zornoza, A., and Hernandez, A. (2013). The effects of virtuality level on task-related collaborative behaviors: The mediating role of team trust. *Computers in Human Behavior*, *29*: 967–974, doi: 10.1016/j.chb.2012.12.020.

Rice, R.E. (1993). Media appropriateness: Using social presence theory to compare traditional and new organizational media. *Human Communication Research*, *19*(4): 451–484.

Scott, C., & Timmerman, C. (1999) Communication technology use and multiple workplace identifications among organizational teleworkers with varied degrees of virtuality. *IEEE Transactions on Professional Communication*, *42*(4): 240–260.

Shin, S.Y., Liu, W., Jang, J., and Bente, G. (2017) The benefits of distance and mediation: How people react to conflicts in video chat vs. ftf. *Computers in Human Behavior*, *73*: 1–8, doi:10.1016/j.chb.2017.03.022.

Short, J., Williams, E., and Christie, B. (1976). *The Social Psychology of Telecommunications*. New York: Wiley.

Straus, S.G., and McGrath, J.E. (1994). Does the medium matter? The interaction of task type and technology on group performance and member reactions. *Journal of Applied Psychology*, *79*(1): 87–97.

Watson-Manheim M.B., Crowston, K., and Chudoba, K.M. (2002). Discontinuities and Continuities: A New Way to Understand Virtual Work. *Information, Technology, and People*, *15*(3): 191–209, doi:10.1108/09593840210444746.

19 Interview with Ichak Kalderon Adizes

A = Ichak Kalderon Adizes; Ra = Rafeket Keret-Karavani; Ro = Arnon Rolnik

Ra: We would like to thank you very much for your time. You are well known for the methodology you developed and the work you are doing with organizations and governments as well.

We would like to talk with you about the implementations that the virtual world have on your work. What is your view on the current and the future trends regarding virtual communication, and what will be its influences on the world of consultancy?

A: I will start with what you called "world of consultancy" before we get into the virtual communication. I hope I created a new field which is not consulting but "organizational therapy." Consulting usually follows the medical analogy, you come to me and I give you a prescription and you are responsible for implementing my advice. In therapy we enable the patient to solve his own problems, we give him the tools to deal with them, and to cope with the environment he is struggling with. The job is to eventually emancipate the patient from external help.

In family therapy we are not treating the individual, we are treating the interactions. This is true for companies. When interactions are stuck, and the energy does not flow easily through the channels correctly, you get destructive conflict which stops the company from dealing with the environment.

I created a methodology that tells me whom to get into the room at the same time, so I can change the culture, the interactions, performance, and behaviors of the organization. This distinction is important when we talk about virtual change management.

Whom do I need in the room depends on what the problem is. Who is necessary in order to solve this problem? Who is holding power or influence over the problem, who is holding it back? Sometimes like in family therapy, it is the mother-in-law. If you are sitting and treating only the husband and wife, you are wasting your time. You need the mother-in-law in the room.

This group can be between two to thirty people. If it is thirty people I cannot do it virtually. The room has too many people and I cannot see the faces of everyone. I need to see the faces, they tell me when I'm stepping on a nerve. I watch the body language very closely, because in my methodology I work with high discipline: who talks when, about what, in what sequence.

My therapy is very systematized so the invited participants areadvancing together in the process of finding a solution. I can get into Zoom session with up to seven people. I take the core of the thirty people. The minimal core will be: the CEO, head of sales, head of human recourses, head of finance and head of operations. That's because there are four major subsystems in any organization: client interface subsystem which is sales and marketing, financial subsystem, the human resources subsystem, and the operation subsystem. Now I have the core representing the subsystems. All problems are caused by disintegration. So when marketing outpaces production, it's a problem. When production outpaces financial capability it's a problem. If disintegration is the source of all problems the solution is integration. They have to advance together. Nobody is left behind.

But I do not start therapy with Zoom because there is no personal relationship that enables me to control them when I'm in Zoom. When the subject matter gets explosive they ignore the camera, they ignore me. I have to establish my authority in-person first. I will not go to Zoom therapy until I feel that I created enough authority.

After we have a first draft solution, an illumination, with the core group, we have to include the others who can undermine the solution this four people arrived at. We go back to the thirty people to accommodate: "What is the problem? How will the solution work out? Why will it work? Why will it not work?" So the thirty will accommodate the illumination of the four to seven, and we are done.

Ra: So, you are saying that you first meet them face-to-face, then you follow up by Zoom meeting and then, when you have the thirty people in the room, it's face-to-face once again.

A: Right. I start with the four to seven first face-to-face. I don't need all the thirty to establish the acceptance of my rules.

Ro: As many other psychotherapists, and you see yourself as a therapist of the organization, you suggest that the first meeting will be face-to-face in order to make sure there is a discipline. While any psychotherapist has the first meeting face-to-face in order to create intimacy, rather than intimacy, you talk about discipline. Am I correct?

A: Yes, you are.

Ra: I would like to ask you about the mutual trust and respect which is a core element in your methodology. Once you established your position and support, and you had two, three, six meeting in Zoom with your client. How using this platform is different (or not) from the face-to-face?

A: No difference, because mutual trust and respect in my methodology is not an intention. It's not an attitude. It is a behavior. I control your behavior by giving you the tools which create the discipline. So, when you follow the rules, the behaviors of mutual trust and respect emerge by themselves.

Here is an example. You and me, Rakefet, are going through a very heavy emotional conflict. When you talk, who is the only person in the world who knows that you finished talking? You. Right? The typical mistake we all do, is when you stop talking I will start talking because I assume you finished. Not true. Because when you stop talking on an emotional subject, you replay to see if what you said is what you wanted to say. So when you stop talking, to whom are you listening? To yourself. So if I'm talking you don't hear me. As a matter of fact I'm interfering with you listening to yourself. I'm annoying you.

So, the "Adizes rule" is when you finish talking you will turn to your right, (people sit in a semi-circle). You have to be conscious that you finished talking. Whoever wants to talk next raises his hand. If they are raising their hand when you are still talking, penalty! Why? Because they are interfering.

Then, you have to call the person by first name, not last name, not nick name, first name. You have to call by first name because when you call by last name it's very formal, it creates distance. I try to break down formality, create a team.

At the beginning people talk long because they don't know if other people are listening. By the third turn they speak very short. People say: "I agree, blablabla … next." You know what is happening? A lot of respect. What happened? Listening! A miracle! Listening! Hear each other. Listening. Respect emerges if you follow the rules and trust emerges thereafter too.

Ra: Actually, we are talking about a very structured methodology, with a lot of rules. My question: does the platform influences in a way on the way you are working? For instance: if you want me to do pushups now (penalty), you were describing a lot of actions that you are doing with the people in the room. What happens when you work with them via video conference? What are the similarities? What are the differences?

A: I might be in the session talking no more than thirty percent of the session. Most of the time they are talking and I'm only watching. I am watching if they are breaking the rules. I only teach the tools, the rules, assign and monitor that tools are being done so I can emancipate the client. As long as they are going in the right direction, I let them go by themselves.

Ra: And it occurs both in the face-to-face and in the video conference as well?

A: Absolutely. In face-to-face they are sitting in horseshoe shape and I pull myself to be a little bit in the back of the first guy in the circle, because I try to prohibit them to look at me. It's almost like in Zoom. I am not there but I'm there.

Ra: So, they are sitting in the room (looking at you in Zoom), and you are the only one who is not in a room. Is that's what you are saying?

A: If they are sitting all in the same room, I need the capability to direct the camera to the one who is talking. When we are sitting in different countries, then it is easier. Why? Because the ones that talks automatically appears on the screen. When they are all in the same room I can see the total group. I can direct whom do I want to see. In Zoom I can see who is talking and I can direct the technology.

Ra: So, actually what you are saying is that this technology allows you to watch and to see each person that talks, which is very helpful because in the consultancy work these cues, like body language, are very delicate and the video gives you a lot of information. You can do your work.

A: Right, and I record every session and I give them the tape so they can watch it. So this is what the technology allows you to do. When you do it person-to-person you cannot record, you can but it's very intrusive.

Ra: Actually, in Zoom we can see ourselves as well, which is definitely not the situation in face-to-face meetings, where we can only see the others. This is also a very critical element. A lot of times, and studies also show it, I'm influenced by the fact that I see myself all the time. I'm very aware of myself. Does this element also influence you? Or do you see it influences you clients?

A: Strangely enough people get so involved in the discussion they forget about the camera, or even me watching.

Ra: Other than the fact that videoconferencing allows you to do work virtually and then you don't have to travel and bear less cost, do you see other benefits? Or if you could, would you have worked only face-to-face?

A: Virtual has advantages face-to-face does not have. Being in-person there, being close, they might try to break the rules. "You are one of us, we ate lunch together, let's go have some dinner." You get co-opted. When I'm in a Zoom meeting there is a very interesting advantage to my authority. I'm on a big screen talking from far away, like speaking from the sky… I have much more authority, so Zoom helps me to keep a distance.

Ra: It is both helping you to keep a distance and yet, form the relationship that you want face-to-face, and then to maintain these relationships in Zoom?

A: Right.

Ro: Since we are talking about meeting that takes place via videoconference, I want to mention the book *Empowering Meeting* written by Shoham Adizes and Nir Ben Lavi based on your methodology. In the book they refer to virtual meetings as well.

A: Great book. I think they mentioned that, for example, in order to follow the rule of talking by the sitting order, we ask participants (who sit separately from each other, in different places) to draw on paper a "horseshoe" setting with the names, so everyone can imagine as if they were sitting in the same room. That way the sequence of who speaks when is kept just like in a physical room.

Ra: The strict methodology and rules were made in order to regulate the spontaneous (often uncontrolled) communication people have, when they sit in the same room. From my experience, meeting in a videoconference while sitting individually in front of the screen, automatically creates different conditions, so it's not only "copy/paste" of the way we facilitate face-to-face.

A: In video it's easier to manage the discussion, because participants can't talk stimulatingly like in the in-person meeting. They talk one by one, using the "horseshoe" for talking in turns. That way the discussion is managed quicker and easier.

Ra: In addition, you differentiate two kinds of meetings in the book: problem solving meetings and implementation meetings. Can I assume that the implementation meetings are more suitable for a videoconference use?

A: Yes, because they run in a top-down manner and require a command and control environment. The problem-solving meetings require a learning environment because their goal is to find solution, and people have to feel free to speak their mind. The meeting is also designed to gain cooperation, so all of this requires a non-hierarchical communication.

Ra: Right, the whole problem-solving meeting is about creating a more fluent and flexible interaction. It's a management challenge considering the less spontaneous communication options.

A: This is the reason I highly recommend to start with the in-person meeting, to set the stage.

Ro: What is interesting is that, we don't know each other personally but toward the end I think we kind of feel you a little bit more, and I want really to thank you.

20 All Together, Now

Videoconferencing in Organizational Work

Ivan Jensen and Donna Dennis

We work together, and we always have, inside, outside, or between organizations, whether old or new. That is the very raison d'être of organizing and organizations. However, thousands of years ago, collaboration as a means of survival was most often limited to or bound by the family, band, tribe or clan, all of which were characterized by synchronous physical and cognitive proximity. Now we live in different times, and rapidly expand professional or commercial boundaries, from the one-person start-up, to the cottage or village industry, across the city, region, continent, or the world. Creating or making anything in the twenty-first century, whether material or immaterial, almost inevitably requires some element of boundary-spanning collaboration. That is challenging, because of the size of organizations, degree of dispersion, and complexity and dynamics (Stacey, 2010; Lojeski, 2010), as increasing and often frequently changing numbers of stakeholders become directly or indirectly involved.

To cope and achieve or maintain both efficacy and efficiency in this setting, let alone wellbeing, we need to collaborate across these boundaries, e.g. between units, divisions, disciplines, functions, national or ethnic cultures as well as customers, suppliers, and freelancing specialists. A prerequisite is the ability to generate, share and make meaning of growing mountains of information; made possible and dependent upon rapidly evolving technologies.

With all this change and complexity, it is easy to overlook the fact that even though technology has recently evolved at a breath-taking rate, basic human interaction and communication has remained fundamentally unchanged for millennia.[1] Human beings have "lazy brains" (Haselager, Dijk, & Rooij, 2008; Gazzaniga, Ivry, & Mangun, 2009) which often drive behavior based on individually or culturally developed heuristics or categories. Thus, through our evolution we have been hardwired to prefer collocation for important communicative-relational activities.

> Our brains like to create order out of the chaos of data coming into them, to make links between information so that our lives make more sense. We feel more comfortable surrounded by order, we feel better inside symmetry, where we can see how everything is connected.
>
> (Rock, 2006: 4)

People are uniquely different, and these differences matter. Every communicative-relational effort is aimed at projecting cognitive, affective, or conative elements of my mind onto yours. We contend that this process is similar in virtual and collocated work *in principle*. However, blocked or incomplete access to dynamic information in virtual work – feedback, dialogue, discussion etc. – will ruthlessly amplify the consequences of the dynamic complexity of the interpersonal space, and thus contribute to uncertainty or inefficiency.

We define virtual work as taking place when dispersed contributors work together towards the achievement of a common goal that none of them could meaningfully, i.e.in terms of time, resources, innovation, and quality, achieve in isolation. Thus, true collaboration as defined by us always involves interdependence, an oftentimes precarious balance between individual autonomy and collective discipline, emphasizing the need for well-oiled communication and relations. It is worth emphasizing here that the reason for virtual work is to utilize diversity – in competence, experience, capacity, availability – that could not otherwise be achieved. Diversity is often, however, also the source of many of the problems that may affect virtual work. With this as our point of departure, we describe primarily the communicative-relational dynamics that enable, complicate, or inhibit collaboration. It is all too easy to offer virtual work as a solution to many problems, based on reduced time for and cost of travelling, but it not infrequently incurs expenses incommensurate with the anticipated savings. However, we firmly believe that productive virtual work is indeed possible when the participants are cognizant of the potential pitfalls inherent in the use of videoconferencing in organizational work (Seibdrat, Hoegl, & Hogler, 2007).

The chapter is informed by theory and the authors' experience through more than three decades as managers for, consultants to, and teachers of individuals and groups within traditional and dispersed organizations. It presents a cognitive approach to understanding a key tool – videoconferencing – of virtual work within organizations. The chapter is written in three parts:

1. Understanding the cognitive nature of collaboration as relevant to virtual work.
2. Introducing the gestalt paradigm as a leader's toolbox for the communicative-relational dynamics of virtual work.
3. Pulling it all together and concluding with a checklist as an aid to focused reflection for leaders and teams using videoconferencing.

The stage is now set. Please imagine that you have been appointed project manager for a virtual development project, with half a dozen project members who represent different professions and cultures and live in geographically dispersed locations. You know that collaboration is dependent on communication and coordination, but what are the challenges, and how will you approach the use of video conferences in this setting?

The Cognitive Nature of Collaboration in Virtual Work and Virtual Organizations

Virtual organizations and distributed work have become common since the late twentieth century, and the trend appears to continue as more and more people collaborate towards a common goal, while separated in *location, time* and *knowledge* (Zemlianski & Amant, 2008; Lojeski, 2010).

- *Dispersion in location* can be just a few hundred yards or less, if the *perceived* distance, organizational affiliation or other factors prevent or significantly reduce face-to-face interaction (Lojeski & Reilly, 2010; Nemiro, Beyerlein & Bradley, 2008).
- *Dispersion in time* has two components:

    1. One is related to *time zones*. For example, if someone in Western Europe collaborates with a person in New Zealand the time difference is 12 hours, which makes it almost impossible to arrange communication within normal working hours. The time difference between the Arabian Gulf and Western Europe is three hours, but because Friday is a holiday in the Gulf, the working hours overlap is only 20 hours per week.
    2. The other is what we call *project time*. Since dispersed collaborators usually work on their different tasks in parallel, they are likely to be at different positions in the task life cycle, which easily becomes a confounding factor. Since time is in finite supply and virtual workers commonly are involved in more projects, there is also often fierce competition for focus and energy from each project (Cummings & Haas, 2012) unless properly managed.

- *Dispersion in knowledge* can be caused by individual cognitive differences, exacerbated by, e.g. professional and cultural, national/ethnic diversity, and management approach to communication, including the choice and use of channels of communication.

Human collaboration is so ubiquitous that we often do not think about the meaning of the concept. In the context of this chapter, however, a more precise understanding is important. We contend that *collaboration* takes place when three or more persons work together to achieve a common goal, for which they hold each other mutually responsible. Thus defined, collaboration is distinctly different from *cooperation* in which each participant – "operator" – produces her/his own output independently, according to a predefined plan. The key issue of *collaboration* is the interdependence between the parties in situations where the common goal, may well be mutually and precisely understood, but not necessarily the challenges and obstacles that we may encounter along the way. The key issue of *cooperation* is the prior definition of the interfaces between the individual operators' output, something which is often not possible when innovation is involved.

Based on our experience, we decompose collaboration as the product of communication and coordination, i.e.

$$\text{Collaboration} \approx \text{Communication} \bullet \text{Coordination}$$

In extreme cases, it is easy to understand that if either of the two factors approaches or equals zero, there is no collaboration; maybe lots of talk but no action, or lots of action but no talk. In other words, collaboration can be understood as the interdependence between communication and coordination.

Communication and Cognition

Communication is and must be an active dialogue-based process involving all the relevant staff, and continued until there is shared understanding, or meaning (Bjørn & Ngwenyama, 2009), of the knowledge content including, as an extreme position, that we "agree to disagree". Thus, communication is an interdependent process. Bjørn and Ngwenyama (2009) argue that "We find that all communication breakdowns are manifested and experienced by the participants at the work process level; however, resolving breakdowns may require reflections at other levels." Cognition can be difficult enough when one is trying to make sense of the world alone, but obviously becomes much more complicated as numbers increase (Weick, 1995; Malhotra, 2000; Klitmøller & Lauring, 2013). Importantly, communication is distinct from "distribution of information", which can be thought of as one-way transmission of information. Regrettably common examples of this difference are: 'I did text you ...', 'but the background material is on the server ...', 'I did send you the agenda information ...', 'I thought that we agreed ...'.

Coordination and Cognition

Coordination, the second factor of collaboration, parallels communication in the interdependence of decision-making and choice of actions between collaborators. In virtual work, the individual often works in isolation and outside a collocated chain of command and is, therefore, to some considerable degree autonomous, self-led. Without the frequent day-to-day interaction of collocated team members, and the resulting myriad of little meaning-making course corrections, the individual member of a virtual team can easily drift significantly off course between the formal video conferences. This requires organizing principles or mechanisms, e.g. a decision-making manager, Standard Operating Procedures, manuals, a Community of Practice. Irrespective of the actual choice of organizing principle, the dispersion in location, time, and knowledge becomes even more dependent upon intra-group communication and meta-communication, particularly when complexity, significant rate of change, and task uncertainty are prevalent. It is the responsibility of the "owner" of the virtual team – possibly through delegation – to ensure that the requisite coordinating mechanisms are in place.

Virtual Work and Information and Communication Technology (ICT)

Virtual work has been around for thousands of years, e.g. between Rome and her commanders in the occupied territories, and between the British Viceroy in India and the Foreign Office in London. The beginning of ICT was really the lighted beacon, the semaphore, and telegraph; with the advent of ICT on top of the Internet, however, prevalence and dispersion of virtual workers and speed of transmission has increased exponentially within the last generation. Gigabit bandwidth availability, mobile phones, social media, cloud computing, big data analytics, machine learning, neural networks, and probably widespread augmented reality just around the corner, are transforming the ICT arena at a breath-taking pace (Mosco, 2017). We will only briefly place videoconferencing in the ICT taxonomy of "media richness" (Daft & Lengel, 1984), which roughly expresses how much information can be transmitted by various media, later expanded to include "media naturalness" (Kock, 2005; Smith, 2014).

Perhaps not surprisingly there are noticeable generational differences in the preferred ICT media depending on what was available at the time the various generations grew up.[2] There are now available several well-performing videoconferencing tools, some packaged with document/file sharing, an internal wiki (like Wikipedia) to assist learning, persistent chats, screen sharing, the option of segmenting users into teams or channels, meeting calendar/organizer, and a T-bot ("chat-robot") that you can talk to for help. These packages can significantly enhance the productivity of teams – and may lead to frustrating information and technology overload and despair for the less IT savvy team members. It may be worth considering introducing "newbies" to virtual work through a simulation game (Gilson, Maynard, & Bergiel, 2013; Devine, Martin, Bott, & Grayson, 2004).

Gestalt and Virtual Work

Above, we have made the assertion that in principle there is no difference between virtual and collocated collaborative work, except that virtual work will suffer disproportionally from absent, insufficient, or inadequate communication and coordination. Why, then, is it more challenging to work virtually if virtual and collocated work is essentially the same, and both contexts are made up of contingent, complex interdependencies between different individuals with their individual cognitions? On an abstract level the answer is simple: a reduced ability to be fully aware of the dynamics within the virtual context, caused by the virtual context and the nature of the available communication media. To illustrate this point, imagine your ability to be fully aware during a collocated meeting if you were blindfolded or had your ears plugged.

Since, however, we cannot normally be aware of that of which we are not aware, supported by the insight of Bjørn & Ngwenyama (2009) that "resolving breakdowns may require reflections at other levels," we need meta-awareness. "Gestalt,"[3] the constituent elements of which we briefly describe in the following, is our preferred awareness and meta-awareness "navigator." With this cognitive and experiential competence, we can become better at constantly moving our own awareness among different domains, the most important of which are:

- content (or task) awareness
- process awareness
- context awareness
- meta-awareness

Although still debated (Blom, 2013), we consider gestalt a paradigm, a complementary synthesis of four main parts. At the end of the description of each, we have added a brief vignette from our practice to illustrate how awareness and meta-awareness may be helpful.

1. *Gestalt psychology* flourished in the first decades of the 20th century as an experimental psychology, attempting to understand the laws behind our ability to acquire and process meaningful perceptions. Gestalt psychology posits that the mind forms a global whole, which we tend to order in a manner that is regular, orderly, and as simple as possible, into "good gestalts" (Ellis, 1997; Rock, 2006). Today, gestalt psychology has been swallowed by cognitive psychology and its neuro physiological knowledge base (Sternberg, 2016). What remains, and importantly so, is that we can never be aware of an objective reality, but only of an already processed, selected image of the world in every moment. We can, however, direct our awareness: think of Rubin's vase, demonstrating the difference between the perceptual figure and ground (Hoffman, 2000; Chabris & Simons, 2011). Our brains hijack our perceptions in every moment (Gazzaniga, Ivry, & Mangun, 2009), but this also applies to higher-level cognitive processing, e.g. the so-called ladder of inference, originally described by Chris Argyris (Senge,

2006). To make matters worse, participants may sometime experience cognitive dissonance due to technical problems, e.g. varying delays between visual and auditory output, or significant pixellation of screen displays.

During a videoconference the manager notes that the group is not making progress towards its objective. She therefore changes focus to process awareness and notices that participants clearly do not see things the same way: differing individual interpretations, and failure to listen carefully to what is actually being said are clues that the group needs to pause and consider the process they are engaged in. The manager pauses the meeting and asks the group to direct their attention to the differences between figure and ground. If the video conference is recorded, team members can see examples of body language they have interpreted as disinterest, energy has dropped, and sub-groups have formed to try to convince one another that their point of view is "right". A pause to consider process is an important skill and can be learned with the help of the manager or facilitator.

2. *Field theory* was formulated by Kurt Lewin (1997). His profound insight is that a person's Behavior, the Person, and his/her Environment are interdependent or, in symbolic notation, $B = f[P, E]$ (f stands for "function of"). Thus, behavior is always contingent, linked to Lewin's notion of the "life space" as that "which has existence in the moment" (ibid.); "existence" meaning that which has attracted or commanded (psychological) *energy*. This view can also be extended to groups, such that B is the group behavior, P the group members, and E is the group environment, like Foulkes' "group matrix" (Foulkes, 1964). One of the important ramifications is that a group cannot be understood merely as a passive aggregation: "The whole is other than the sum of its parts" (Sansone, Morf & Panter, 2004). This also relates to the question of causality; in groups, as indeed with individuals, it cannot be linear or deterministic (Couldry & Hepp, 2016).

It is easy to understand that subgroups may form around any theme, issue, identity element, need etc. if it is associated with more (psychological) energy than the overall team task. A subgroup, therefore, can be short-lived or more enduring depending on the theme around which it forms. The theme of "functional sub groups" is dealt with by Agazarian (2004), and "difficult groups" by Weisboard (Weisboard & Janoff, 2010). It is a general human trait that we tend to momentarily polarize members of the groups or subgroups to which we belong into "us", and non-members into "them" (Johnson, 2014; Berreby, 2005). Subgroups relevant to virtual work not infrequently form around professional affiliation, ethnicity, organizational affiliation, role, function, status. Another facet of the virtual field is trust, which should be encouraged and talked about as early as possible; it is initially often fragile and in need of reinforcement and calibration (Crisp & Jarvenpaa, 2013). The complexity of a given virtual field is obviously dependent upon the number of team members and their diversity (Jensen & Jackson, 2007) and for this reason alone, team size should be restricted; there does not appear to be one number cast in stone, but five to six may be optimal (Lim & Klein, 2006), probably corresponding to the vaguely defined optimal number for collocated teams (HBR Guide to Making Every meeting Matter, 2016).

The manager and team are in the midst of merging two teams into one, increasing the complexity of team interactions. Video conferencing allows the new team to look at the new situation and begin to restructure their interactions. The manager is particularly focused on what goes on at the level of the team. They all decide to reconfigure the team in such a way that sub-groups can be utilized, avoiding large group meetings when possible. With smaller groups meeting they can increase their knowledge of one another, the experience they bring with them, and their efficiency. They also agree on the interface and gate-keeper functions between the (sub) teams.

3. *Phenomenology* is the final part of the gestalt paradigm, grappling with important questions of self, consciousness, and identity, how existence becomes experience (Zahavi, 2014). It exists as two somewhat overlapping domains: as a philosophy and as a methodology. It is the latter that is most figural in gestalt work in organizations in which a person is understood as an embodied and socially and culturally embedded being-in-the-world. Precisely for this reason, considering the cognitive processing that takes place every second, the interdependence between subject and environment, as well as responsibility and choice, we need the phenomenological focusing on the here-and-now as well as, in Husserl's words, "the things themselves" (Husserl, 2014). Thus, peeled out of categories, biases, prejudices etc. through "bracketing" or "epoché", i.e. the systematic procedure of "phenomenological reduction", we are assumed able to suspend judgment

regarding all other beliefs, and this way examine phenomena as they are originally given to consciousness.

> The manager of this team, as with many other virtual team managers, is coping with members that are spread across several time zones and cultures. She has learned that an important skill is to develop her own curiosity on – awareness of – how the team members understand and interpret what is happening, constantly reminding team members to relate to what was actually said or done, rather than on their un reflected, instantaneous thoughts and feelings. The use of recorded video conferencing allows team members and manager to replay if sufficiently important misunderstandings inhibit the way the team engages.

4. *Humanistic existentialism* became an element of gestalt thinking primarily through the influence of Jean Paul Sartre (Sartre, 2007) and Simone de Beauvoir. The axiom of existentialism is that "existence precedes essence," that we are "condemned to freedom," and that all human beings bear the responsibility for the choices they make in life, without which life is absurd (Sartre, 2007). Man's ultimate responsibility is to become truly himself, stripped of illusions and vanity, because only this way can he make the best contribution to humanity.

> In one on one meetings the manager encouraged team members to consider work and career goals and the choices they are making. The dialogue focuses on their intentions and what impact they are having on team members. During group video conferences the manager notes examples of how she can reinforce team member accountability – when and how they choose/make decisions and take responsibility for their choices.

Putting It All Together

We have argued that virtual and collocated work in principle are equivalent, and that virtual work inevitably and forcefully exposes any communicative-relational shortcomings. Thus, it would be tempting to emulate as closely as possible the collocated work context, but this would defy the raison d'être of virtual work: the ability to utilize geographically dispersed team members from different disciplines while avoiding travelling time and cost. However, both collocated and virtual work is about collaboration – communication and coordination – and it is equally important in the two settings to prepare the foundation and ground rules by attending to the basics: communication and coordination. This is relevant to both leaders and members of virtual teams. On a somewhat abstract level, it is about creating shared understanding of mission, vision, strategy, and values as required, as well as shared understanding of not just content but also meta-communication and meta-coordination

Having come this far, it would be tempting to roll out a long list of do's and don'ts but that may well be a distraction from the skilled, awareness-directed approach we are advocating. The leader needs to develop and hone the meta-awareness that will allow him/her to oscillate between context, content and process focus in the here-and-now of every moment.

Leading and leadership in collocated and virtual work are in many ways not too different. One aspect is, however, often different: leaders of virtual work lead people who are of necessity largely self-led, due to the dispersion, and resultant isolation, in location, time and knowledge. This calls for a humble understanding of the complementarity between leader and the self-led. Inspiration for this can, e.g. be found in "translucence" – the "'triangulation of visibility, awareness, and accountability" (Bjørn & Ngwenyama, 2009) – and the "need to learn, relearn and unlearn" (Caulat, 2012). Leaders of virtual teams need to be particularly aware of the potential 'Bermuda Triangle' – in which things magically disappear – between:

- A precise and mutually understood goal, what needs to be achieved
- What is done, and how it is done, as well as the professional and personal autonomy of all involved
- The group's needs and constraints

Members of a virtual team are more dependent upon a crystal-clear understanding of who needs to talk to/interact with whom about what when and how. They cannot calibrate their individual cognitions around the water cooler, in the canteen, when running into one another in the corridors, or at other meetings. Nor does distribution of information necessarily of itself create shared understanding. This requires awareness of what *actually* is, rather than what our brains may lead us to believe. A virtual team, therefore needs to have some meta-awareness; ideally evenly distributed across the team but under all circumstance with the team leader. It may be wise to designate a facilitator for videoconference meetings, whose task it is to keep an eye on the process of the meeting, rather than its content.

Three caveats belong here:

1. It is non-delegatable responsibility of the formal leader of a virtual team to explicitly stake out the requisite 'playing field' or 'ground rules' for the team at the very beginning, bearing in mind that this will limit, at least to some degree, the autonomy of the team members. Examples of this may be:

    - checking into meetings a few minutes ahead of time
    - clear objectives for every meeting
    - no multitasking, e.g. by receiving phone calls, reading mails, or texting under the table during the meeting
    - muting your microphone when not speaking to reduce/eliminate background noise
    - *everybody* contributes something, however little, at each meeting
    - background material and agenda are always distributed *prior to* each meeting
    - decide who compiles the minutes of the meetings, if required etc.
    - the directed attention onto each speaker in the video conference should be disturbed as little as possible. Normal binaural hearing, for example, enables us to precisely locate sounds and contribute to discriminate individual voices. Videoconference sound is usually 'mono', however, so we lose much of the ability to locate individual voices in the presence of background noise or when several participants speak at the same time. This may be aggravated by the fact that we cannot necessarily get visual clues, e.g. lip-reading, facial expressions, body language etc. from video conference software that cannot track who is speaking
    - participants in video conferences should all be virtual, with no face-to-face participants, as there is a pronounced tendency for these to dominate meetings.

2. Differences concerning the relationship between a formal leader and his or her reports may be influenced by cultural norms, e.g. the "power distance," "individuality," and "uncertainty avoidance" indices of Hofstede (Hofstede, 2016) as further elaborated in the GLOBE study (House, Hanges, Javidan, Dorfman, & Gupta, 2004). Some team members may have expectations of the relation between leader and subordinate that are not commensurate with yours. For example, if you as a low-power-distance leader have team members from one or more high-power-distance or low-individuality cultures you cannot necessarily expect dissenting answers to a question like "Do we all agree on …" Similarly, do not expect enthusiastic support for a "Let's try it and see what happens" approach from team members from cultures with high uncertainty avoidance. Differences between professional cultures may be equally troublesome, e.g. between medical doctors and IT specialist collaborating on a tele-health problem. If relevant, it may be wise to articulate

this possibility from the start, so that any subsequent team dysfunctionality stemming from this can be dealt with in a non-punitive manner.Significant uncertainty in the virtual interpersonal space can become quite existential and lead to subgroup formation around those who perceive each other as "birds of a feather", silo thinking, or even withdrawal (Jensen & Jackson, 2007). This can be quite stressful for some or all, and seriously impair the team work if energy and focus is directed more towards maintaining or defending individual identities than towards the team goal. The ultimate subgroup consists of only one person, me, and if the subgroup pressure becomes sufficiently strong I often encapsulate myself in my professional role; again, a position that does not promote teamwork. One way of counteracting the tendency to "ivory tower isolation" and promote the development of team identity and spirit is to schedule regular, brief meetings that emulate collocated presence, with the sole purpose of attending to the social landscape and wellbeing of the team, rather than the virtual project.

3. Video conference technology and software has developed significantly and can utilize an impressive array of ancillary functions. But all it takes is one camera, microphone, or internet connection that is not working as intended before an entire team is wasting valuable time waiting for somebody to sort out the problem. If the first video conferences of a virtual team are marred by technical problems, it will be hard work to get the team members to be committed to this way of working. Therefore, prior to going live, we strongly urge you to arrange an individual hands-on session with each team member with the sole purpose of testing every bit of equipment, and the competence to use it, at both ends.

In conclusion, we began this chapter with axiomatic assumptions about human communicative-relational behavior, some of its components, and a basic belief that *in principle* there is no difference between collocated and virtual work. *In practice*, however, virtual work ruthlessly amplifies the consequences of the dynamic complexity, flaws, incomplete knowledge, uncertainty, or lack of shared meaning in the interpersonal virtual space. Communication and Information Technology is important as enablers in virtual organizational work but may paradoxically also contribute to some of its challenges. This means that both leaders and staff must be constantly on the lookout for and able to address inadequate communication and coordination or, in other words, be capable of meta-dialogue. We have illustrated points of reflection for some of the important videoconference and leadership choices to be made along the way. We firmly believe that videoconferencing is here to stay, and can make significant, valuable contributions to virtual work in many different contexts when used appropriately, i.e. maintaining awareness of and effectively dealing with any potential pitfalls. In an appendix we have included a checklist that can be used to inspire meaningful questions, reflections, and a gap analysis for leaders and staff who want to dive into or look for ways to improve existing use of videoconferencing.

Appendix

Virtual Work Checklist and Gap Analysis

Please reflect on the following indicators of effective virtual team communication and coordination. This is not about right or wrong, but only about *what is*. The value of the checklist stems from the team's shared understanding of what we do well, and what we might do better. Be prepared to use the checklist again as the virtual work progresses.

Rate the effectiveness of the leader and the team on each of the dimensions of virtual teams by using these scores:

4= Strongly Agree 3= Agree 2= Disagree 1= Strongly Disagree

You can also use this document for a gap analysis by indicating where you and the team are (A), and where you would like or need to be (B), for example on a scale from 1 to 5 ...

Table 20.1 Virtual work checklist

Leader	Team	A	B
Technology			
We have the Information and Communication Technology (ICT) we need			
We have been trained and are comfortably competent using our ICT			
Goals			
We know how our individual goals align to team/organization goals			
We pursue our individual and team goals with energy, drive, and a need to finish			
We have a shared vision on the team			
Communication			
We communicate with each other openly and honestly			

(Continued)

Table 20.1 (Cont.)

Leader Team A B

We display genuine curiosity and interest in the perspectives of others

We have virtual "water cooler" or "morning coffee" meetings in between task-dedicated meetings

We have a high level of participation at our meetings

We listen to different ideas with an open mind

We have fun on this team

Coordination

We cooperate and coordinate with one another

We show respect for different cultures

We are flexible and adapt to time zone challenges

Subgroups

We have no inner circles or other subgroups on the team

We are all on this team because of our individual competences

Output and outcome of virtual work

We deliver on time, on quality, and on budget

We analyze our successes and failures for clues to improvement

Leadership

We experience a good balance between professional autonomy and leadership direction

Note: Used with Permission © 2018, Donna Dennis, Ph.D. and Ivan Jensen, MD., Gestalt International Study Centre.

Notes

1 *"Plus ça change, plus c'est la même chose"* (The more things change, the more they remain the same); the quote is attributed to French writer Jean-Baptiste Alphonse Karr, a one-time editor of *Le Figaro*.
2 See https://pages.avanade.com/rs/857-NHG-455/images/Avanade-Office365-neue-Tools-Mehrwert.pdf
3 "Gestalt" is a German word that has no immediate English equivalent; it can be used as a noun and verb meaning roughly "form or shape" or "to give form or shape to". Today, "gestalt" may denote gestalt psychology, gestalt therapy and (organizational) work on gestalt grounds.

Reference

Agazarian, Y.M. (2004). *Systems-Centered Therapy for Groups*. London: Karnac Books.

Berreby, D. (2005). *Us and Them: Understanding Your Tribal Mind*. New York: Little, Brown and Company.

Bjørn, P., & Ngwenyama, O. (2009). Virtual team collaboration: Building shared meaning, resolving breakdowns and creating translucence. *Information Systems Journal, 19*: 227–253.

Blom, S. (2013). *"Identy Work" in the Context of Organizational Change: A Gestalt Perspective*. Derby: University of Derby.

Caulat, G. (2012). *Virtual Leadership: Learning to Lead Differently*. Faringdon: Libri Publishing.

Chabris, C., & Simons, D. (2011). *The Invisible Gorilla: How our Intuitions Deceive Us*. New York: HarperCollins Publishers.

Couldry, N., & Hepp, A. (2016). *The Mediated Construction of Reality*. Cambridge: Polity.

Crisp, C., & Jarvenpaa, S. (2013). Swift trust in global virtual teams: Trusting beliefs and normative actions. *Journal of Personnel Psychology, 23:* 45–56.

Cummings, J., & Haas, M. (2012). So many teams, so little time: Time allocation matters in geographically dispersed teams. *Journal of Organizational Behavior, 33*: 316–341.

Daft, R., & Lengel, R. (1984). Information richness: a new approach to managerial behavior and organizational design. In L. Cummings, & B. Staw (Eds), *Research in Organizational Behavior*. Homewood, IL: JAI Press.

Devine, D.H., Martin, K., Bott, J., & Grayson, A. (2004). Tinsel Town: A top management simulation involving distributed expertise. *Simulation and Gaming, 35*: 94–134, doi:10.1177/1046878103258193

Ellis, W.E. (1997). *Gestalt Psychology*. Gouldsboro, ME: The Gestalt Journal Press.

Foulkes, S.H. (1964). *Therapeutic Group Analysis*. London: George Allen & Unwin Ltd.

Gazzaniga, M.S., Ivry, R.B., & Mangun, G.R. (Eds). (2009). *Cognitive Neuroscience: The Biology of the Mind*. New York, NY: W.W. Norton.

Gilson, L., Maynard, M., & Bergiel, E. (2013). Virtual team effectiveness: An experiential activity. *Small Group Research, 44*: 412–427.

Haselager, P., Dijk, J. v., & Rooij, I. v. (2008). A Lazy brain? Embodied embedded cognition and cognitive neuroscience. I. P. Calvo, & T. Gomila (Eds), *Handbook of Cognitive Science: An Embodied Approach*. Oxford: Elsevier.

HBR Guide to Making Every Meeting Matter. (2016). Boston: Harvard Business Review.

Hoffman, D. (2000). *Visual Intelligence: How We Create What We See*. New York: W.W.Norton.

Hofstede, G.H. (2016). *Culture's Consequences: Comparing Values, Behaviors, Instiitutions and Organizations Across Nations*. Thousand Oaks, CA: SAGE Publications.

House, R.J., Hanges, P.J., Javidan, M., Dorfman, P.W., & Gupta, V. (Eds). (2004). *Culture, Leadership, and Organizations*. Thousand Oaks, CA: Sage Publications.

Husserl, E. (2014). *Ideas for a Pure Phenomenology and Phenomenological Philosophy I*. Cambridge MA: Hackett Publishing Company, Inc.

Jensen, I., & Jackson, P. (2007). Social Uncertainty in virtual organizations: A preliminary ontology of the constituent elements. In J.J. Klobas, *Becoming Virtual: Knowledge Management and Transformation of the Distributed Organization*. Heidelberg: Physica-Verlag.

Johnson, B. (2014). *Polarity Management*, 2nd edition. Amherst, MA: HRD Press.

Klitmøller, A., & Lauring, J. (2013). When global virtual teams share knowledge: Media richness, cultural difference and language commonality. *Journal of World Business*, *48*(3): 398–406.

Kock, N. (2005). Media richness or media naturalness? The evolution of our biological communication apparatus and its influence on our behaviour toward e-communication tools. *IEEE Transactions on Professional Communication*, *48*(2): 117–130.

Lim, B., & Klein, K.J. (2006). Team mental models and team performance: A field study of the effects of team mentalk model similarity and accuracy. *Journal of Organizational Behaviour*, *27*: 403–4018.

Lojeski, K.S. (2010). *Leading the Virtual Workforce: How Great Leaders Transform Organizations in the 21st Century*. Hoboken, NJ: John Wiley & Sons.

Lojeski, K.S., Reilly, R.R. (2010). *Leading the Virtual Workforce: How Great Leaders Transform Organizations in the 21st Century*. Hoboken, NJ: John Wiley & Sons.

Malhotra, Y. (2000). *Knowledge Management and Virtual Organizations*. London: IDEA Group Publishing.

Mosco, V. (2017). *Becoming Digital: Toward a Post-Internet Society*. Bingley: Emerald Publishing, Ltd.

Nemiro J., Beyerlein M., Bradley L., & Beyerlein S. (2008). *The Handbook of High-Performance Teams: A Toolkit for Collaborating Across Boundaries*. San Francisco: Jossey Bass.

Rock, D. (2006). *Quiet Leadership: Six Steps to Transforming Performance at Work*. New York: Harper-Collins.

Sansone C., Morf, C.C., & Panter, A.T. (Eds) (2004). *The Sage Handbook of Methods in Social Psychology*. Thousand Oaks: SAGE Publications.

Sartre, J.-P. (2007). *Existentialism and Humanism*. Slingsby: Methuen Publishing Ltd.

Seibdrat, F., Hoegl, M., & Hogler, E. (2007). How to manage virtual teams. *Sloan Management Journal*.

Smith, R.S. (2014). Collaborative bandwidth: Creating better virtual meetings. *Organization Development Journal*, *32*(4): 15–38.

Stacey, R. (2010). *Complexity and Organizational Reality: Uncertainty and the Need to Rethink Management After the Collapse of Investment Capitalism*, 2nd edition. New York: Routledge.

Sternberg, R.J. (2016). *Cognitive Psychology*, 7th edition. Andover: Cengage Learning.

Weick, K. (1995). *Sensemaking in Organizations*.Thousand Oaks, CA: Wiley.

Weisboard, M., & Janoff, S. (2010). Keeping difficult situations from becoming difficult groups. In S. Schuman, *The Handbook for Working with Difficult Groups: How The Are Difficult, Why They are Difficult and What You Can Do about It* (s. 1–16). New York: Jossey-Bass.

Zahavi, D. (2014). *Self and Other: Exploring Subjectivity, Empathy, and Shame*. Oxford: Oxford University Publishing.

Zemlianski, P., & Amant, K.S. (Red.). (2008). *Virtual Workplaces and the New Nature of Business Practice*. Hershey, PA: Information Science Reference.

21 A Reflexive Account

Group Consultation via Video Conference

Nuala Dent

Using myself as a reflexive subject, this chapter explores my experience of consulting with three groups using video conferencing platforms. These studies include: consulting with a global group of tertiary students on task and process; coaching a group of female academic leaders in Saudi Arabia; and facilitating reflective inquiry with a team of therapists in Australia. As well as delving into the particulars of each scenario, the chapter will look more broadly at themes, patterns, similarities and/or differences across the scenarios.

The chapter will consider how technology affects the task, the interplay of physical and online places, and the impact of these on the way group members and the group-as-a-whole are internalised and worked with. My central argument is that groups require a psychic space for thinking and the challenge for groups that meet via video conference is to discover how such a space can be created and sustained.

The term "face-to-face" means "to be in each other's sight or presence." Traditionally used to denote a meeting of people in the same physical place, it can also describe people who meet on video conferencing platforms. The ambiguity regarding usage of the term is unsettling and may reflect a deeper uncertainty about the impact of technology on the ways in which we meet, communicate and work or about the meaning of presence. What does it mean to be in each other's presence through the medium of a digital technology platform?

I search for words to distinguish these different face-to-face meetings. I could identify them as "physical" and "virtual" but this implies one is real and the other not-real. To describe a video conference meeting as "online" suggests that a meeting where all members are in the same room is "offline," upsetting traditional notions about what is required to be present to each other and engaged with the task. Not discounting this paradox, for the purposes of this chapter I will use "face-to-face" to denote a group meeting in the same physical place and "online" to denote a group meeting via technology and the medium of computer/electronic device.

My first experience of research into online groups was the analysis of the dynamics of a large study group that met over a four-week period via an online text-based discussion forum. One of the key hypotheses from this analysis is that the online experience may "amplify the pressure on members to conform to group norms, to not question the group think in an attempt to avoid annihilation" (Dent, 2010: 30). This led me to another opportunity for inquiry into the dynamics of an organization's online workspace. In this context, a new organization with a global membership sought to explore members' engagement with its online platform, which aimed to promote collaborative working arrangements. Themes of (in)visibility and (dis)connection emerged.

> As remote participants, we are only seeing the part of the system that is presented to us … akin to sensory deprivation. We see that which is on the screen, but the camaraderie, background noises, eye contact, body language, break time conversations are absent. We are often in isolation, at computer screens, in a variety of settings, time zones, climates etc., and with subsequent varying levels of energy to engage with the task. It is easy for us to "hide" in the group and project onto our computers. Without any external feedback, these act like mirrors and we may consequently introject our projections and feelings (such as disconnection, isolation, disengagement, apathy, powerlessness), and these feelings may become exacerbated.
>
> (Jennings and Dent, 2012: 4)

This chapter aims to develop a deeper understanding of the dynamics that come into being when using video conferencing for group consultation and how disruptions impact the creation and/or finding of psychic space. It is written using a systems psychodynamics lens (Coplin, 1967), an interdisciplinary approach that combines psychodynamic principles derived from object relations theory as it applies to group functioning, with the growing body of principles and techniques that emerged from the fields of "group dynamics" research and practice.

> Each member of a group inhabits three realms of reality. First, he inhabits his private world of thoughts and dreams, uncommunicated and largely uncommunicable. Second, he inhabits a world that is shared by others conceived of in terms of time and space about which a good deal of agreement can be gained without much difficulty. This is the ordinary world of common sense that is objectively perceived. And third, he inhabits a world of shared creations of the mind, phantasies, attitudes, values, assumptions and misgivings, that have little conclusive to show for themselves objectively, but by virtue of being "held in common" have a great influence on the life of the group members and are in that sense extremely real.
>
> (Gosling, 1977: 868)

In simple terms, it is the study of groupings and phenomena (Long, 2013). It looks beyond the obvious to the underlying dynamics and considers how these dynamics are connected.

Three Scenarios

1 Consulting to a Group of Tertiary Students: Finding the Psychic Space with the Optimal Resources of Space and Time

In 2012, I was contracted to work with a group of students enrolled in a new blended tertiary study program on organizational analysis. Classes were offered through a combination of physical five-day workshops and online seminars, individual supervision in the form of role analysis, small learning groups, discussion forums, and online library over a three-year period.

I had the opportunity to attend the first face-to-face seminar before the online work began. My earlier research and experience indicated that a physical meeting would be important for the ongoing work in the online space. I spent five days in the same physical space with the students, getting a sense of them, letting them "get into me." My embodied experience created a connection to the students that proved helpful in my work with them online and gave me a greater sense how my role might contribute to the journey of study they were embarking on.

As consultant to a small online learning group, I had the dual task of consulting to group process as well as to the students' learning tasks. The group comprised seven mature age students, geographically dispersed across Europe, Asia and Australia. We met for two-hour sessions every four weeks, in a "virtual classroom" in a "virtual" school. The classroom offered video and/or audio conferencing, a visual representation of everyone in the room, shared whiteboard/presentation space, and public and private chat.

The Experience

This was a new program, and a new way of working for all staff on the program. In working with groups, a decision was made that we would consult in pairs. This alleviated some of my anxiety of working in this new way. I did not have to be omniscient. I could trust my co-consultant to pick up what I couldn't see, hear, think or feel in this online environment.

My co-consultant and I aimed to create an intentional "work group" (Bion, 1961b), using a reflective process to promote awareness of fantasies and covert actions that might either detract from or support the work. We developed a way of working where, between our sessions with students, we would meet to reflect and develop working hypotheses. By working hypothesis I mean "The best fit one is capable of making of the complexity of reality, ready to be replaced with another that better approximates what the truth might be" (Lawrence, 2006: 39). I propose this work we did in our consulting pair provided a containing function for the work with the group; it acted as a "container" (Bion, 1984) to take in and hold the disruptive feelings that arose in the group sessions.

The working hypotheses were shared and tested with students as we came to understand some of the dynamics at play, notably the anxiety related to learning which fostered an over-dependency on the teachers, that is a "basic assumption dependence" mentality (Bion, 1961a), and the oscillation between connection/disconnection in the online environment. Students spoke of feeling connected in the sessions but disconnected between them. They often arrived feeling ambivalent and left feeling re-energised. It made me wonder about the optimum amount of time required between sessions to maintain a sense of connection with others, a continuity of being part of the group. In Winnicott's terms, what would be "good enough" (Winnicott, 1971), that is, what active adaptation was required to meet the students' needs. In the staff group, there was consensus about the challenges of connection, but program costings meant the design could not be changed at that time. Despite this, we were able to work intentionally on the task of learning through experience.

The geographic spread and multiple time zones presented an ongoing challenge to find suitable times that worked across these zones and fitted with people's schedules. And the reality was that it was morning for some people, evening for others; some people were readying for sleep while others were gearing up for the day. Joining the sessions from multiple countries and devices meant that the internet connection was often unstable and disrupted our capacity to think. We developed "work arounds." One way was to turn the video off to decrease this instability and rely on audio and chat to do the work. Fortunately, we could still "see" who was in the room, represented by names next to microphones. We used these as cues. When a person was about to speak, the microphone would pick up their inhalation and represent it visually. Sometimes, when the internet connection was particularly bad and there was a lot of echo, we would ask people to mute if they weren't speaking. However, without the sounds of breathing and background noise, we found we would lose sense of who was in the room. At various times, some people could hear but not be heard, or vice versa, and the group (or someone in the group) would narrate the conversation by text using the chat function of the classroom. This became quite innovative, with people using different colors as visual identifiers.

A particular learning for me is related to the physical place from which we connect to an online group. I remember one session in the evening as I was working from home. I had asked my family not to disturb me. They were in another part of the house while my dog was whining outside the door, wanting to be let in. I tried to ignore the dog because I felt that to acknowledge him would be stepping out of my work role into my family role. As the dog became more insistent, my anxiety grew. We were not using video in this session and I had muted my microphone so as not to disturb the group. I found myself caught between two roles, two worlds. I was simultaneously in a work environment and at home, a consultant and a pet owner. To ignore the dog, felt like a pretence of sorts, a fantasy. Once I realized this, I explained my situation to the group, bringing my dog into the room. This revelation could be described as the surfacing of an "unthought known," an experience known to me, about which I was previously unable to think (Bollas, 1987). My action shifted something in the group, and they too brought something of the experience of their physical environments into the shared space. Prior to my acknowledgement of the situation, nobody online "knew" about the dog and yet, I believe it was "known" at an unconscious level. This highlights the need for me that, when online, we accept the reality of where we are (physically) and consider how this might impact our engagement.

I worked in this system for two years and, over time, the challenges of maintaining engagement grew and began to outweigh the benefits of being involved in this work. Working with students for two hours every four weeks was not enough to sustain the sense of connection that I had when we started. I did not meet them in the same physical place after the first workshop, though they came together with other staff fairly regularly for the duration of the program. To remain connected, for example through attendance at online seminars or by reading and commenting in discussion forums, required a much bigger investment of time and energy than I had the resources to commit or was contracted to do. In the end, it was unsustainable and I resigned from the position. This suggests that, when compared to a face-to-face setting, an online environment may require a greater investment of time and energy to create and maintain a psychic space that supports learning through experience.

2 Coaching a Group of Academic Leaders: Finding the Psychic Space Across Cultural Differences

In 2014–2015, I coached a group of women in Saudi Arabia. This was part of an executive leadership program commissioned by a women's university in Saudi Arabia for their senior leaders. The program comprised face-to-face modules, online seminars and individual and group coaching over a twelve-month period.

I was contracted to work with a small group of five leaders, to provide both individual and group coaching online, and to work with them during a face-to-face module in Saudi Arabia. My first interaction with each participant was about two months into the program. By this time, they had completed their first module and a 360-degree leadership assessment. My first contact was individual online sessions to meet each of them and debrief their leadership profile. This was followed soon after by a face-to-face five-day intensive module, then six more online individual coaching sessions and two group coaching sessions over the next eight months.

I was anxious going into the first session, having little knowledge of the people, their culture or their expectations. We had been advised to "go slowly." I thought a lot about transference and anticipating they would be wearing niqabs (face veils), I wondered what visual cues there might be to work with. My supervisor reminded me that I would have my own experience, the feelings evoked in me, as data. This was helpful and while there were the inevitable frustrations with technology (particularly so in Saudi Arabia as many of the digital platforms were blocked at that time), these initial sessions were quite satisfying. The women did not wear any head covering, required only in the presence of males. One woman needed an interpreter, but the other four had completed their doctorates overseas and were fluent in English. They were interested and eager to learn about themselves, and even more to learn about me. I sensed a great desire for contact with western culture.

The Experience

We found Google Hangouts to be the most stable platform for our online meetings. I had encouraged them to find somewhere quiet where they wouldn't be disturbed for these meetings. They chose to meet with me on Fridays, a non-work day for them, and mostly logged in from home. Those with children were often distracted by family matters, as I had been by the dog, and we worked around this. I would hear people calling out in the background, children wanting attention. We were sometimes joined by babies or toddlers, cuddling with mum as she spoke with me about her challenges and aspirations at work.

The group were working on a shared learning task and would present their findings at the conclusion of the program. The purpose of the group sessions was to think with them about how they were working together yet it felt almost impossible to work on the task. The internet connection was not stable, consequently we worked without video. One person did not speak English so there were times when the group spoke in Arabic and the energy seemed to change. They sounded relaxed and I enjoyed the lyrical nature of their discussion. In English, it was more laborious. The group wanted to focus on connecting with me and each other as female confidantes, whereas I wanted them to work with the concept of person-in-role and to consider role-relatedness in relation to the task. I wondered if their reluctance to join me in this was an attack on my role as consultant to the group. Alternatively, it could be related to the Saudi Arabian culture, that we needed to do the work of connecting and approach the task in an indirect manner.

It is helpful here to consider the definition of role as "the patterning of ideas by which a person organises their behaviour in relation to a specific situation" (Reed, 2000). Reed goes on to identify role as having both psychological and social aspects:

Psychological – the person "constructs" a set of behavioural patterns so that they can act in the situation to achieve the desired goal
Sociological – the expectations and intentions of other people in the system about how the person should conduct themselves

These two aspects influence how a person-in-role manages themselves in relation to their current circumstances. I suggest that in this case, it is the importation of a western paradigm to a middle-eastern culture which may have created profound/intolerable anxiety and mobilized "basic assumption" mentality (Bion, 1961a), where members unconsciously act to avoid thought or feeling related to the task.

The program was designed to teach women how to take up leadership as it is thought about in western society and yet, in Saudi Arabia, women have little opportunity to do this. This is a patriarchal society where women are subjugated to men and often do not have a sense of their own agency. As well as gender, there are issues of competition in relation to power. These women came from families with differing status in a country that is a kingdom, not a democracy. At an unconscious level, the group may have been enacting basic assumption "me-ness" mentality, working on the tacit assumption that the group was to be a non-group (Lawrence et al., 1996).

While I was able to work with individuals in their one-on-one sessions on the paradox of western leadership in this context and their experience of group dynamics, these were unable to be worked with in the group sessions. That is, between the consultant and group members, we were unable to create the psychic space to bring together our fears and fantasies about female leaders in the reality of their world.

After the initial burst of energy, it seemed, over time, more difficult for participants to maintain engagement with some people not turning up to their final individual coaching sessions. This may have been a result of the length of time since we'd met face-to-face, or it may have been linked to the overall program, which seemed to fizzle towards the end, with the presentation ceremony (where they would share their findings) postponed twice, and ultimately delayed by two months. This may be related to a struggle, at an institutional level, to locate a psychic space to think about cross-cultural issues in relation to the program. This points to a need to consider the implications of working cross-culturally over time and in an online environment, and what might be required to find and create the optimal space for group coaching.

Reflective Inquiry with a Team of Therapists: Finding the Psychic Space with the Right Technology

In 2015–2016, as part of an action research project, I conducted reflective inquiry with a team of eight therapists in regional Victoria, Australia. The organization provides clinical services to children who have experienced trauma and are in the care of the child protection system. The research focuses on the experience of working in a partially distributed team, defined as a team that is spread across geographic locations and that has two or more people in at least one location. The aim of the research is to understand the interface of face-to-face and online ways of working and how this impacts team functioning. The sessions which are the subject of this chapter were not completely computer-mediated but a blend of physical and online, conducted via the organization's internal video conferencing system.

Prior to these sessions, I had interviewed each staff member and observed team meetings. I had led two face-to-face reflective inquiry sessions: in the first, staff members shared how they saw themselves as a team; and, in the second, I shared my experience of the team.

In the first computer-mediated session, I was in head office with the manager, while the team logged in from two other locations. This was followed by another face-to-face and computer-mediated reflective inquiry sessions, and then two computer-mediated review sessions. These were facilitated from one of the regional offices with the manager in attendance and members from the other office joined via video-conference.

The team were willing participants in the research and engaged with me in the inquiry. However, I found myself continuously frustrated by the technology. This was in stark contrast to the team's acceptance of its limitations.

The Experience

In preparation for the first computer-mediated session, I invited participants to share photos of their office for use in a social photo matrix. The social photo matrix method promotes the understanding of the unconscious in organizations by the group freely associating to photos of participant's workplaces (Sievers, 2008). I assembled a random collection of photos from each location into a presentation to share digitally. I arrived at the office with the presentation on my laptop, and on a memory stick. I came prepared with a computer cable to connect to the video conferencing display only to discover that there seemed to be nowhere to connect the cable. The manager tried to share the file on an internal shared drive, so it could be viewed locally in each location, but the team could not access the file. Instead, I found myself holding my laptop up close to the webcam so people in other locations could see and associate to the images. This felt ridiculous; it was difficult for me to hold my role and hold the team to the task of free associating. As well as exposing some of my assumptions it seemed the system was trying to tell me something about the experience of, or the value placed on the usefulness of, technology in that workplace. Joseph writes on the use of countertransference as a means of understanding the patient's individual defensive mechanisms in the psychoanalytic setting:

> If the analyst struggles … to give detailed interpretations of the meaning of individual associations, then she is living out the patient's own defensive system, making pseudo-sense of the incomprehensible, rather than trying to make contact with the patient's experience of living in an incomprehensible world.
>
> (Joseph, 1989: 446)

In systems psychodynamic research, countertransference phenomenon provides the researcher with understanding of group and system defenses against anxiety. I propose my experience was a "living out" of the team's experience of technology; experience unable to be felt or expressed. They need technology to support their work as a team, but the organization provides technological systems which are limited in their capability and consequently impact the team's capacity to work together.

Learning from this, in the first review session I decided to keep the instructions simple and asked that they provide drawing and tactile materials for use during the session. We used the video conference as the team would usually use it during team meetings. I shared my findings and then invited the staff members to work with their colleagues in their own location to create, individually or as a group, something which reflected their experience of participating in the research. Most people engaged in the activity, though some found it difficult to relax into it. I set a time boundary and, when we returned, I led them in a reflection where, with good humor, they shared their creations in front of the webcam and/or took photos which they shared using their mobile phones. This felt like a more "real" reflection of how technology is used in the organization and of the reality that they are more like two teams (based on location) than one team. We, the team and I, as a system, had found a way to work productively towards the shared task of reflecting on the experience.

However, in reflecting on the reluctance of some participants, I wondered how it was related to their work. In the location where I was, the manager and team leader were present and participants seemed less able to "play." This activity might evoke an unconscious anxiety related to their work with traumatized children. In some way, play might mean to relinquish the "adult" role and be in touch with the "child" experience. This seemed harder to do when people were with others in their reporting line. Or it could have been related to being in the same location as the researcher. What was my role in this? I pondered whether I had asked too much of them so, for the next session, instead of asking them to draw/create, I decided to provide images for them to choose from.

I prepared an electronic visual image deck (like a deck of cards, only with images) that could be viewed on the computer. People would be invited to choose one they were drawn to in response to the question "What is your experience of the research?" Then, together, the group would free associate and delve deeper into the experience.

I sent a link for the digital file to the manager ahead of time, explaining that I wanted to use it as part of the session. She assumed that everyone had received it so had not thought to do anything about having it ready for the meeting. Again, the technology was unable to be made use of in the way I had intended. I had brought hard copies with me and was able to facilitate a face-to-face activity with people in the room, however people elsewhere were unable to participate. I was struck again by, and wondered about, the manager's role in this. I had previously noted a basic assumption "dependency" (Bion, 1961b) mentality of the team towards the manager and wondered if my experience was a parallel. Was I operating in a "dependency" mentality towards the manager; wanting her to make it work, when the reality was she was not particularly interested in technology? Or was the team operating in a "dependency" mentality towards me, hoping that through my research I would identify and solve the issues related to working across locations? While it seemed crazy-making at the time, on reflection it seemed predictable. I could have pre-empted this by sending hard copies ahead of time to each location. This reflects something I had previously noticed in this workplace, a double handling of information, storing documents in both digital and electronic form; speaking to a lack of trust or confidence in the technology. In an inquiry by Jennings and Dent (2012) into the user experience of a virtual platform, this lack of trust is understood as related to problematic boundaries:

anxiety inherent in trusting the virtual space, as it is in many ways boundaryless – no time boundaries and no territory boundaries (everywhere and nowhere) ... we think the lack of trust in virtual platforms as a medium is an ongoing challenge to remote engagement, and will be until we are more comfortable with technology...The combination of unknown human elements and technological elements makes for inexhaustible experienced possibilities.

(Jennings and Dent, 2012: 5)

This resonates with my experience of this team; that there is an inherent discomfort with technology in relation to their work and this is acted out in the way they use technology to interact with each other. It raises the question about what would be the optimal use of technology to create the psychic space required for group reflection and sense-making.

Looking for Patterns

Each group I worked with had a different purpose, and there were variations related to the number of people, gender, locations, time zones and technology platforms. As explored earlier in this chapter it is my experience that place, technology and culture can have a significant impact on group mentality and the capacity to work co-operatively on a shared task. An interesting commonality that I'd like to put forward is a characteristic of psychic space related to physical proximity as experienced in very small face-to-face groups.

A prominent characteristic of the psychological field is related to the physical proximity of members to each other, i.e., to all of the other members, not just to one's neighbors. This characteristic is manifested in the self-consciousness of members about how close their hands are to those of their neighbors, whether their feet are likely to touch those of a member opposite, how big a shift backwards of their chair they can make without appearing notably hostile. Your neighbors' breathing becomes a prominent feature of your awareness; if you want to cough you must do it into someone's face unless you make a deliberate maneuver not to. Eye contact is telling when present, awkward when absent and always under keen surveillance as to its intensity and duration. It would seem that in this way the very small group is constantly faced with the problems of intimacy, particularly intimacy as a danger to be avoided.

(Gosling, 1983: 868)

In all three scenarios, when using video there seemed to be an amplification of these "very small group" characteristics regardless of group size. Despite the lack of physical proximity geographically, there is something intimate about the online group that can intensify a person's self-consciousness. It is as though, in the online group, there is no place to hide or disappear. If you're sitting at a computer, the camera shows a close-up of your face. Your microphone picks up subtle (and not so subtle) sounds, background noises. Instead of seeing the group-as-a-whole, you see the group in fragments represented by the small, pixelated, individual videos, not unlike multiple dyadic relationships occurring simultaneously. I contend that similar to Gosling's description of very small groups, this experience can be overwhelming and make it difficult to think. This characteristic of online group video interaction is one which merits further investigation.

In contrast, when there is no video, I find my attention is less divided and I can focus more on the group-as-a-whole, be aware of and work with transference and countertransference. Western writes that we need a psychic internal space in which to think, and that this is "initially formed by the creation and management of a physical external space" (Western, 2017: 208). As consultants to online groups, while we cannot manage the physical space of each participant, we can encourage them to manage their physical boundaries, for example, to find somewhere quiet where they won't be disturbed, use earphones and turn off other applications on their device. If we think of the online space as akin to a place, we can give consideration to how we manage boundaries related to this, such as the choice of platform, agreement on how to work in the space, assignment of roles, for example, moderator, note taker, timekeeper, and pay attention to and work with, rather than against, those elements that was can't control, such as the internet connection.

This links with a theme that is common across all the scenarios, a frustration with technology and subsequent struggle to identify and work with the transference in the moment. I've been curious for quite some time about our relationship with technology and how, in a sense, we reify it or treat it as a single material thing with a homogenous, undifferentiated character. This makes it easier for us to imagine it as an extension of the self that can be perfectly controlled (Wynn and Katz, 1997) or, alternatively, split off as the "other." At a societal level, it may be that we have a "basic assumption" pairing mentality with technology/internet, hoping our interaction with it will produce the magic of connection with others in different geographic locations. However, the connection is often unsatisfactory and short-lived and we return to feelings of hatred (fight/flight), despair returns (dependency) and we find a reason to pair again. This is similar to the cyclical pattern that Bion (1961b: 152) described in relation to "basic assumption" pairing.

To move from "basic assumption" to "work group" mentality, the systems psychodynamics approach stresses the importance of paying attention to physical and psychical boundaries. Time, territories, role are strictly maintained (Hayden and Molenkamp, 2004) to provide a secure-enough psychic space or "container" for the work. Winnicott (1971) calls this a transitional space, one that exists on the boundary between the inner world of feeling, fears, wishes and fantasies and the "real" world of roles and relationships, authority and accountably, between what is subjectively conceived and objectively perceived. Paradoxically, it is both created and there to be found.

To find and/or create a psychic space for thinking, consultants need to work with the group to consider how they bring themselves to the work in an online place. The primary process for groups to find a common identity is through a common task. I have found that inviting participants to share something of their preoccupations regarding their physical environment and local context, has helped the group internalise the "other" in the room, in that it enables them to "recognise a certain 'sameness' amongst themselves that ties them together and brings with it some feelings of loyalty and solidarity" (Long, 2002: 3). The task of creating the online place, is an iterative one, and a necessary part of the work each time the group meets because the group, and the psychic space of the group, is dynamic, alive and ever-changing.

Concluding Thoughts

In writing this chapter, I had to face to my own ambivalence about online groups, risking dismantling what I know about physical groups, in order to explore this emerging space. I am relieved to find that systems psychodynamics concepts are useful, not obsolete, for thinking about the dynamics. Bion (1961a) proposed that "groupishness" is the propensity of individuals, similar to other herd animals, and that it is instinctive and available to be mobilized even when the group is dispersed. My experience of working with groups online supports this theory.

One limitation of my experience is that it is not fully/solely online as in each case I have met participants in the same physical place at the beginning of the work. I have found that a physical meeting can help anchor my experience and sense of connection in the initial stages of the work. However, the sense of connection is not sustained over the long term; this being more dependent on the frequency of meetings. It may be that online groups need to continue to meet regularly in the physical space to support inter-relatedness. Alternatively, it may be that the role of consultant or researcher requires a greater anchoring and sense of connection to enable the work with participants (an exploration of their experience is beyond the scope of this chapter).

I propose that through acknowledging preoccupations in the consultant's and group members' local contexts, we can bring together many different physical places to create a shared online place. In this shared place, we can then find ways to work across differences and create a space for thinking and learning. As I write these concluding remarks, I'm aware of the danger of generalizing, because events are defined, predicated and/or determined by the social context. I conclude with the thought that this reflexive account is, for me, simultaneously a point of arrival and a point of departure. My hope is that it creates a space for others to join in further exploration.

References

Bion, W.R. (1961a). Experiences In Groups. In Bion, W.R. (Ed.) *Experiences in Groups and Other Papers*. London: Tavistock Publications.

Bion, W.R. (1961b). Group Dynamics. *Experiences in Groups, and Other Papers*. New York: Basic Books.

Bion, W.R. (1984). *Attention and Interpretation*. London, Karnac Books.

Bollas, C. (1987). *The Shadow of the Object: Psychoanalysis of the Unthought Known*. London: Free Association Books.

Coplin, H.R. (1967). Introduction. In R. Gosling, D.H. Miller, D. Woodhouse, & P.M. Turquet (Eds) *The Use of Small Study Groups in Training*.

Dent, N. (2010). *Integrating Face-To-Face and Virtual in the Study of Group Relations*. Master Of Applied Science (Organisation Dynamics) Masters, RMIT.

Gosling, R. (1977). Another Source of Conservatism in Groups. *Group Analysis*, 10.

Gosling, R. (1983). A Study of Very Small Groups. In J.S. Grotstein (Ed.) *Do I Dare Disturb the Universe: A Memorial to W. R. Bion*. London: Karnac Books.

Hayden, C., & Molenkamp, R.J. (2004). Tavistock Primer II. In S. Cytrynbaum, & D. Noumair A. (Eds) *Group Dynamics, Organizational Irrationality, and Social Complexity: Group Relations Reader 3*. Jupiter, Florence: A. K. Rice Institute for the Study of Social Systems.

Jennings, C., & Dent, N. (2012). Grubb Guild – Report to Action Inquiry Task Group 31 January 2012. Unpublished.

Joseph, B. (1989). Transference: The Total Situation. In M. Feldman, & E. Bott Spillius (Eds) *Psychic Equilibrium and Psychic Change: Selected Papers of Betty Joseph*. London: Routledge.

Lawrence, W.G. (2006). Organisational Role Analysis: The Birth of Ideas. In J. Newton, S.Long, & B. Sievers (Eds) *Coaching in Depth: The Organisational Role Analysis Approach*. London: Karnak.

Lawrence, W.G., Bain, A., & Gould, L. (1996). The Fifth Basic Assumption. *Free Associations*, 6, Part 1.

Long, S. (2002). The Internal Team: A Discussion of the Socio-Emotional Dynamics of Team (Work). In R. Weisner, & B. Millet (Eds) *Himan Resource Management: Contemporary Challenges and Future Direction. An Interactive Digital Book On CD Rom*. Wiley.

Long, S. (2013). Socioanalytic Methodology. In S. Long (Ed.) *Socioanalytic Methods: Discovering the Hidden in Organisations and Social Systems*. London: Karnac Books Ltd.

Reed, B. (2000). An Exploration of Role: As Used In the Grubb Institute. In T. G. Institute (Ed.). London.

Sievers, B. (2008). Perhaps it is the Role of Pictures to Get in Contact with the Uncanny: The Social Photo Matrix as a Method to Promote the Understanding of the Unconcious in Organisations. *Organisational & Social Dynamics*, 8(2): 234–254.

Western, S. (2017). Where's Daddy? Integrating the Paternal and Maternal Stance to Deliver Non-Authoritarian Leadership For The Networked Society. *Organisational & Social Dynamics*, 17: 198–221.

Winnicott, D.W. (1971). *Playing And Reality*. London, Routledge Classics.

Wynn, E., & Katz, J.E. (1997). Hyperbole Over Cyberspace: Self-Presentation and Social Boundaries in Internet Home Pages and Discourse. *The Information Society*, 13: 297–327.

22 Practical Considerations for Online Organizational Consultancy

Rakefet Keret-Karavani and Arnon Rolnick

In this chapter, we will present recommendations to the meeting leader, having in mind the key question:

> How can I manage the online meeting to best achieve the defined goals?

For this purpose, the chapter will be divided into two parts:

1. Principles for meeting *planning*:

   - Deciding when a meeting should be held through videoconference, and when it should not.
   - Consider the space from which participants connect to the meeting: different options and their organizational meanings.
   - Preparing participants.

2. Principles of meeting *management*:

   - Setting.
   - Maintaining focused attention.
   - Creating active participation.

A major part of the discussion is relevant to any meeting, co-located as well as virtual. There are indeed management principles that are appropriate for any situation in which it is necessary to lead a group from A to B. However, it is important to pay attention specifically to two points:

1. Technology is one more factor that shapes the experience of the session and can affect its results.
2. Video conference medium changes the perception of phenomena known from collocated meeting, sometimes more salient and other times subtler.

Readers who use videoconferencing as a daily communication tool, can find value in this section as well. Oftentimes it is worthwhile to "take a step back" and examine the automatic manner we do things.

At the end of this section we will address meetings that are intended for learning and development, such as management development, team development, etc., followed by recommendations for this type of content and process.

1 Planning Principals

a Is Videoconference the Right Medium for the Meeting?

When the meeting deals with complex issues that require interaction and involvement, the video platform is a very good solution, since in these situations we seek to get as much information about our interlocutors. The goal of these meetings usually includes: problem solving, decision making, conflict resolution, product/strategy development, presentation of a new idea, etc.

On the other hand, it is not advisable to include issues that require lengthy analysis of the data. When one wants to work on a document/report/presentation, screen sharing with the necessary information provides all the needed communication. Adding the option of participants' images is interfering, as there is a frequent need to change between viewing the people and viewing the document. These switches distract, draw away attention, waste time and cause frustration.

b Space

In "space" we refer to two aspects: sitting together/alone, and the location from which one connects to the meeting.

Here are various meeting's formations, and some of the possible effects:

- All participants sit together around a camera with one large screen, and the meeting leader (manager/consultant) is somewhere else. In this formation there are only two locations.

  - *This option visually demonstrates the manager/consultant's externality to the group.*
  - *When seen on a large screen, it enhances the perception of leader's distance from the team and might strengthen authority as well.*

- Some of the participants and the meeting leader share a screen together, while other participants sit independently.

  - *This visually reflects the power relations of what is often considered headquarters ("the big site") with the small ones.*
  - *Exposes the relationships between the manager and the collocated employees, whether they are close, tense etc.*

- Some participants share one screen together, some sit independently and the meeting leader sits independently as well.

  ○ *This visually reflects the power relations of what is often considered "the big site" with the small ones, creating subgroups.*

- Each participant, including the meeting leader, sits independently in front of a screen.

  ○ *This "flattens" the image of the organizational structure, blurring the visibility of power relation and hierarchy.*

  ○ *Allows space for each participant, concretely: to see and be seen, hear and be heard, and symbolically: everyone has his own place and representation on the screen.*

Each of the above formations affects the dynamics among the participants, and between the participants and the meeting leader. As a meeting leader, when you plan the meeting, you are invited to ask yourself:

- Is the *team's scattering image* on the screen, visually represent a message you want to emphasis, or something you want to change? For example: the "togetherness" of a particular site? The importance of another site? Maybe the interculturality of the headquarter employees? If so, gathering the collocated participants in one room is an effective option. On the other hand, if you want to prevent some of the participants from feeling isolated, it is recommended not to have some participants sit together and some to connect individually.
- Is there a *culture* where sitting together/alone significantly affects the interaction? For example, sitting together make them more responsive? Or sitting alone allows them to be involved much more?
- Is there a planned *content* that one sitting arrangement or another is more suitable? For example: if the meeting is going to deal with a conflict between two sites, each sub-team sitting together in their site will probably enhance the fight dynamic: the image of "us and them" will be vivid. In that case you may consider asking participants to connect individually. Another example is when we want to have an informal meeting, getting to know each other personally, asking participants to connect from home.

c *Preparing Participants*

Change Management: From Audio Meeting to Videoconference Meeting. If the decision is to start using video in meetings which previously used only audio (via telephone/using the software without a camera turned on), this is a change that participants may perceive as an invasive act ("maybe they do not trust me and want to see what I'm doing?"), or simply annoying ("now I will not be able to do whatever I want while talking").

Therefore, it is necessary to explain that the rationale for using the camera is the need for interaction, involvement and concentration in the meeting.

Change Management: From Sitting Together to Sitting Individually. If the decision is to move from a sitting together in a room to individual sitting, it is a significant change that has to be managed. People will not give up the experience of sitting together so quickly.

As discussed in the last paragraph, the joint sitting of the collocation participants often creates discomfort among the others who sit alone, and opens the door to a dynamic of "inequality." This phenomenon is especially significant when participants come from different cultures. The most common case is when the conversation is in English, which for some (if not all) participants is not their mother tongue, and an internal debate begins in the local language about the speaker's words … while the speaker does not know what is going on. Even when all the participants share the same culture, it often feels like those sitting together create a "coalition" versus the others who sit alone. It doesn't take more than a whisper or an exchange of looks in order to create a feeling of "inside" and "outside."

Often there is a challenge for participants who work together in the office to connect to a meeting from a quiet place, especially in organizations that work in open space and lack meeting rooms for a quiet conversation. People usually find it easier and more comfortable to sit together, and do not make the effort to create the conditions to connect individually.

A good practice is to talk individually with the participants before the first joint meeting, using the same software to be used in the meeting. This meeting is aimed to understand whether the participant has prior experience with the software, to what extent s/he feels comfortable with the medium etc. In addition, it is advisable to discuss the setting and rules with the participants, both in the preliminary meeting and, of course, on the first meeting.

Here are some recommendations for the various formation options.

When some participants sit together and some alone:

- For those sitting together, stress the importance of having one conversation, ask to avoid side talks, and to speak the language in which the conversation is being conducted.
- For those sitting alone, acknowledge that it might require some time/effort to step into the discussion and emphasize the importance that they express their opinion.

When each participant sits individually:

When participants have no previous experience:

- Invite for a meeting using the selected software: give preliminary explanation of the system, ensure that there is proper equipment, and coordinate expectations about setting.
- Although the meeting is virtual, and in principal might be done "on the road" (literally...), it should be taken seriously and take place in a quiet private space.
- Request to open the camera as it is essential in order to involve the team (unless otherwise agreed upon).
- Ask to use a laptop/desktop that allows all participants to see a large, comfortable image of everyone.
- Make sure that there is a strong Internet connection, high quality camera and microphone.
- Emphasize adherence to time.

A useful practice is to give the participant examples of possible disruptions and ask what can enhance their proactive participation and focused attention.

When participants have partial or daily experience:

- Invite for a meeting using the selected software, and ask how positive the experience was. Were there any inhibitors? (Management factors/technology factors/environmental conditions).
- Ensure that there is high quality equipment and coordinate expectations about setting.

Since a closed quiet room is essential for an effective meeting, if participants connect from work, it's imperative to assess the conditions the organization can provides both technologically and physically. For example: Is there a proper space (quiet office or conference room)? If not, is it legitimate to connect to the meeting from outside the organization (maybe from home)? These kinds of preparations save a lot of nuisance and unnecessary frustration. It also signals to the participants that the meeting leader takes this meeting seriously.

2 Principles of Meeting Management

An effective meeting is one in which participants are focused and involved in what is happening. Considering the various characteristics, we have described throughout this part, it can be concluded that the videoconference medium challenges the participants' ability to concentrate and engage. When sitting together in front of one screen, as mentioned above, different social dynamics develop and might take away the attention. When sitting independently one has tempting options to do other things online or offline. Compared to audioconference, videoconference allows for greater connection and involvement, but compared to collocated meeting, the managerial challenge is still high.

a Setting

Organizational virtual meetings challenge boundaries more than collocated ones. Setting is a critical factor for any successful group process, but is twice as important here, since there are a lot of disruptions in the virtual context.

Setting provides a clear and known purpose, defined time and space, concurrent technological equipment and agreed documentation methods and etiquette.

A predetermined setting makes the conduct of the meeting dependent on the situation and not on a person, thus reducing ambiguity and creating clarity and calmness.

In a screen view, there are two characteristics to consider:

1. *Screen display options*. The various videoconferencing software has several *screen display options*. For example: In Zoom there is *speaker view* where the speaker looks big on the screen and the rest of the group is in small squares (so the speaker's image is seen bigger), and *gallery view* where all the images are in equal size. Most people are not aware of this feature, and the common situation is that each partici-pant will have a different screen display depending on his computer's default.

   Why do we point it out? The "gallery view" creates a group feeling and is more egalitarian, since we constantly see everyone at the same time and at the same size. However, such a display may also be overwhelming, as there is a lot of "information" from many facial expressions, changed body language, and different backgrounds.

   The "speaker view" allows one to concentrate more on the speaker and the content s/he conveys. At the same time, some participants who see themselves on the big screen, find this view as an inhibitor to an active participation.

   The meeting leader is advised to consider the meeting's goals and decide whether the nature of the interaction and of the participants require uniformity of the screen display.

2. *Self-image*. Usually, as a default, the participants see their own image, and some attention is diverted to it.

   - In professional/management team meetings, it is recommended to ask participants to "hide" their image to avoid distraction, and to make a bigger space on the screen for other images.
   - In learning and development meetings (section B2 below), it is recommended that participants see themselves, since self-image

viewing raises self-awareness and serves feedback and reflection processes.

b Holding Attention

When the Purpose of the Meeting is an Organizational Task (team meetings/project meetings, etc.).

It should be noted that this part refers to constantly repeated meetings, however there are principles that are worthwhile maintaining even if it is a one-time meeting.

CLARITY

Setting and definitions that match expectations: on the practical level – reducing misunderstandings, and on the emotional level – creating trust. We create clarity against the ambiguity generated by technology and the frequent disruptions.

It is highly recommended that the first meeting be devoted to presenting the rules that the meeting leader wants to assimilate, and a joint discussion with the group on the rules of conduct they decide to set together.

SOME RECOMMENDATIONS FOR KEY ISSUES THE MEETING LEADER MAY WISH TO CONSIDER

- Punctuality, appropriate environmental conditions, and technological equipment.
- Introduce the "Mute" button and when it will be used.
- Request participants to speak briefly since there is an attention limitation, due to the medium's nature.
- Prepare participants for the option of asking them to shorten their speech in order to advance the meeting.
- Give instructions on what to do when facing technical problems to minimize disrupting the meeting.
- Relate to cultural differences: explain the platform has different characteristics, and therefore as the meeting leader you will take some actions. It's advisable to say you are aware that these actions might be less acceptable/convenient for people of a particular culture, but it is intended to promote the meeting. For example: a direct approach of questions might not be the first choice for the Far-East cultures.
- Explain that it takes time to get used to the medium and to synchronize as a group.

- How do we want to regulate the conversation? (Taking turns by raising a hand? Rounds? Spontaneously?)
- What is required to maintain attention? (For example: Is it legitimate to ask the meeting leader in a private message to accelerate the discussion? etc.).
- What can engage the participants in the session?
- Suppose participants and/or the meeting leader want to indicate that some change is required: shortening speech, returning to the topic after discussion has shifted etc. What is acceptable?
- Should the meeting be recorded? If so, to what purpose and where is it kept?

RECOMMENDED PRACTICES FOR MANAGING A MEETING

Some practices which might be considered too "controlling" in a room, can be very useful in videoconference, at least in the first few meetings until the team is synchronized with the medium and with one another.

- Start with some "Ice Breakers".
- Use direct questions to involve people.
- Ask for a round of references every once in a while.
- Make short summaries to collect the inputs of participants.
- Use "survey" or other tools when appropriate for opinion/comments/ ideas.

When the Purpose of the Meeting is Learning and Development

Meetings aimed at personal development, teams/organizations development are focused on the exploring management and leadership concepts, cultivate interpersonal skills, develop effective team relations, and more.

To achieve those goals, participants are asked to get into a different state of mind from the mode they have in daily organizational meetings. During a facilitated process, they are raising the awareness of their own perceptions and actual behaviors, they receive and give personal feedback, and generally deal with the *behavioral and emotional aspects* that affect them in the role. Participants rarely deal with emotional processes in the organizational setting, yet these are often the basis for all communication and business actions that follows.

Hence, it is important to clarify that during these meetings the focus is on regulating relationships, in order for work to become as effectively as possible.

Leading these meetings requires a high level of group facilitation skills, to professionally navigate the group process as well as the personal ones. In most cases those meetings are facilitated by an external facilitator/consultant, or a trained in-house consultant. A common example is when a team starts working together, often the team's manager asks a consultant to conduct a process of team building, to structure policies that are the basis for the team's work.

This part of the section is intended for an external consultant/advisor, though a manager who wants to conduct such processes with the team will find things relevant as well.

First of all, the considerations we discussed in the previous section are all relevant in such a meeting.

Since, as mentioned before, the content of these meetings focuses on behavioral and emotional aspects of relationships (and not on a business task), we want to raise the participants' awareness to the delicate signs we constantly communicate to one other consciously and unconsciously. It will help them to pay attention to what they transmit to others, and what others might transmit to them. This is not different from in-person meeting. Yet, the medium of videoconference makes situations appear different than it would have in an in-person meeting, sometimes more salient and other times subtler.

This is the reason why we recommend the facilitator to use two separate devices: one with a big screen of a desktop/laptop showing *gallery view* and a second small devise (laptop/tablet etc.) showing *speaker view*. The two devices allow the facilitator to see all the participants in large unchanging images, while following the speaker closely. It enables the facilitator to "be closer" to the speaker and tentative to the visual information, and still be in touch with the group-as-a-whole dynamics.

Modeling Behaviors

By the term "modeling" we refer to the facilitator's behavior, leading by example and setting the tone for expected group's behaviors.

Verbalize as often as possible the aspects that *influence* the relationships as they are *formed in video*. Often participants are not aware how their behaviors are seen on the screen, and the possible implications. For example: how does it feel for others when one's attention is away, as they can see the person's head turning away (to his mobile phone?) or eyes moving on the screen (surfing the Internet?). The facilitator's modeling can be a useful practice, relating unjudgmentally to participant's presence and asking him/her: "In video communication we can't always be sure if we have the attention of each other. Please let know, where you are right now?"

Other example is the quality of the participant's image. Factors like dark environment, improper camera position, using mobile phone's small screen instead of laptop/desktop etc. are *not* just technical accessories that influence one's image *visibility*, but critical aids which actually "transfer" one's presence. In addition, often times "technicalities" tell us something about unspoken issues as well, like being ambivalent regarding the participation in the meeting etc.

Videoconference shows closely everyone's facial expressions. The facilitator might show specific interest in the facial expression and ask, what does it reflect?

When the facilitator refers to the participants' actions, expressions etc. in an interested non-judgmental way, it helps to involve people while making them conscious to their behavior.

Practical "To Do" Considerations

- It is highly recommended that each participant sits individually for the reasons listed above.
- Send reading/viewing/listening materials before and after the meeting, so that the meeting will be devoted to interactive parts of discussions and dialogue.
- Choose software suitable for the atmosphere you want to create and the message you want to convey. For example, there are instructional-educational programs in which, apart from participant's images, various learning aids are regularly displayed on the screen. There are programs where participants' images are displayed on the entire screen. A screenshot of the first type will transmit more of a class message, while the second screen image creates more of a workshop atmosphere.
- Make use of a variety of sharing tools through which participants can bring their personal and emotional world to create openness.

Epilogue

Arnon Rolnick and Haim Weinberg

Online Session
By Roni Frischoff

Only the desk knows
underneath an interpretation
a barefoot caress

We reach the end of our journey, in which we and other authors shared our experience with various formats of online therapy and struggled how to connect technology and therapy/consultation. We tackled questions about human relationship and their meaning for therapy and consultation. These questions are based not only on our experience but also on long-term accumulated knowledge, which we tried to summarize as well in this book. However, technology, and specifically Internet applications, change in such an accelerated pace that it is difficult to stay updated and acquainted with all the innovations. While concluding the book, we are aware that very soon, even before the book is published, new technologies will show up. Just as one example, after writing the book and mentioning the obstacle of the body's absence online and after commenting on the still position of the camera, we learned about a new technology in which the camera can move and show more of the surrounding and of the body of the participants. We also discovered a camera that represents the eyes of the observer (the therapist, for example), showing the client(s) the direction that the therapist is looking at. It seems that very soon, online presence will be enhanced through Virtual Reality technologies, so we humbly admit that we cannot foresee all the technological creative innovations that might assist and advance remote therapy. Even so, we think that in this book we succeeded touching principle dilemmas related to "distant" human encounters and addressed possible solutions to them.

Most of the work of psychologists, counselors, psychotherapists, and mental health professionals is based on their understanding of human behavior and interpersonal processes. In each of these professions intimacy and trust is crucial. Inserting technology into the clinic, and particularly entering cyberspace, challenges these important perspectives.

In his bestseller *Lessons for the 21 Century* (2018), Yuval Noah Harari writes that "humanist religions" typified the previous century, facilitating the blossom of liberalism and the importance of the subjective experience, focusing on self-esteem issues. However, the twenty-first century is typified with a new religion: Dataism. Its followers put their faith in information by encouraging us to see it as the only true source of value. Perhaps we, as mental health professionals, should be careful not to blindly follow this new religion and to become aware of the dangers in technology and its innovations?

On the other hand, giving up on the endless possibilities that open through remote meetings, and avoiding experimenting with new methods and creative formats of therapy and consultation seem no less extreme. This ambivalence reminds us of similar dilemmas that many scientists faced when developing new revolutionary technologies. For example, Marie Curie, who won the Noble prize twice, researched uncontrolled radiation. Her achievements included the development of the theory of radioactivity and led to using radiation for better medical diagnoses (e.g. using X-rays) but also to hazards of radiation disease (she herself died from exposure to radiation in the course of her scientific research). Another example is Albert Einstein, whose revelations in the field of Physics enabled the achievement of nuclear fission some years later. It is interesting that in the early thirties of the previous century he exchanged letters with Freud, asking him how to prevent war. Several years afterwards he suggested to President Roosevelt to establish laboratories for researching Uranium, contributing to the development of the Atomic bomb. It seems that any scientific development can bring both blessing and curse.

The editors of this book are very attentive to the ambivalence towards technology that is typical of therapists and counselors. For our book, we chose writers who believe in the importance of the interpersonal encounter as a central part of the consultation process, but also writers who dare sailing to new territories and discover the new world of remote therapy. Our bottom-line conclusion is that Progressivism cannot be stopped. We should harness it for the benefit of human race. Just as we can harness the nuclear power for positive outcome, we can recruit the Internet and remote therapy to expand and improve our services and therapeutic processes. Indeed, in each of the sections in this book, we tried to expand the scope of possibilities, risks and solutions in the field of online therapy and consultation.

In this book, we mentioned modern psychological theories from relational and intersubjective neurobiology field. Those approaches show how people are born into and are wired for relations and for the other's face and voice. This book was written and edited with a deep belief that the need for the other is embedded in our existence. As mental health professionals we believe in the human spirit and are convinced that we can harness technology for the sake of moments of meeting – even from a distance.

Index

Entries in *italics* denote figures; entries in **bold** denote tables.

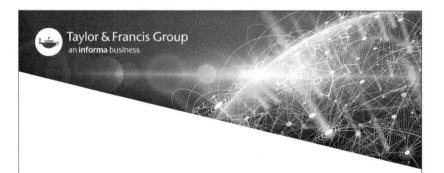

Lightning Source UK Ltd.
Milton Keynes UK
UKHW022215230720
367080UK00008B/65